P9-ECO-218

Colorado

Jon Klusmire
Photography by Paul Chesley

COMPASS AMERICAN GUIDES
An Imprint of Fodor's Travel Publications, Inc.

Colorado

Copyright © 1993 Fodor's Travel Publications, Inc.
Maps Copyright © 1993 Fodor's Travel Publications, Inc.
Second Edition

Library of Congress Cataloging-In-Publication-Data
Klusmire, Jon, 1956-
  Colorado / by Jon Klusmire : photography by Paul Chesley. — 2nd ed.
    p. cm. --
  Includes bibliographical references and index
  ISBN 1-878867-35-0 (pbk.) : $16.95
    1. Colorado—Description and travel—1981- —Guide-books.
I. Title. II. Series.
F774.3.K57 1993
917.8804'33—dc20

Editors: Kit Duane, Don Pitcher, Julia Dillon   Designers: David Hurst, Christopher Burt
Series Editor: Kit Duane   Map Design: Eureka Cartography, Bob Race
                                                     Photo Editor: Christopher Burt

First published in 1992 by Compass American Guides, Inc.
6051 Margarido Drive, Oakland, CA 94618, USA

Production house: Twin Age Ltd., Hong Kong   Printed in Hong Kong

Cover: Durango and Silverton Narrow Gauge Railroad

COMPASS AMERICAN GUIDES ACKNOWLEDGES the following institutions and individuals for the use of their photographs and/or illustrations: Colorado Historical Society, pp. 21, 24, 39, 58, 92, 94, 101, 103, 104, 108-109, 110, 175, 196, 200, 227, 228; the Museum of Western Art in Denver, pp. 25, 29, 57, 132-133, 172; Denver Public Library, Western History Department, pp. 143, 170, 171, 249; Pueblo Library District, p. 81; Center of Southwest Studies, Fort Lewis College, Durango, p. 192. Mural on pp. 156-157 used with permission from the Peabody Museum at Yale University. U.C. Berkeley paleontologist Mark Goodwin contributed the essay on p. 155.

THE AUTHOR ACKNOWLEDGES all those chambers of commerce across Colorado whose information helped immeasurably in the preparation of this book. I also want to thank Abbott Fay, one of my former history professors, for the time he spent listening to my initial brainstorming and for reading the finished manuscript.

The staffs at the Colorado Historical Society; Denver Public Library, Western History Collection; the Museum of Western Art; and Colorado Ski Museum were all accommodating. Likewise for the crew at my local library, the Glenwood Springs Branch of the Garfield County Library.

*This book is dedicated to my grandparents, Eldo and Gladys Klusmire,
who brought the Klusmire clan to Aspen in the 1940s, and to my Uncle Bob,
a man who never met a shot of whiskey he couldn't drink, a horse he couldn't ride,
or a bull elk he couldn't shoot and haul down a mountainside.*

C O N T E N T S

Topical Essays

Maps

MAP INDEX

Literary Excerpts

FACTS ABOUT COLORADO

Centennial State

CAPITAL: Denver
ENTERED UNION: Aug. 1, 1876
FIRST EUROPEAN SETTLEMENT:
San Luis in 1851

STATE FLOWER: Rocky Mountain columbine
STATE BIRD: Lark bunting
STATE TREE: Colorado blue spruce

POPULATION (1991): 3,376,669

		FIVE LARGEST CITIES:	
White*	88.2%	Metro Denver	1,848,319
Hispanic	12.9%		(incl. Boulder)
Black	4.0%	Colorado Springs	290,500
Asian	1.8%	Pueblo	102,400
American Indian	.8%	Fort Collins	79,400
*Includes some Hispanic		Greeley	60,536

GEOGRAPHY:

Size:	104,091 sq. mi. (269,576 sq. km), 8th largest
Highest point:	Mt. Elbert 14,433' (4,400 m)
Lowest point:	Arkansas River enters Kansas 3,350' (1,021 m)
Highest temp. recorded:	118° F (48° C) at Bennett on July 11,1888
Lowest temp. recorded:	-60° F (-53°C) at Maybell on Jan. 1, 1979
Wettest place:	37.41" (935 mm) at Savage Basin, San Miguel County
Driest place:	6.96" (174 mm) at Manassa, Conejos County

ECONOMY:

Major industries:	Tourism, aerospace, defense, electronics, agriculture
Chief crops:	Corn, wheat, hay, sugarbeets, barley
Minerals:	Gold, oil shale, construction sand and gravel
Per capita income:	$19,440

FAMOUS COLORADOANS:

Molly Brown, Scott Carpenter, Jack Dempsey, Mamie Eisenhower,
Douglas Fairbanks, Scott Hamilton, Lowell Thomas

AUTHOR'S PREFACE

AT FIRST BLUSH, I THOUGHT WRITING THIS BOOK WOULD BE a mere finger exercise at the old word processor. Hey, I was born here, lived here all my life, have a degree in history, am a working journalist, have forgotten more about Colorado than most people know, and was more than ready to write the guide of guides: no hagiography here, no siree, the real stuff, the good stuff, nothing but the truth, babble babble, dribble dribble, mutter mutter.

Fired with enthusiasm and hubris, I started. But something happened to my bluster and bombast as I dug into the state I thought I knew so well.

Thankfully, this isn't another "been everywhere twice, talked to everyone once," Colorado guide. My goal is not to inform the reader if lox and bagels are available in Ordway or to rehash the history of the Centennial State and its people. Instead, what I have tried to do is provide an interesting glimpse of a fascinating state, to give the reader a feel for what made the state what it is and what it wants to be.

But this is also intended to be a guidebook, albeit a more selective guide than some of the encyclopedic items already available. Thus, it includes a solid selection of information to help you discover and enjoy a good cross-section of Colorado's famed attractions.

What I set out to do after I uncovered favored and unique restaurants, motels, and fishing holes was to discover the links between how the past helped shape the present and how the past and present—whether embodied by the Mining Law of 1872 or the international oil market of the 1990s—might combine to signal the future.

It didn't take me long to realize that I had indeed forgotten a lot about Colorado, that some of my assumptions were a bit outdated, that my home state proved to be a whole lot more interesting and intriguing than I had remembered.

Fortunately, Paul Chesley's photos meant I wouldn't have to keep finding new combinations of words (how many times can you say breathtaking?) to describe Colorado's indescribable scenery. Instead, I'll just let his work speak for itself.

Tracking down comfy beds, T-bone steaks, good elk hunting, and the fastest ski lift while trying to explain the essence of what makes Colorado Colorado proved to be a tremendous challenge. Don't feel too sorry for me though. It was also a delightful challenge that gave me a grand excuse to tour the state and spruce up, dust off, or throw away my pet theories about how Colorado evolved into the intriguing and internationally renowned place it has become.

I certainly had a wonderful time doing that, and I hope the fruits of my efforts will provide the reader an entertaining look at a state that certainly holds plenty of entertaining and educational surprises for any visitor, or even for a certain, once cocksure, lifelong resident.

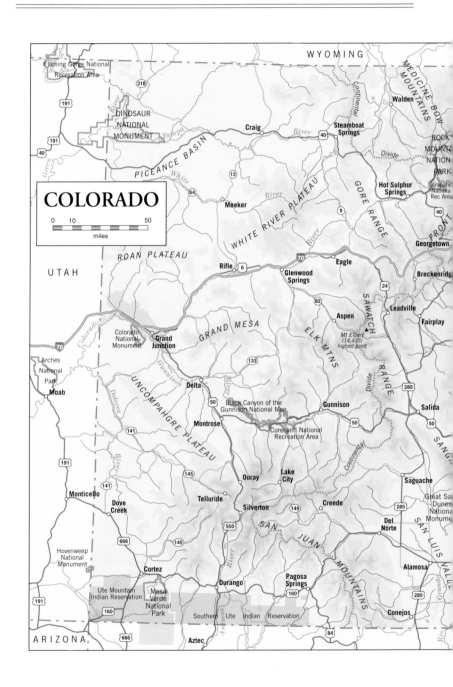

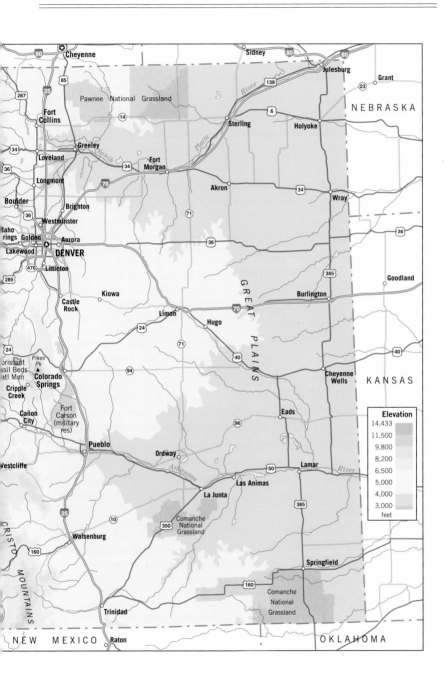

INTRODUCTION

COLORADO IS A SPRAWLING WESTERN STATE whose Rocky Mountain spine of towering snowcapped peaks is bracketed by a vast prairie on the east and a dry, windswept desert on the west. To the south, mystery reigns.

All of Colorado provides postcard images. If a picture is worth a thousand words, pictures of many Colorado scenes are worth a thesaurus. And even that can't describe the beauty, tranquility, and almost spiritual feel that can overtake mere mortals when escaping into the millions of acres of Colorado plains, mountains, and deserts.

Whether it's the stability of small town life on the plains, brightly clad skiers busting through piles of "champagne powder," or a sunrise splashing color across a desert moonscape, nature can provide visitors to Colorado more than enough goosebumps.

Goosebumps aside, there's more than postcard images in Colorado. There is also the Oil Shale Capital of the World, the world's highest town (railroad, paved road, and suspension bridge), enough natural hot springs to soak away half the world's fatigue, the world's biggest underground hole filled with military brass (and we're not talking ammo dump), and the sweetest peaches this side of paradise.

Although this book can't reproduce the taste of those peaches, it can give you a taste of and feel for the parts that make Colorado a unique whole, while pointing out each area's sights, scenes, and history. As with any story, there are characters, and Colorado is full of them, from the first optimistic gold miners and silver barons to the current crop of peach growers on the Western Slope.

Before most people get to the Rocky Mountains, they cross or fly over Colorado's eastern plains. Running right up to the mountains, the plains are flat as a pancake, and full of wheat, tractors, and tornados. (If Dorothy and Toto had flown back from Oz and wakened in eastern Colorado, they'd have thought they'd landed in Kansas.)

The string of cities along the Front Range of the Rockies popped to life to supply the booming gold and silver towns deeper into the mountains. Once the gold and silver boom busted, the Front Range cities worked to become bastions of civilization in an untamed land, and then found themselves in the right spot at the right time to become the federal government's western hub.

A forest dressed in its finest foliage.

The Colorado mountains remain the state's biggest draw and biggest bragging point. The mountains first beckoned the mountain men and fur trappers who truly explored the rugged backcountry. Next came the gold and silver miners who scattered throughout the state, from Boulder to Durango, in search of the minerals of which Victorian dreams were made.

Today, millions of acres of national forest, national parks and recreation areas, and public land draw visitors from around the globe. Whether it's to fish, backpack, bike, camp, hunt, or just try to get back in touch with land that has not been scarred or trampled by civilization, Colorado is more than accommodating.

The same is true for the state's famed mountain resorts. Entire communities have been created from scratch to itch the urge to ski. Mining towns down on their ore learned how to mine powder or historic charm instead of minerals. The transformation has been dazzling. Formerly dilapidated Victorian downtowns now boast everything from living history to the latest fashions.

Traveling toward the western side of the Rocky Mountains, it's possible, within a couple of hours, to drive from a 10,000-foot (3,048-m) mountain pass down to sprawling farm and ranch land where the myth of the West with its fiercely independent farmers and ranchers is still alive and well. From there it's on into a hot western desert full of rattlesnakes and wind-carved rock formations.

Turning south, the traveler finds more subtle transformations, in mysteries of the past and mixtures of cultures. It was here that ancient Native American artisans created stunning cliff dwellings, and it was through this area that Spanish explorers traveled in the fifteenth century searching for the legendary Seven Cities of Gold. Later, a colonial Spanish/Hispanic culture, emanating from Santa Fe to the south, flourished and was eventually challenged by American settlers arriving from the east. Among other things, the Americans decided that southwestern Colorado was just the spot for the state's indigenous Ute Indians. As a result, the area is a true melting pot of people and heritage.

A common bond is shared by all Coloradoans: a reliance on natural resources and the surrounding environment for a livelihood. That, in turn, has created and is still creating another enduring Colorado feature: cycles of boom and bust. First it was gold, then silver, then coal, oil, oil shale, and uranium. Colorado still contains valuable minerals waiting to be mined, but today those hoping to recover them often find themselves in conflict with those whose livelihood depends on preservation of Colorado's environmental treasures. That the representatives of these two treasure troves collide on a regular basis keeps things interesting, if not downright exciting.

Thanks to its history and its people, Colorado is a state that is used to remaking itself whenever it has to. It is an amazing testament to the state's bountiful natural resources and resourceful citizens that it has been able to adjust and survive in an ever-changing world, while retaining its famous, almost magical reality.

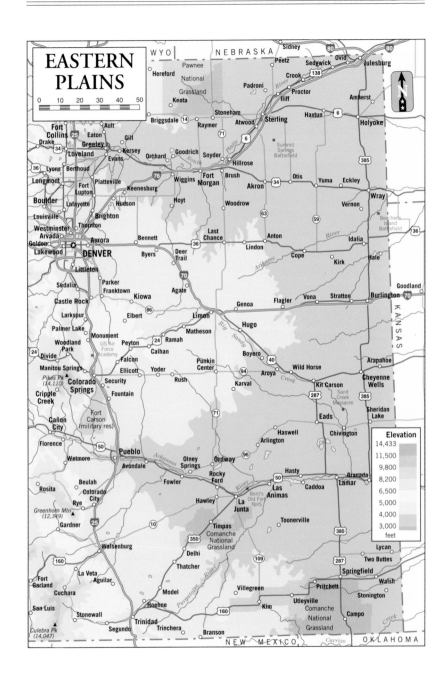

EASTERN PLAINS

THE SILENCE IS PALATABLE AS YOU TRAVEL across Colorado's eastern plains, either on two-lane, straight-as-a-string state highways; on Interstate 70, which cuts through the middle of the state; or on Interstate 76, which angles across the northern plains from Nebraska to Denver. Acre upon acre of corn, wheat, soybeans, and silence are your only companions.

The first trappers, explorers, and gold seekers traveling across America's Great Plains probably broke that silence with swear words and vile oaths about this Great American Desert which was just an obstacle to overcome and appeared to be a totally worthless pain in the butt. (Ride a mule a for a month; you'll understand.) Your seating arrangements are probably much more comfortable, but one look at a map might lead you to agree that the plains are to be sped through with a minimum of stopping and a maximum of miles per hour.

Don't be so hasty. Not only will you be missing a large part of the state's history and more than a few significant attractions, you might also bypass some of the last bastions of real American small-town life, a life that has survived the frantic freeways, crammed shopping malls, crime, stress, and anxiety that you are speeding away from.

■ BENT'S FORT AND THE SANTA FE TRAIL

The men who set out into the Colorado Rockies between 1820 and 1840 came in all shapes, sizes, colors, and nationalities. They were the mountain men and fur trappers who, with a horse to ride and another to carry their traps and scant provisions, truly explored Colorado's mountains. Frenchmen, Americans, Mexicans, and Indians all plunged into the state's frozen streams to supply the beaver pelts that fashioned fashionable men's hats from New York to Paris.

The trappers would head out into the mountains in the fall, trap all winter, and return, if lucky enough to keep their own pelts on their own heads, with enough beaver "plews" to sustain them for the rest of the year.

The fickle finger of fashion finished off the beaver trade about the same time the trappers finished off the beavers. By the 1840s, with silk hats riding high on sophisticated heads, the beaver business was dead. Another animal's shaggy, fashionable head, however, reared up just in time to coat the southern plains with commerce. Buffalo robes replaced beaver pelts in the world of fashion and the traveling trappers' carnival called the "rendezvous" was replaced by permanent trading posts and forts to take advantage of the buffalo robe trade.

Bent's Fort was one of the most successful trading posts in the West during the buffalo robe stampede. Built in 1833 on the American side of the Arkansas River between present-day La Junta and Las Animas, its thick adobe walls, secure lodging, and store of trading goods made it a welcome sight to anyone coming out of Colorado's southern mountains or across the plains on the **Mountain Branch of the Santa Fe Trail.**

Brothers Charles and William Bent and Ceran St. Vrain operated the original fort and several others for 17 years. They were successful in part due to innate business sense, and in part due to their ability to respect the cultures and peoples upon which their trade depended.

This was a heady time. Until the Mexicans won their independence from Spain in 1821 and freed themselves from colonial domination, Santa Fe was prevented by the King of Spain from trading with the United States. Once Spanish rule ended, land and trade opened up, and the effect was electrifying.

Authenticity is the stock and trade at Bent's Old Fort.

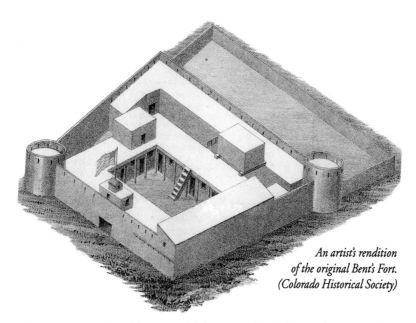

*An artist's rendition
of the original Bent's Fort.
(Colorado Historical Society)*

It was a time when skin color didn't matter, Spanish or American political shenanigans were old news with no practical effect, paperwork was unheard of, governments' approving or disapproving hand was invisible, and you didn't need lawyers and accountants to seal a deal or assure that promises once made were kept. All you needed were mutual respect for those you encountered, an appreciation of their labors and wares, a little haggling, a firm handshake, and a shot of trading post whiskey, which in its earliest incarnation was grain alcohol flavored with red pepper. (Does that give you a clue to the derivation of the word "firewater?")

The male Plains Indians, not white hunters, killed the buffalo, and the women prepared the robes, thus good relations with the Indians were a necessity. Fair trading and the marriage of William Bent to Owl Woman, a Cheyenne, cemented the Bents' tie to the Natives. Neither could the Bents indulge in disrespect or disregard for the American, Mexican, and Spanish traders and travelers who plied the Santa Fe Trail.

Once inside the *placita* (the open courtyard inside the fort's walls), nationalities and cultural differences were forgotten, for a time at least, to be replaced by security, commerce, and companionship.

Maybe that's why, over 100 years and millions of politicians, lawyers, and bickering bureaucrats later, **Bent's Old Fort National Historic Site** has become one of Colorado's première tourist attractions. It's also a nice rest after fishing, floating, or hunting along the Arkansas River. (See "GREAT OUTDOORS" for more on the area's recreational possibilities.)

Within sight of plains and mountains, visitors can amble through the fort's gates into the *placita* and back into a simpler time. Volunteer interpreters dressed in buckskins and sombreros man the trading post, which is filled with all the goods needed to refresh an average mountain man or weary traveler on the way to Santa Fe. You can rest in the shade under the adobe awning that rings the inside of the fort, cuss the end of the beaver empire with the bearded trapper next to you, ply some information about a rapid route across the Rockies from a nearby mountain man, or just sit and wonder what life was like when a man's word was his bond, his handshake his seal, his life unmolested by contracts, lawyers, accountants, and politicians.

■ COMANCHE NATIONAL GRASSLAND

If that reflective mood remains after a trip to Bent's Fort, you can travel back to La Junta on Colorado 194, then take Colorado 109 or US 350 through the **Comanche National Grassland**. Here you can see how the Great American Desert looked before the plow turned under the buffalo grass and native plants that were once a part of the plains' barren beauty. Let your mind wander back to the time when all a man needed was a horse to hunt and fight from, buffalo meat and robes, his family and his tribe, and respect for the Creator who provided all of life's necessities. Unfortunately, fierce competition, a little war with Mexico, a gold rush in the Rockies, and the arrival of thousands of settlers made sure the peaceful days of collaboration on the plains between the whites and the Indians ended.

The trials and tribulations of the gold-seekers rushing to California, Nevada, and Colorado from the late 1840s to the 1860s are both humorous and tragic. Even those with scant sense realized winter was the wrong time to trek across the prairie, so summer was the only traveling season. Few tried it alone. Many were never heard of again. Horses and mules were the preferred beasts of burden, but humans tried to fill those horseshoes by pushing wheelbarrows or carts themselves,

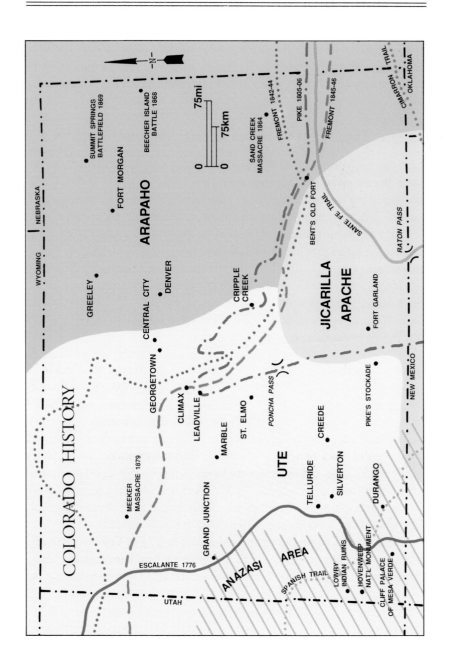

COLORADO HISTORY

ANAZASI AREA

UTE

ARAPAHO

JICARILLA APACHE

and some even tried crude backpacks, a much ridiculed choice. One enterprising soul decided to make the wind do the work by attaching a sail to a regular wagon. It worked for a while before unceremoniously sinking miles before making port.

■ SETTLERS VERSUS INDIANS

Generally, until after the Civil War, Colorado's plains were just an obstacle to overcome. But the sodbusters, those not seeking quick riches—but merely farmland—saw something else under the buffalo grass sod: fertile soil. And on Colorado's eastern plains, they saw something even more important: water for irrigation.

As the sodbusters got closer to the Rockies they noticed a difference from the pancake-flat plains they had crossed. Before hitting the mountains, they started encountering everything from little streams to sizable rivers coming off the eastern side of the Continental Divide. For instance, over 50 smaller streams or rivers feed the Arkansas River before it crosses into Kansas. Between the Arkansas and the South Platte, another score of streams flow through the plains, and the South Platte is also fed by dozens of streams great and small.

Sod houses and solid citizens settled the plains for farming. (Colorado Historical Society)

"The Chinook Wind" by Harvey Dun. (Museum of Western Art)

In 1860 the federal government squeezed the Cheyennes and Arapahos into a triangular reservation between the Arkansas River and Sand Creek, about 40 miles (64 km) west of the present-day Kansas border and 30 miles (48 km) north of the Arkansas River. The once free-roaming hunters got a measly 40 acres per family, along with machinery, money, and instruction on how to pull the plow. Some younger braves roamed from the unfenced, unguarded reservation, attacked an occasional supply wagon, and didn't quite seem to respect the whites' generosity or boundaries.

Those forays, and the fear of more of them, helped convince many settlers that the plains would never be "safe" until even the vaguest threat of Indian attack was removed. That meant removing all the Indians.

This determination led to breaking the silence of the plains with booming cannon fire, crackling rifle shots, chilling war hoops, and the screams of wounded and dying men, women, and children.

Those sounds of conflict have long since been swept away by the wind, but are recalled by the names now proudly taken by many counties and towns on the eastern plains. Names like Pawnee, Cheyenne Wells, Kiowa, Arapaho, Comanche,

EATING DOG WITH THE INDIANS

*T*he lodge of my host, Kongra Tonga, or the Big Crow, presented a picturesque spectacle that evening. A score or more of Indians were seated around it in a circle, their dark naked forms just visible by the dull light of the smouldering fire in the centre. The pipe glowing brightly in the gloom as it passed from hand to hand around the lodge. Then a squaw would drop a piece of buffalo-fat on the dull embers. Instantly a bright glancing flame would leap up, darting its clear light to the very apex of the tall conical structure, where the tops of the slender poles that supported its covering of leather were gathered together. It gilded the features of the Indians, as with animated gestures they sat around it, telling their endless stories of war and hunting. It displayed rude garments of skins that hung around the lodge; the bow, quiver, and lance, suspended over the resting-place of the chief, and the rifles and powder-horns of the two white guests. For a moment all would be bright as day; then the flames would die away, and fitful flashes from the embers would illumine the lodge, and then leave it in darkness. Then all the light would wholly fade, and the lodge and all within it be involved again in obscurity.

As I left the lodge next morning I was saluted by howling and yelping from all around the village, and half its canine population rushed forth to the attack. Being as cowardly as they were clamorous, they kept jumping around me at the distance of a few yards, only one little cur, about ten inches long, having spirit enough to make a direct assault. He dashed valiantly at the leather tassel which in the Dahcotah fashion was trailing behind the heel of my moccason, and kept his hold, growling and snarling all the while, though every step I made almost jerked him over on his back. As I knew that the eyes of the whole village were on the watch to see if I showed any sign of apprehension, I walked forward without looking to the right or left, surrounded wherever I went by this magic circle of dogs. When I came to Reynal's lodge I sat down by it, on which the dogs dispersed growling to their respective quarters. Only one large white one remained, who kept running about before me and showing his teeth. I called him but he only growled the more. I looked at him well. He was fat and sleek; just such a dog as I wanted. "My friend," thought I, "you shall pay for this! I will have you eaten this very morning!"

I intended that day to give the Indians a feast, by way of conveying a favorable impression of my character and dignity; and a white dog is the dish which the customs of the Dahcotah prescribe for all occasions of formality and importance. I consulted Reynal; he soon discovered that an old woman in the next lodge was owner of the white dog. I took a gaudy cotton handkerchief, and laying it on the ground, arranged some vermilion, beads, and other trinkets upon it. Then the old squaw was summoned. I pointed to the dog and to the handkerchief. She gave a scream of delight, snatched up the prize, and vanished with it into her lodge. For a few more trifles I engaged the services of two other squaws, each of whom took the white dog by one of his paws, and led him away behind the lodges, while he kept looking up at them with a face of innocent surprise. Having killed him they threw him into a fire to singe; then chopped him up and put him into two large kettles to boil. Meanwhile I told Raymond to fry in buffalo-fat what little flour we had left, and also to make a kettle of tea as an additional item of the repast.

The Big Crow's squaw was briskly at work sweeping out the lodge for the approaching festivity. I confided to my host himself the task of inviting the guests, thinking that I might thereby shift from my own shoulders the odium of fancied neglect and oversight.

When feasting is in question, one hour of the day serves an Indian as well as another. My entertainment came off about eleven o'clock. At that hour, Reynal and Raymond walked across the area of the village, to the admiration of the inhabitants, carrying the two kettles of dog-meat slung on a pole between them. These they placed in the centre of the lodge, and then went back for the bread and the tea. Meanwhile I had put on a pair of brilliant moccasons, and substituted for my old buck-skin frock a coat which I had brought with me in view of such public occasions. I also made careful use of the razor, an operation which no man will neglect who desires to gain the good opinion of Indians. Thus attired, I seated myself between Reynal and Raymond at the head of the lodge. Only a few minutes elapsed before all the guests had come in and were seated on the ground, wedged together in a close circle around the lodge. Each brought with him a wooden bowl to hold his share of the repast. When all were assembled, two of the officials, called "soldiers" by the white men, came forward with ladles made of the horn of the Rocky Mountain sheep, and began to distribute the feast, always assigning a double share to the old men and chiefs. The dog vanished with astonishing celerity, and each guest turned his dish bottom upward to show that all was gone. Then the bread was distributed in its turn, and finally the tea. As the soldiers poured it out into the same wooden bowls that had served for the substantial part of the meal, I thought it had a particularly curious and uninviting color.

"Oh!" said Reynal, "there was not tea enough, so I stirred some soot in the kettle, to make it look strong."

Fortunately an Indian's palate is not very discriminating. The tea was well sweetened, and that was all they cared for.

—Francis Parkman, Jr., *The California and Oregon Trail, Being Sketches of Prairie and Rocky Mountain Life,* 1849

Neeso Pah, or Chivington. Or names like Sand Creek and Beecher's Island, the two major "battles" on the eastern plains which eventually led to the Indians' final removal.

But Sand Creek and Beecher's Island were as different as night and day; the first being the era's equivalent of throwing the Christians to the lions (with a Methodist minister doing the throwing), the second being one of the most astounding displays of stamina and courage during the Indian Wars and an example of superior technology (firepower) being the key to military victory.

The Cheyennes and Arapahos settled into the Sand Creek reservation and from 1860 to 1863 things went pretty smoothly except for a little horse stealing and minor conflicts. The Civil War had slowed the flow of settlers and in 1864 Indian raiding and rowdiness grew as roving bands struck along the Arkansas River Valley. In June, some Indians killed the Hungate family a mere 25 miles (40 km) south of Denver. When the five white, scalped, and mutilated bodies were brought to town for display, terror and outrage struck. The city was certain that complete annihilation by hordes of Indians was imminent.

Arapaho and Cheyenne leaders met with Territorial Gov. John Evans (Colorado became a U.S. Territory in 1861), state officials, and military leaders. The Indians left the meeting seemingly satisfied and went back to their camps to prepare for a peaceful winter. They hadn't counted on political maneuvering or the power of public opinion. The white officials made conflicting reports of the meeting and the public and press wouldn't drop demands for outright warfare.

■ SAND CREEK MASSACRE

In August, Governor Evans, being a sensitive politician, said anyone who wanted to fight Indians could volunteer for 100 days in the Third Colorado Militia. Commanding the militia was Col. John Chivington, a Methodist minister who had served with distinction during the Civil War. With no Indians on the warpath, it appeared no action would take place before the 100-day enlistment ended, and Chivington's troops began to be ridiculed as the "Bloodless Third."

When Evans—who was pushing for statehood because a mere territory couldn't handle murderous Indians—left for Washington, Chivington decided it was time for action to satisfy the public demand for a "Bloody Third." He moved his troops

BLACK ELK SPEAKS

*W*e made these little gray houses of logs that you see, and they are square. It ... is a bad way to live, for there can be no power in a square.

You have noticed that everything an Indian does is in a circle, and that is because the Power of the World always works in circles, and everything tries to be round. In the old days when we were a strong and happy people, all our power came to us from the sacred hoop of the nation, and so long as the hoop was unbroken, the people flourished. The flowering tree was the living center of the hoop, and the circle of the four quarters nourished it. The east gave peace and light, the south gave warmth, the west gave rain, and the north with its cold and mighty wind gave strength and endurance. This knowledge came to us from the outer world with our religion. Everything the Power of the World does is done in a circle. The sky is round ... and so are all the stars. The wind, in its greatest power, whirls. Birds make their nests in circles, for theirs is the same religion as ours. The sun comes forth and goes down again in circle. The moon does the same and both are round. Even the seasons form a great circle in their changing, and always come back again to where they were. The life of a man is a circle from childhood to childhood, and so it is in everything where power moves. Our teepees were round like the nests of birds, and these were always set in a circle, the nation's hoop, a nest of many nests, where the Great Spirit meant for us to hatch our children.

But the Wasichus (whites) have put us in these square boxes. Our power is gone and we are dying, for the power is not in us anymore.

—John G. Neihardt, *Black Elk Speaks*, 1932

"What an Indian Thinks," by Maynard Dixon. (Museum of Western Art)

into position around the Sand Creek Reservation on Nov. 29, 1864, and, without warning, gave the order to attack. That's all the citizen soldiers needed to hear. They ran amok. It wasn't an attack. It was a slaughter. During an all-day battle (which shamed Chivington because the Indians were-outnumbered and out-gunned) no Indian prisoners were taken. Whether armed or unarmed, any Indian, including the women and children running from the scene, were summarily tracked down and killed.

Some Coloradoans thought the move long overdue and applauded the "battle," including the killing of the children. "Nits make lice," was one oft-used quote that justified such cold-blooded action. The nation didn't see things in such glowing terms. Congress reprimanded Chivington and called the action "a foul and dastardly massacre which would have disgraced the veriest savages." Famed scout Kit Carson said of Sand Creek:

> *Th*e pore Injuns had our flag flyin' over 'em, that same old stars and strips that we all love and honor . . . then here come along that durned Chivington and his cusses. They'd bin out huntin' hostile Injuns, and couldn't find none no whar . . . . So they just pitched into these friendlies, and massa-creed them—yes sir, literally massa-creed them in col' blood, in spite of our flag thar—women and little children even . . . And ye call these civilized men Christians; and the Injuns savages, du ye?

The Indian response to Sand Creek was immediate. Violence broke out all along the frontier from New Mexico to Montana. More than 20 stage stations were destroyed; the town of Julesburg, Colorado, was burned to the ground; and hundreds of people died on both sides over the next two years.

Today, on Colorado 96, north of the town of Chivington and Chivington Reservoir, a Kiowa County road leads to a small monument marking the Sand Creek Massacre.

■ BEECHER'S ISLAND

The final major Indian battle in Colorado was a far different story since it was a battle in every sense of the word. The Arapaho and Cheyenne had been officially moved to Indian Territory in 1867, but still had hunting privileges and the spunk to raid isolated farms or supply wagons, which kept the public wary of "the Red Menace."

In September of 1868, about 1,000 Indians met a patrol of 50 Army scouts under Capt. John Forsyth, who quickly took refuge on an island near the Arikaree Fork of the Republican River, about 11 miles (18 km) west of the current Kansas border and about 15 miles (24 km) south of Wray. (This island was later named Beecher's Island in honor of a soldier killed in the attack.) The scouts delivered withering firepower thanks to a new weapon: the Spencer rifle. Instead of the old single-shot muzzle-loader of Civil War fame, the Spencer used a single cartridge, and thus could be reloaded and re-fired much more quickly. After holding off the Indians for nine days and killing famed Chief Roman Nose, the scouts were rescued by the Tenth Cavalry Regiment, an all-black force based at Fort Wallace, and took their a place of honor amongst the era's Indian fighters.

By 1870, the Indians were permanently banished to reservations, the bison herds were rapidly dwindling, and settlers had begun plowing under the virgin prairie.

■ GREELEY

In 1872, Colorado set up a Board of Immigration—a forerunner of the modern chamber of commerce, to attract settlers by publicizing the state's virtues. The word "publicizing" doesn't quite express the vigor of the board's approach. How about screaming to high heaven about what a Garden of Eden this place called Colorado was? That's better.

Anyway, the publicity, willingness of emigrants to set out to newly opened land, and Americans' general feeling that things are better just over the horizon attracted settlers. It also attracted an unusual number of "colonies" or "cooperatives" in which members would share work, profits, and decisions to create a successful town.

These idealists decided this new land, especially in the northern plains near the Front Range, was the perfect place to start new communities and generally show the world just exactly how to run a perfect little farming town. **Greeley** was the most famous, and successful, of the utopian endeavors.

In 1869, a tour of the West by Nathan C. Meeker, the Agricultural Editor of the New York *Tribune,* convinced him that Colorado was perfect for a cooperative

(following pages) Irrigation greened "The Great American Desert."

farm colony. The *Tribune* was owned by Horace Greeley, and Meeker took Greeley's advice to "Go West Young Man, Go West." A public meeting in New York lined up followers willing to pay $155 a head to take part in the effort, of which Meeker was elected president. (For more about Meeker see "WESTERN SLOPE.")

The promised land was purchased near the confluence of the Cache la Poudre and South Platte rivers. The settlers started arriving in the spring of 1870, imposed a total booze ban, and established the settlement of Greeley.

The big guy, Horace Greeley, came out to visit and encourage the operation. Whether it was his encouragement, a virtual absence of hangovers, or just outstanding land and plenty of irrigation water, the town of Greeley started to prosper. Extensive irrigation led to outstanding crops and an almost unheard of experiment in those days of the open range: fencing cattle off the land. Of course, a cynic or two thought the $20,000 fence was merely an effort to keep the sinners from non-utopian communities away from the saints at Greeley. Intermingling, however, took place, especially in the colony of Evans, begun in 1871 just to the south. In its saloons one could usually find a Greeleyite temporarily testing or tasting where the grass was truly greener.

Soon Greeley had a buffalo hide processing plant, museum, library, and lyceum, and by 1880, when the colony's charter had expired, the original utopianists had created the beginnings of present-day Greeley (which, by the way, retained its anti-booze law until after World War II). Not every colonist thought Greeley was a utopia. Many arrived, looked around, and left; or arrived, tried to live within the rules, then left for other plains towns or to homestead their own farms.

■ MORE UTOPIAS SPROUT

The **Longmont** colony, started in 1871 about 30 miles (48 km) north of Denver, was another success story, thanks to support from rich New Yorker, Elizabeth Thompson. But good management, ample irrigation water, and hard-working colonists didn't hurt either.

Fort Collins, 30 miles (48 km) north of Longmont, another colony started at this time, is still spreading the good word. In 1879 it secured Colorado State Agricultural and Mechanical College. Farmers soon reaped the benefits by getting the

ROUND 'EM UP, HEAD 'EM OUT
ACROSS THE PLAINS

You'd think anyone with about 30 percent of their brain cells in working order could figure out that the stupidest and most expensive way to get Texas cattle to Eastern markets would be to drive them northwest across the prairie to railheads in Colorado and Kansas where they would then be shipped back east. Why not angle those herds toward Chicago and be done with it? But there were good reasons Texas cattlemen decided to undertake epic northwest cattle drives from the 1860s to the 1880s.

One reason was that during the Civil War, the Union Army held the northern Mississippi River. In 1863, the fall of Vicksburg, Mississippi, effectively closed off the southern market for Texas cattle. Besides, no self-respecting Texas Rebel would sell anything to those damn Yankees. Thus arrived the great Texas cattle glut. Prices were a joke, even if buyers could be found. Meanwhile, without Texas cattle, beef prices back East soared. That's why Rebel cows started making their way to Colorado in earnest in 1864.

But even after the war, the direct route from Texas east wasn't the most profitable. It was impossible to drive thousands of cows through established, usually fenced, farmland, and pay every farmer for every chomp of corn consumed.

The great, open plains, on the other hand, featured miles of fenceless range and all the prairie grass a cow could eat. So it was cheaper to start from Texas in March with skinny cows and head north across the plains, letting the cattle arrive at the railhead with plenty of meat on their bones (some claim this easy eating started the federal grazing subsidies that have kept the cattle industry fat to this day, at taxpayers' expense).

Great herds—often numbering in the thousands—kept coming, especially when the train reached Denver in 1870. But getting there wasn't always that easy. The drovers had to avoid those pesky homesteaders and their fences, find water every few days, and face truly life-threatening, not to mention profit-reducing, troubles. As usual, as soon as it was apparent money could be made in cattle, large operators and corporations arrived to dominate the scene. Colorado cattle barons accumulated huge acreage and herds along the Arkansas and South Platte rivers. Some real barons from England and Ireland also invested heavily in the Western cattle industry, and the international connection helped provide the cash to create corporate farming.

continues

(following pages) Cattle ranching is still the backbone of the high plains economy.

By the 1880s the open range era started to wane. Overgrazing occurred as the cattle vied for less and less grass. More homesteaders were irrigating the plains and fencing their property (in 1874, an effective barbed wire machine allowed farmers to fence on the cheap). To this day, the rule is you have to fence cattle and sheep OFF your property. If 300 cows come through a hole in your fence and eat all your hay, what a bummer, fix your fence.

By the mid-1890s the open range was pretty much closed, but it lingers in two significant ways. Stories recalling the open range and cattle drives immediately put all Americans' brain cells on hold, especially John Wayne fans. Those days are indelibly etched on America's collective vision of the West.

Everyone knows the story: a rancher facing financial ruin turns into a tough but fair trail boss, assembles an unlikely crew of misfits, drunks, and amateurs to herd his thousands of cattle across the plains. They fight the weather, Indians, each other, and finally meld together as a team, make it to the railhead, get drunk, say their emotional (for men) good-byes, and head off into the sunset and the next drive.

More importantly for Colorado, the cattle industry gave the state one more economic leg to stand on and boosted Denver's importance as a regional transportation hub. And the open range is really alive and well, now it's just described as national forests and Bureau of Land Management land.

The proliferation of cattle spreads large and small led to the creation of stockmen's associations in the 1880s. Originally started to coordinate roundups and institute a rational branding system, the associations quickly became powerful political forces. And they were instrumental in promoting the idea that cattle had a "right" to graze public land. On the Western Slope, the cattlemen fought not only the railroads and legislature, but the sheepmen. The name "Night Riders" gives you a pretty good clue about the cowboys' methods when sheepmen were the target.

The sheepmen's and cattlemen's associations, which today display only minor undercurrents of antagonism against each other, are still kicking and still have the ear of more than one local, state, and national legislator. You can hear them behind the podium, in Meeker, Denver, or Washington, D.C., recalling the heritage of the open range before launching into a biting chant about the vital importance of protecting cattle and sheep grazing rights on that huge public trough called federal land.

most from their land by using information from the school's farmer/scientists about better irrigation and dryland farming techniques, crop rotations, profitable cash crops like sugar beets, and effective mechanization. Today, the school's extension agents still dispense the latest agricultural information and advice to farmers and ranchers throughout the state.

Longmont and Greeley were the exceptions to the rule when it came to colonies. Most colonization efforts were launched by companies in New York and Chicago that pulled cash out of innocents' pockets and sent them to barren stretches of Colorado. Several ethnic varieties of colonies were tried, and failed. The Mormons (in the San Luis Valley), the German Colonization Society (Colfax), and a Jewish settlement (Cotopaxi) all met the same fate—they failed as utopias but lived on as towns.

Sterling, which straddles Interstate 76 in the middle of the northeastern plains, was founded in 1873–74, but quickly dumped idealism and embraced pragmatism. The townsfolk offered to move lock, stock, and barrel, and toss in 80 acres of free land, if the Union Pacific Railroad would locate a division point for its line three miles (five km) northeast of the original town. The railroad accepted and the whole town picked up and moved to the new location.

Intensive tillage contributed to dust storms, such as this one outside of Lamar in 1937 during the Great Depression. (Colorado Historical Society)

Some aspects of farm life never change.

Ironically, while the utopionists were busy trying to use "civilization" to create a utopia, they overlooked the type of utopia Mother Nature laid at their feet: the prairie itself. Today, a bit of that natural utopia is preserved in the **Pawnee National Grassland,** located north of Colorado 14, which links Fort Collins and Sterling. No plows slashed through the buffalo grass and other native prairie plants. Creeks still run free, and during the four seasons the wind, rain, snow, and sunshine still play on the natural prairie much as they did when the wagonloads of wide-eyed optimists rolled through on their way to their version of utopia.

By the turn of the century the colony craze had cooled. Towns had been established, the good land claimed, the bad abandoned, and favorable court rulings had secured a steady supply of irrigation water. By 1907, six million acres of Colorado farmland had been irrigated, most of it on the eastern plains.

In the decades that followed, all that was left for those who found themselves in the small towns dotting the eastern plains was the choice between staying and putting down roots and making this land theirs and their children's, or bolting from the serenity and set ways of the eastern plains for bigger, more exciting environs.

■ IT'S THE REAL AMERICA: SMALL TOWNS OF THE EASTERN PLAINS

In between the plain's main arteries—the interstate highways and the Arkansas River—are small farm towns sheltering anywhere from a couple dozen to 10,000 residents and accessible only by those straight-as-a-string blue-line highways. They are intriguing, sometimes mysterious, usually misunderstood. Often they operate under a different set of rules than their urban counterparts, and they can, among those who know them well, quickly generate deep, almost mystical affection or a cold sneer of contempt.

Along the interstate highways are some plains towns urging motorists to pull off for some gas, a meal, and maybe a night of rest. But most of the plains towns are untainted by tourism. Conversely, plains towns also remain free of tourism's benefits—cultural events, upscale eateries (cuisine, not food), art galleries, and international fame.

The eastern plains towns have experienced a natural, slow evolution and are peopled by those who have found something special, something intriguing in the way of life sustained in an intimate community. The people who choose to live in small towns infuse them with civic parallels of their own personalities.

The common characteristics of most small towns are cited by fans and foes alike as either the basis for a passion for such a way of life, or dread of the same.

■ WHERE NEIGHBORS STILL CARE

Fans celebrate the small town as a final remnant of "real America," an America where neighbors still care about neighbors and the good of the community, a community where "values" are more than stock market quotes. They are places where:

- If you need to go to the bank you can park in the middle of the street, run inside, do your business, trot back to your car and wave at the cop driving by, who just waves back and shakes his head a little.

- Where you usually lock your doors at night, but if you wake up at midnight and realize you forgot, you don't sit upright in bed and break out in a cold sweat.

- Where the blaring of the fire siren to call out the volunteer fire department sends people racing out of the Elks Club meeting. Or the Rotary Club. Or the chamber of commerce.

- Where you don't have to go to town council meetings because you already stopped the mayor on the street and gave him an earful.
- Where, without the help of the local newspaper, you know what's happened, what should have happened, and what probably will happen, because that's what always happens.
- Where on most summer weekdays the cheering of the spectators at the slow-pitch softball game drowns out the traffic noise on the main drag.
- Where half the population makes the trek, convoy style, to root for the high school team at state championships.
- Where you shop downtown, even if it costs a little more than the big city mall, because, well, just because it's your downtown.
- Where it takes 15 minutes to work your way through the coffee shop because you have to say "hi" to everyone and generally get caught up.
- Where it's easy to appreciate and benefit from a family's roots because they are generations deep.

■ WHERE LIFE'S *TOO* SLOW

On the other hand, to the foes of small towns, life seems stifled—a stodgy anachronism. They see them as mere backwaters, as holding tanks for those who didn't have the talent or gumption to swim in a bigger pond. For these people small towns are places where:

- The police decide on the spot who should spend the night in jail, who should go home and sleep it off, and when a bus ticket to Denver solves a transient problem.
- Where playing golf with the town judge or poker with the police chief can keep little "indiscretions" under wraps and keep the scales of justice tipping the right way, toward the "right" people.
- Where the same group, usually of men, seems to always get elected to town council. And they include the president of the Elks. And the Rotary. And the chamber of commerce.
- Where there is nothing else to do on a weekday summer night but play slow-pitch softball or cruise the main drag.

- Where everyone that counts plays high school sports and 30 points in a basketball game just might improve a student's comprehension of the Civil War.

- Where shopping means filling out catalog order forms and waiting for the UPS truck.

- Where the coffee shop crew knows all about that intimate nightcap you enjoyed with your new flame. And the sight of a local's car in the parking lot at the Dew Drop Inn informs everyone in town whose spouse is away on business or visiting relatives.

- Where if you don't have grandparents buried in the town cemetery, you're going to be a newcomer for quite a while.

So which is it? Shangri-la or Living Hell? Here's one hint: small town life must be pretty appealing or there would be more ghost towns on Colorado's eastern plains than in its mineral-rich mountains, which are full of them.

Speaking of life in the slow lane, try a stagecoach ride.

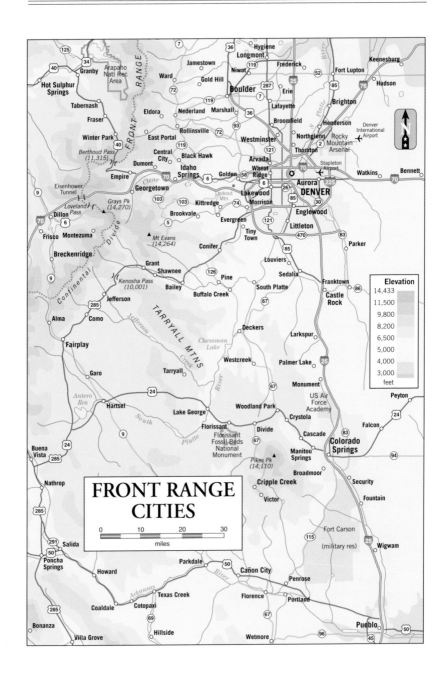

FRONT RANGE
CITIES

0   10   20   30
miles

FRONT RANGE CITIES
DENVER, BOULDER, COLORADO SPRINGS, PUEBLO

WHEN PRESIDENT DWIGHT D. EISENHOWER FLEW INTO DENVER in the mid-1950s on his way to do a little fishing, the media followed. Their stories and photos revealed a surprise to the nation: the cities along Colorado's Front Range had evolved from a string of rough frontier towns into unique, modern cities primed to lead the West into the future. That attention also alerted the nation to the special combination of attitude and natural allure of Front Range cities that would eventually be dubbed "quality of life."

■ URBAN HISTORY

Until World War II, Colorado's Front Range cities—Denver, Boulder, Colorado Springs, and Pueblo—weren't much to brag about. Towns at the base of the Rockies had existed in part to supply mines, miners, and prospectors. Later they supported smelting, minting, or other forms of finagling gold and silver into "useful financial instruments" or hornswaggling investors into thinking a piece of paper with a mine's name on it would make them rich. Which was not bad work, if you could find it.

Despite the best efforts of civic boosters and the newly minted mining tycoons, the urban scene resembled little more than the squalid, ramshackle slums of older, more established eastern cities. The gold and silver barons tried to dress up the drab little cities with stately brick mansions and plush hotels, but those bits of Victorian refinement swam against the tide in a sea of mud streets and slap-dash building. During most of the nineteenth century, Colorado's "cities" seemed to be frontier outposts at best and muck holes at worst, full of hayseeds, bums, fools called prospectors, and much of the nation's undesirable or immoral population. By the early twentieth century, urban Colorado, if more respectable, was still a backwater.

■ MOVING INTO THE MODERN ERA

Mining made **Denver** the state's transportation and financial center, so it remained a city to be reckoned with. "Quality of life" was probably an alien term to Robert W. Speer, but as mayor of Denver in 1904, he knew it was lacking. First he tackled small things, like cleaning up Cherry Creek, building sewers and storm drains, and actually laying out streets and lining them with trees. Bigger items were next, like dotting the town with parks and starting a Greek-style Civic Center Auditorium. Thus a little quality was added to life in Denver.

Then came "Cow Town" days, a tag Denver sought during the 1880s, was glad to have during the Depression, and became well deserved after the Monfort family, in 1930, came up with a new way to raise and fatten cattle. Instead of letting cows roam around eating whatever range grass was handy, the Monfort clan penned them up and stuffed them with hay, corn, and grain. Thus was born the modern cattle feedlot wherein a skinny calf could become a fattened calf in no time. And in no time all those cattle were being shipped through the cow town of Denver.

Denver's railroad yards expanded into a spaghetti-like swirling of tracks and spurs to accommodate huge stockyards. Although Denver never matched Chicago's

Stockyards fueled the growth of the city after the mining boom faded.
(opposite) Downtown Denver has always aspired to great heights.

DENVER IN 1865

*I*n that period Denver was appropriately called the "City of the Plains." Situated sixteen miles from the base of the nearest Rocky Mountain peak, and six hundred and fifty miles from Atchison, Kansas, the nearest town to the east, . . . its population numbered about five thousand souls. Here was to be found the illiterate man—but a grade above coyote—lawbreakers of every kind and from every land, to men of culture and refinement.

Here it stood, a typical mining town, a monument to the indomitable energy of man in his efforts to settle that barren and almost endless plain and open to the world the Rocky's unlimited hidden gold. Here were brick structures modern for that day, the brick being made from the soil of the territory; a United States mint, a church, a school house, large warehouses, stores, and the home of the *Rocky Mountain Daily News,* which kept one partially in touch with happenings in the faraway states. Isolated from the outside world, it was an ideal place of refuge for those anxious to escape the outraged law. Knights of the green cloth held full sway. Men in every walk of life gambled. A dead man for breakfast was not an uncommon heading for the menu card, the old tree on the west bank of Cherry Creek furnishing the man. Society was just a little exclusive and to gain admission the pass was, "Where are you from?" and in some cases, "Your name in the east?"

Desperadoes made one attempt to lay the city in ashes and certainly would have accomplished their purpose had it not been for the timely action of the Vigilance Committee in hanging the ring-leaders. When the guilt of a suspect for any crime was in doubt, he was presented with a horse or mule and ordered to leave between sun and sun and never return.

—Charles E. Young
Dangers of the Trail in 1865

"brawny shoulders" when it came to stockyards, it wasn't exactly a 98-pound weakling either. The city welcomed the jobs, although the accompanying, er, well, aroma, wasn't listed in chamber of commerce brochures.

By the 1970s, Denver had decided to go upscale, and it's been trying to live down its cow town image ever since.

The college town of **Boulder** (University of Colorado) just kind of chugged along, thanks to an ability to lure Eastern "adventurers" wanting a taste of the West along with a taste of Plato and beer.

Colorado Springs, thanks to General William Palmer and Pikes Peak, *was* one huge chamber of commerce brochure. A true tourist city, it relied on a flow of visitors, rather than natural resources, for its livelihood.

Down south a bit farther, **Pueblo** took almost everything in stride because it was a steel town whose furnaces stayed hot, thanks to Colorado Fuel and Iron (CF&I) and the coal and coke fields near Trinidad. As the first fully integrated steel mill in the West, the Pueblo works had a jump on the competition, a jump that kept it ahead of the crowd for almost 70 years and kept Pueblo a stable, blue-collar city.

■ THE MILITARY ZEROS IN

Colorado had its share of military installations before World War II—Denver's Fitzsimmons Army Hospital and the Lowry Air Base—but when the bullets started flying, so did Colorado's economy. Colorado Fuel & Iron Company steel mills and coal mines started cranking. The Denver Arms Plant shot out conventional bullets in huge numbers, and the Rocky Mountain Arsenal created a new type of killer—chemical weapons and bombs.

Military bases cropped up everywhere or were dramatically expanded all along the Front Range. Buckley Field, Peterson Air Field, La Junta Army Air Field, Pueblo Army Air Base, and Camp Hale all joined the king of the military hill, Camp Carson—covering 60,000 acres between Denver and Colorado Springs—which trained over 150,000 men before the war ended. Another type of "installation" also called Colorado home, but is not mentioned today with much pride. Near Granada on the eastern plains, thousands of Japanese Americans were interned in a relocation camp for the duration of the war.

Cheek and jowl with the military men were the arms makers, led by Martin Marietta Aerospace, which started building intercontinental ballistic missile systems in Denver in 1956. The military-industrial connection continued apace as the Korean and Vietnam wars kept the bullets flying and paychecks coming into the 1970s. The 1980s promised more. President Ronald Reagan pumped cash into the military machine and the "Star Wars" program was to be launched at the Air Force Space Operations Center at Colorado Springs, which opened in 1983.

(top) Making Titan missiles the Martin Marietta way.
(above) The "Star Wars" control center at Martin Marietta.

Like many previous Colorado booms, the brakes may be applied to the Front Range's military gravy train, and once again, Coloradoans' hands aren't on the controls. And once again, there will be environmental skid marks, the largest left by the Rocky Flats Plant. Years of toxic pollution from producing chemical weapons and nuclear weapons triggers have made the plant a toxic time bomb. (It *is* slated for cleanup, however.)

As the 1990s got underway, the U.S. felt less threatened. The Cold War was won, lost, or called a draw, and chunks of the Berlin Wall became curiosities. Cutbacks at several Army bases and private weapons plants seemed imminent. Then the Persian Gulf War armed Congress, the Pentagon, and the military-industrial complex with a slew of new options, debates, and arguments ultimately relevant to Colorado's military connection.

PEACETIME DUTY

THE B-52, LONG A SYMBOL OF THE FREE WORLD'S STRATEGIC BOMBARDMENT STRENGTH, IS CURRENTLY SERVING ON ALERT STATUS AT STRATEGIC AIR COMMAND BASES IN THE CONTINENTAL UNITED STATES AND GUAM. IN ADDITION TO ITS NUCLEAR ALERT POSTURE, THE B-52 IS ALSO USED IN A CONVENTIONAL CONTINGENCY ROLE PERFORMING SUCH MISSIONS AS AERIAL MINE-LAYING, SEA SURVEILLANCE, AND SURFACE SHIP AIR INTERDICTION.

WARTIME SERVICE

FROM JUNE 1965 TO AUGUST 1973, B-52s OPERATING FROM KADENA AIR BASE, OKINAWA; ANDERSEN AIR FORCE BASE, GUAM; AND UTAPAO ROYAL THAI NAVY AIRFIELD, THAILAND; FLEW OVER 126,000 COMBAT MISSIONS IN SOUTHEAST ASIA. THE EXTENSIVE B-52 BOMBING RAIDS AGAINST TARGETS IN NORTH VIETNAM IN DECEMBER 1972 KNOWN AS "LINEBACKER II" BROUGHT THE NORTH VIETNAMESE TO MEANINGFUL DISCUSSIONS IN PARIS THAT LED TO THE RELEASE OF THE AMERICAN POWs IN FEBRUARY 1973.

The U.S. Air Force Academy trains fighters for duel duties.

■ DENVER

■ BOOMS AND BUSTS

When the nation was suffering through the assorted energy crises of the 1970s and early 1980s, Denver was delighted. Situated in the heart of a region overflowing with coal, natural gas, oil, and uranium, not to mention the nation's biggest pile of oil shale, Denver saw itself in the hub of a monster boom. It was almost as good as the gold and silver days.

Skyscrapers popped up so quickly in downtown Denver it was suggested the state bird should be the elevated building crane instead of the lark bunting. Most major energy companies set up regional offices, uncounted independent and smaller oil, gas, and energy companies also flocked in, and Denver became a high-flying energy boom town. Oil prices kept rising as fast as Denver's skyscrapers, bulldozers kept digging away at oil shale, drilling rigs kept popping up and drilling down, and Denver kept soaring.

The energy bust, of course, eventually came, but when Denver performed a slow swan dive into it, Denverites didn't gnash their teeth, whimper, whine, and do real swan dives off half-finished skyscrapers. Instead, they took things into their own slightly burned hands and started to prepare for the twenty-first century.

Besides, the whole world hadn't collapsed. Denver still had more federal workers than any city but Washington D.C., and the half-empty skyscrapers created a impressive skyline dramatizing the already dramatic backdrop of the Rocky Mountains. The military-industrial connection was still there, as were the regional transportation, communication, medical, supply, and financial firms. Then, the city undertook two massive civic projects: a new downtown convention center to go with its revitalized downtown, and a huge new international airport.

■ EXPLORING HISTORIC DENVER

Denver is a city of brick homes, tree-lined streets, and a settled, comfortable feel. This is a city where roots have taken hold. But, before you set out to explore Denver, get a good street map, especially of downtown, or you'll think you're in some mega-scale maze of one-way streets, three-way intersections, triangular buildings, and general confusion. The city was laid out at the confluence of the South Platte River and Cherry Creek, making the concept "grid system" a joke.

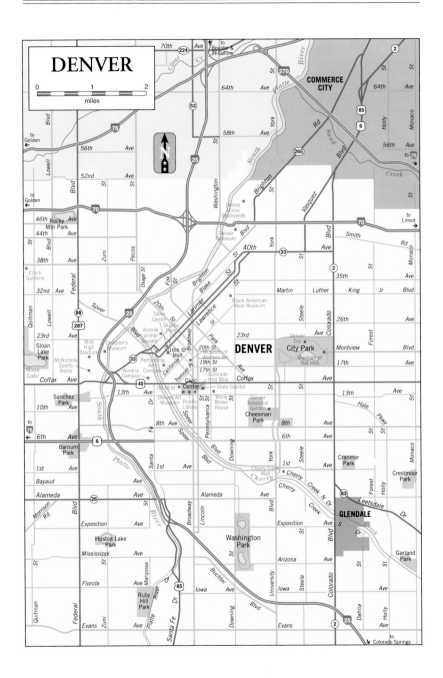

DENVER

0   1   2
miles

If driving into downtown, a good option is to get as close as you can and walk around instead of driving around and around and around. A better option is taking the free shuttle bus, which drops you off a block away from either historic Denver or modern Denver.

Historic Denver is wrapped up nicely in an easy stroll around the **Civic Center** area (at the intersection of Broadway and Colfax avenues, which both have off-ramps on Interstates 70 and 25). The first thing to catch your eye at the corner of Broadway and Colfax is the gold-domed **State Capitol Building**, built in 1894. It features opulent appointments that would make a silver baron blush, and the world's entire supply of rose onyx in the interior. Free tours are offered on weekdays, and if you can make it up a 93-step staircase you'll be treated to a stunning view of the Rocky Mountains and the rest of Denver.

Two square blocks of parkland, an ad hoc compilation of gardens, Western sculptures of bucking broncs, fountains, and Mayor Speer's Greek Revival outdoor theater separate the Capitol from the **Denver City and County Building.** This building looks a little Greek, too, with its column-filled facade and guard columns around each wing.

The **United States Mint** is just a block farther west at West Colfax and Cherokee. This Italian Renaissance-style monolith and its four-and-a-half foot thick walls was built in 1904 and has become an extremely popular tourist attraction. Weekday tours are free, but not samples of its wares, which include the nation's second largest stash of gold bullion. One theory for the mint's popularity is that it's reassuring to see the federal government is at least trying to make some cold, hard cash, in the form of six billion coins a year, even while it is spending money faster than the mint can make it. "Hey, at least we're trying to keep up," the folks at the mint must say. Loop back around the park toward the Capitol, and you run into museum row, with four attractions within three blocks.

Denver Art Museum, (100 W. 14th St.) jars the historical perspective, and even most people's artistic perspective. Ten stories high, it looks like the architect let a kindergarten class cut various size windows anywhere and everywhere into the building's 28 sides. (The windows were placed as they are to reveal "living art," looking from the inside out.) It's eye catching, but is it art? Inside are what many consider to be the world's finest examples of Native American art.

Byers-Evans House will ease modernist malaise. Built in 1883 for William Byers, founder of the *Rocky Mountain News,* and then occupied by John Evans, the

Denver's early architecture: authentic Mission style and imported Greek.

state's second governor, the home gives a glimpse of the good life lived in post-World War I Colorado (13th and Bannock).

Denver Public Library, at 1357 Broadway, can hand you the entire West. The mere thought of the library's renowned and irreplaceable Western History collection sends historians of the West into Pavlovian pantings. Stored in the archives are priceless source documents on Western history ranging from diaries and letters to photos, paintings, and sketches. Official government documents such as treaties and state constitutions and legal briefs are on hand.

The Colorado History Museum (13th and Broadway) provides a visual look at the state's progress using a wide variety of displays and attractions. Some of the finest examples of Anasazi pottery available are on display, along with detailed dioramas depicting frontier forts, buffalo hunts, and mining techniques. On a larger scale are the full-scale pieces of mining equipment, a covered wagon, a sod house, and a huge model of Denver as it was in 1860 before it was razed by fire. A 150-year time-line and research library let you trace the state's history and dig as deeply as you want into the people, places, and events that shaped Colorado.

The **Museum of Western Art,** at 1727 Tremont Place, has a fine collection of Western art, including more than 125 paintings and bronze sculptures tracing the development of the Western frontier from the Fur Trapper Era through World War II. The collection is housed in the historic "Navarre" building, once a bordello and gambling hall to which silver barons and cattle kings traveled surreptitiously through a sub-floor tunnel from the Brown Palace Hotel across the street.

The Navarre Building houses an inspiring collection of Western art. (Courtesy Museum of Western Art)

"On the Platte River near Denver" by Worthington Whittredge, 1865, is just one of the many fine paintings on display at the Museum of Western Art.

■ UNSINKABLE MOLLY BROWN

Two blocks behind the state capitol, Pennsylvania Street runs atop just the slightest of hills, and it was here that the financiers and miners who struck it rich in Colorado's gold and silver rush came to build mansions (and to literally put themselves above the muddled and muddy mass of Denver society). Of the score of remaining elegant nineteenth-century homes that line the avenue, one stands apart, not only because of the two sculpted lions guarding its opulence, but because of who happened to call it home: the Unsinkable Molly Brown.

A Missouri native, Molly Tobin hit Leadville in the early 1880s. It took a few years, but in 1886 she finally snagged her man: James J. Brown, superintendent of the Little Johnny Mine. Brown's mere one-eighth share of the mine's wealth made him a millionaire and allowed the couple to move to lavish digs, complete with sculpted lions at the entrance, in Denver's most stylish neighborhood. Molly decided to conquer Denver's close-knit upper crust, the so-called "sacred 36," only to be constantly rebuked. Denver's prominent families thought she was not merely a social climber, but a social leaper, if not a broad jumper, and took great delight in snubbing her.

That's why midnight, April 14, 1912, was lucky for Molly. That's when the *Titanic* sunk and she boarded lifeboat number six. Rallying the scared survivors, she scared the hell out of the helmsman, took a turn at the oars, shared her clothing with those colder than herself, and became the heroine of the *Titanic* tragedy, or so said the newspapers of the day.

At any rate, she was generally credited with extraordinary effort and general gutsiness throughout the whole affair. After that, the doors of Denver society grudgingly swung open for the now "Unsinkable" Molly Brown, and she reached the high point of her life.

Things got messy after that. Jim Brown died in 1922, leaving no will, just legal entanglements. Her riches might have been slowly shrinking, but her bravado never did. She kept swaggering through exclusive hotels in Palm Beach, New York, and Europe in lavish, if not exactly stylish, clothes.

She still remembered Leadville, though, by offering to supply the town's children with mittens and presents during the Depression. She didn't have enough money for the gifts, but her family members quietly fulfilled the promise.

The Unsinkable Molly Brown died in 1932, her splashy wardrobe in tatters, bills for back-rent and other legal problems still dogging her, but not depressing her truly unsinkable determination to never give up the grand life she had, for the most part, created for herself.

"The Unsinkable Molly Brown" afloat in Victorian finery. (Colorado Historical Society)

■ EXPLORING MODERN DENVER

Denver created something for itself in the **Sixteenth Street Mall,** a mile-long pedestrian-thronged, bustling business-lined bit of urban renewal. Shuttle buses ferry visitors the length of the street, which mixes a little old with a little new amid its ambiance.

Comfortably nestled in amongst the imposing glass and steel skyscrapers of downtown Denver is the historic **Brown Palace Hotel,** on 17th and Tremont at the top of the mall. This now-stubby sandstone triangle of a building is a living reminder of gold and silver's glory days, complete with upright, uniformed bellmen, Victorian art deco delights, and a nine-story atrium topped with Tiffany stained glass that was the talk of its day when it was built in 1892. The hotel hasn't lost its sheen a century later.

The D&F **Tower** is another bit of history poking its head into the skyline. At a whopping 325 feet (96 m), it was the tallest building west of the Mississippi in 1910, and is now the centerpiece of **Skyline Park,** beyond which mega-modern is spoken at the **Tabor Center.** Three levels of glass, chrome, towering skylights, a 550-foot-long (168-m) greenhouse, and every other modern architectural trick set the scene for the center's 70 shops and restaurants.

Larimer Square (1400 block of Larimer) mixes the best of both worlds. Larimer is Denver's oldest street, and for a while in the 1960s it looked its age. Now its Victorian buildings have been restored, and visitors can stroll past, through, and into an eclectic sprinkling of establishments from coffee houses and outdoor cafés to unique shops and bistros. Don't miss the **Tattered Cover Bookstore,** one of America's biggest and best retail book outlets—1st Avenue opposite the Cherry Creek Mall.

■ DENVER DIVERSIONS AND DAY TRIPS

Denver is not just a downtown; its many diversions can keep you busy for days. **City Park,** on Colorado Boulevard just north of Speer Blvd., contains enough to keep kids and adults entertained for a day. **The Denver Zoo,** one of the nation's top ten, has innovative natural habitats and fine new exhibits. **The Denver Museum of Natural History,** also in the park, features good old Colorado dinosaurs and over 90 other dioramas displaying North America's plants and animals. The museum also hosts national traveling historic exhibitions, as well as a fine mineral display, including "Tom's Baby," Colorado's largest gold nuggets. **The** IMAX **Theater,** with its four-and-a-half by six-and-a-half-story screen brings everything into

sharp focus, as does the **Charles C. Gates Planetarium,** which features the solar system in multimedia splendor and laser shows that are, shall we say, hot.

Elitch Gardens and **Lakeside Amusement Park** need no introduction to roller-coaster fanatics. Both parks have the real thing: wooden roller coasters that rattle and groan as much as the riders. They're the vomit comets of choice among aficionados of the sport. Both parks offer the usual amusement park fare for those a bit more faint at heart.

Perhaps the most popular day-trip tour from Denver involves the 12-mile (19-km) drive to Golden on US 6. The tour people foam at the mouth to take trips to the **Adolf Coors Brewing Company** in Golden, the world's largest single beer brewing facility. If you're of age, you can sample the company's products, to a point, of course.

Tiny Town is just that, a tiny little town composed of over 50 hand-crafted miniature buildings and featuring a steam-powered locomotive which hauls tiny passengers around the place. The town is scrunched into scenic Turkey Creek Canyon, which makes the drive worth it even if you can't fit into the train. In Denver, take US 285 (Hampden Avenue) west and out of town for about 10 miles (16 km) and turn left at the Tiny Town sign onto South Turkey Creek Road and look for little things to appear.

Denver boasts some some imaginative "street art" as well as a wealth of "fine art" in its many museums.

(opposite) The ornate atrium inside the historic Brown Palace Hotel.

PROFESSIONAL SPORTS

When describing fans of Denver's professional sports teams, the word "rabid" is usually where most people start before proceeding to detail, if possible, the further depraved depths of passion said fans display. Part of the reason for the fans' unabashed, unquestioned love affair with their pro sports teams is that pro sports came to Denver late and, in the case of football and basketball, through the back door. It wasn't until the 1960s that the football Broncos arrived, originally as part of the American Football League, and the basketball Nuggets came to life with the American Basketball Association. Only after the two renegade leagues merged with their more well established counterparts, the NFL and the NBA, did the city earn an aura of respect in the nation's sporting eyes. As for baseball, Denver endured decades of AAA minor league baseball before the Colorado Rockies were born in 1993 as a National League expansion team. With such a short sports history, every fan is an expert, every game monumental, and every move by every team becomes instant fodder for Monday morning quarterbacks, or point guards, or left fielders.

You can contact Denver's big league teams for information about schedules, seating availability (scalping tickets is illegal and the Broncos always and the Nuggets generally sell out their games, so good luck) and special discount packages at the following phone numbers and addresses:

Denver Broncos
(303) 433-7466 for tickets
Denver Broncos Ticket Office, 1900 Eliot Street, Denver, CO 80204

Colorado Rockies
(303) ROCKIES for tickets
Colorado Rockies Baseball Club, P.O. Box 120, Denver, CO 80210-0120

Denver Nuggets
(303) 893-DUNK for tickets
Nuggets Ticket Office, 1635 Clay Street, Denver, CO 80204

Both the Broncos and the Rockies play at Mile High Stadium at 1805 Bryant Street in Denver. The Nuggets play at McNichols Arena, 1635 Clay Street. Both Mile High and McNichols are in the same general area, at the intersection of Colfax Avenue (I-70 Business Loop) and Federal Boulevard (Highway 287).

Real people hang out.

Buffalo Bill's Grave and Museum is just 20 miles (32 km) west of Denver on Interstate 70 on Lookout Mountain. Buffalo Bill, the West's best known frontiersman and showman, didn't really want to be buried there, as the folks remind anyone who asks in Cody, Wyoming, and North Platte, Nebraska, where Bill had ranches and lived. But he died at a relative's house in Denver, and well, civic pride and a little quick talking landed Bill atop the hill. The museum contains posters, guns, outfits, and other remnants from Cody's Wild West Show, along with exhibits on frontier life and the Pony Express, which had a station in Julesburg on the eastern plains.

Buffalo Herd Overlook, also on Lookout Mountain, gives you a chance to observe, take photos of, or generally marvel at the beasts which once roamed the Great Plains by the millions. The city of Denver maintains the park in a natural setting.

Mount Evans and **Echo Lake** are what the Rocky Mountains are all about, and they are located just 40 miles (64 km) west of Denver on Colorado 103 off Interstate 70. Once the road is cleared of snow around the end of May, you can drive right to the top of this 14,260-foot (4,335-km) peak and breathe the rarified air usually reserved for those with large lungs and climbing gear. At the base of the mountain, Echo Lake mountain park features picnic spots, fishing, and views of the lofty, generally snowcapped surrounding peaks.

Some of the West's most famous **gold mining towns** are within an hour's drive of Denver. Central City, Breckenridge, Georgetown, and Silver Plume, to name just a few, were once boomtowns, and have recently been reborn with their golden history intact. See the following chapter, "ROCKY MOUNTAINS," for more about them.

■ BOULDER

When prospectors hit a legitimate mother lode on Gold Hill, just west of town, Boulder found itself leading the state into the 1860s' gold boom. A steadier source of employment, however, quickly became the center of Boulder—Colorado University—which has since kept the city on an even keel. When the computer age dawned, Boulder became home to a fast growing, high-tech explosion that has made it one of the nation's top computer and high-tech startup zones.

(previous pages) Wildlife dioramas at the Denver Museum of Natural History are certain to both please and educate the kids.

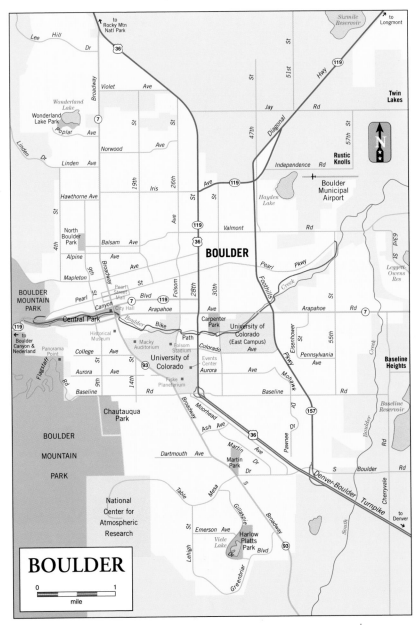

BOULDER

0   1
mile

(following pages) The Flat Iron Mountains rise abruptly above the city of Boulder. Howling chinook winds of hurricane force occasionally blast out of the canyons and over the city.

Then there's the sports boom. Boulder became home to national and international stars such as runners Frank Shorter, Arturo Barrios, and Ingrid Kristiansen; cyclists Davis Phinney and Connie Carpenter; and triathletes Mark Allen, Mike Pig, and Scot Molina—just to get a list started.

Why is Boulder such hot training ground?

Well, the pleasant winters allow for year-round training (with a little spunk and the right gear, that is); the altitude (5,363 feet or 1,630 m) makes the air seem thicker almost anywhere else; and a large athletic community provides support, world-class training partners and, because stars are so commonplace, some anonymity.

Combine a beautiful setting, university eggheads, computer nerds, a horde of outdoor-loving athletes, and an environmentalist on every corner and you have quality-of-life becoming almost a religion in Boulder. A little touchy-feely for some, a bit far-out for others, seemingly extreme by some standards, but jealously guarded and paying off for Boulder, regardless.

Although Boulder is basking in its celebrated lifestyle and computerized boom, its eyes are open. New machines, enthusiastic speculation in startup companies, international competition, corporate shenanigans, general national economic health, and all the other factors that have busted more than one Colorado boom could take a bite out of byte-world too. But there will still be the university, the athletes, the quality-of-life lovers, the air, and the mountains.

■ EXPLORING BOULDER

Those who enter Boulder via US 36 are greeted by a big mall, but entrances to cities can be deceiving. Keep going. Hit Baseline, turn off at Broadway, and you're heading for the heart of Boulder.

The **University of Colorado**, with its solidly academic-looking brick buildings topped by red tile, and tree-lined walkways, is the first attraction. A second is the frenzy of college students trying to look cool while rushing to their next class. By comparison the lunch bunch at Colorado Springs' Air Force Academy looks a bit rigid. **The Hill** is a concentration of shops and cafés catering to the college crowd when they're feeling less frenetic. This is the place to relive your college days or bemoan the fate of the nation at the thought that what you're seeing is our "best and brightest."

Pearl Street Mall, farther down Broadway in the middle of downtown, is the king of the hill when it comes to people watching. This pedestrian mall is always alive and usually bizarre enough to bring a grin or an incredulous look from some. Entertainment runs from sidewalk jugglers and singers to painters to organized concerts and educational seminars. Food ranges from basic burgers to such foreign-sounding stuff that you don't dare ask about ingredients. This combination of Berkeley and Haight Street, plus a few Bermuda-short types from Des Moines thrown in to add some color, makes the mall a "don't miss."

A unique feature of Boulder is that it has brought the outside inside town. The **Boulder Creek Bike/Pedestrian Trail** winds through town from east to west and delivers a refreshing dose of the outside to all the urbanity. **Boulder Canyon** though, is what makes the eyes of climbers and hikers really light up. Just minutes west of town from either Pearl Street or Arapahoe Avenue, the canyon's rock walls and formations offer world-class rock climbing and dozens of hiking trails.

Those not wanting to sweat their way into the wilds can take a number of scenic drives through the foothills and hit high-mountain scenery on one end, history on the other. West of Boulder on Colorado 119 is **Nederland,** an old gold

Ya' gotta love Boulder's neon nightlife.

mining town starting to modernize while retaining small-town charms. Take Colorado 72 north and you will eventually end up at the resort town of Estes Park and **Rocky Mountain National Park**, or stay on 119 south and you'll find yourself in the revived gold rush towns of **Black Hawk** and **Central City**. (See "ROCKY MOUNTAINS" for more on these historic settlements.)

■ COLORADO SPRINGS

Colorado Springs has always been an exception to its Front Range brethren, because it was designed from the very beginning to attract tourists. Broad boulevards—neatly laid out to accommodate the carriages of the rich and stylish of the late 1800s—and the fine Broadmoor Hotel were all part of a plan to turn the town of Colorado Springs into a European-style vacation spa and resort.

Those efforts, proximity to Pikes Peak and the Garden of the Gods, as well as such visitor amenities as the first golf links west of the Mississippi, made Colorado Springs the Front Range's original tourist city.

Colorado Springs kept the tourists coming thanks to spirited promotion. Pikes Peak became the nation's most famous mountain, even though it isn't Colorado's highest or even its most dynamic-looking peak. Assuring the peak's fame was the second oldest car race in America: the **Pikes Peak Hillclimb**, organized in 1915. Only the Indianapolis 500 is older, but Indy lacks 156 hairpin turns up a gravel mountain road.

Colorado Springs took its quality of life to the bank for over a century, but it also realized it couldn't rest atop Pikes Peak twiddling its thumbs while waiting for more bankable deliveries. So it began courting the military, and in the post-World War II era, the military delivered. The military brass liked the view of Pikes Peak so much it virtually encircled the town with bases, airfields, and command posts. Colorado Springs scored the **North American Air Defense Command Center** (**NORAD**) in 1957. This little enterprise entailed digging a huge cave deep into Cheyenne Mountain from which to operate the nation's nuclear wars come hell or commie nukes. The Air Force Academy came to town in 1958 and those crafty Colorado Springers quickly repeated their Pikes Peak performance and turned the Academy and its unique chapel into one of the state's largest tourist attractions. A real double-dipper, in other words.

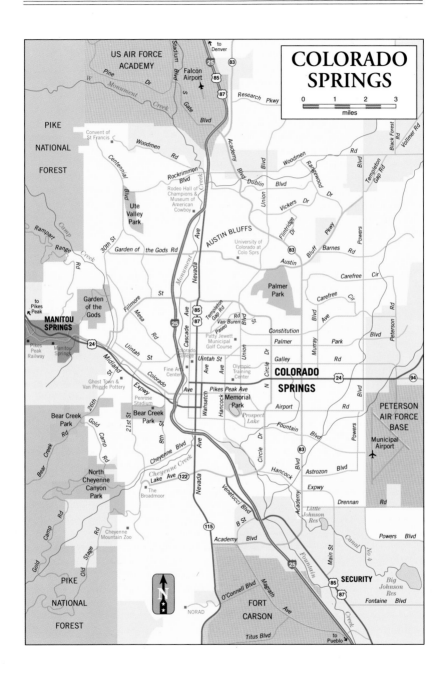

COLORADO
SPRINGS

0   1   2   3
miles

(top) Colorado is attracting high-tech industry such as this Honeywell chip manufacturing facility near Colorado Springs. (above) Air Force cadets drilling their honor code.

Double back-flips occupied the city as it worked to become the nation's Olympic city. The U.S. Olympic Committee, headquarters for the Olympic training centers, and 20 sports national governing bodies now call Colorado Springs home. With Colorado Springs' track record, it seems a safe bet that the city, thanks to its diverse economic base, will keep huffing and puffing along into the future.

■ EXPLORING COLORADO SPRINGS

U.S. Air Force Academy, located north of the city off Interstate 25, doesn't necessarily draw visitors who yearn to see young men and women with snappy uniforms and sabers, although at lunchtime that's the scene. The **Cadet Chapel,** with its 17 spires pointing 150 feet (45 m) skyward, is the place's truly inspiring sight.

Garden of the Gods wasn't named so for lack of inspiration; it's provided by naturally carved red-rock formations. You can either drive through for a quick look or take one of the many trails to get a feel for its mix of strange and fascinating rocks, earth, and plants. Just before you leave Colorado's version of Eden, there is an unmolested 1,350 acres of park containing windswept rock formations and sandstone towers with names like "Kissing Camels" and "Weeping Indian" jutting

"AMERICA THE BEAUTIFUL"

Katherine Lee Bates probably didn't give much thought to, or receive much inspiration from, the miles of prairie she traveled through on her way to Colorado in the summer of 1893. She was not writing a guidebook and she probably had no burning interest in the latest grain-producing techniques of the day.

Instead, she was a well-respected professor of English Literature at Wellesley College, in Wellesley, Massachusetts, who was making the time-consuming, arduous, cross-country journey to spend a summer as a visiting professor at Colorado College, located in Colorado Springs.

Like most visitors to Colorado Springs, she was urged to make a trip to the top of the legendary Pikes Peak. The trip was not exactly a wilderness adventure or a physical challenge since a cog railway and carriage road had been ferrying sightseers to the summit for the past three years. Bates succumbed to the urgings and found herself atop the most famous mountain in Colorado.

From that perch she could see the miles of planted prairie stretching eastward. She looked into the distance in every direction across the top of the Rockies and saw nothing but beautiful skies. And then there were the dark, brooding Rocky Mountains themselves, towering to the north, south, and west.

Poetic inspiration did not hit, it slam-dunked this matronly English teacher from back East. Her poetic mind was sent reeling by the combination of Colorado's Rocky Mountains jutting almost straight up from the flat eastern plains to touch the sky with their ragged peaks. This unique combination, this stunning juxtaposition, seemed to sum up not only the West, but the entire nation.

She eventually found the right words to express the feelings that swept through her on top of Pikes Peak that day:

> *Oh beautiful for spacious skies,*
> *For amber waves of grain:*
> *For purple mountain majesties*
> *Above the fruited plain—*
> *America, America, God shed his grace on thee,*
> *And crown thy good with brotherhood*
> *From sea to shining sea . . .*

Surprisingly, the poem "America the Beautiful" did not appear in print until 1911, when it was the featured poem in one of Bates' many books of poetry. By then she had published ten other books of poetry, and would eventually pen a total of 15 volumes before dying in 1929 at the age of 70.

However, as soon as "America the Beautiful" was released, it was set to music. It became Bates' most enduring and inspirational work, and many consider it this nation's real national anthem.

Garden of the Gods is Colorado Springs' most popular attraction.

Fanatic Air Force Falcon football fans jam Falcon Field.

from the flat ground. You can either drive through for a quick look or take one of many trails to get a feel for this geological oddity.

U.S. Olympic Center, near the heart of downtown, is where about 350 inspired athletes sweat out gold medal dreams. The 37-acre complex hosts over 500 programs, including training camps, seminars, clinics, and anything else loosely tied to our nation's Olympic effort.

NORAD's Cheyenne Mountain complex west of the city and its huge cave blocked by 25-foot-thick (eight-m) doors are reassuring, but not as inspiring as a chapel or weight lifter unless you like the feel of having foreign military target men put a red X on your town.

Broadmoor Hotel, still Colorado Springs' centerpiece, occupies about 3,000 acres between Cheyenne Mountain on the west, the city to the north, and Interstate 25 and Fort Carson on the east. The original hotel has been augmented by every conceivable type of visitor service and attraction to become a formidable resort complex complete with everything from a ski hill to three golf courses. The place has garnered more resort review stars than all the area's military brass com-

A wall fresco in Manitou Springs depicts an Indian weaver.

bined. (Also see Broadmoor Hotel under "Accommodations" in "PRACTICAL IN-FORMATION.")

Pikes Peak Highway and **Manitou Springs** rest west of town on US 24. Manitou Springs actually has a spring from which bubbly water is bottled, and it is the hub of all the action up Pikes Peak, from the road races, marathons, a cog railroad, and plain old drive to the peak in the family car. Manitou also boasts of some **cliff dwellings** built by the locals, but at best the effort just whets your appetite for the real items in Mesa Verde National Park. **Florissant Fossil Beds National Park,** on the other hand, is the real thing. Real fossils in real fossil beds on a 6,000-acre park off US 24.

Before Perrier, there was Manitou soda.

■ PUEBLO: A STEEL CITY

The folks in Pueblo, Colorado's "Steel City," have had a chance to prove that they can be pretty steely-eyed in the face of adversity.

Located south of Colorado Springs along Interstate-25, and north of the prolific coal fields around Trinidad, CF&I's steel plants were stoking Pueblo's

PIKE DIDN'T HAVE A PEAK EXPERIENCE

All the fame, notoriety, and mountain-naming generated by a little hike through Colorado by a man named **Lt. Zebulon Pike** is a little hard to understand if you just look at the bare outlines of his famous expedition of 1806.

After successfully crossing the Great Plains and meeting with various Plains Indian tribes, Pike and his crew couldn't seem to get much right once they got inside the borders of present-day Colorado.

When they first sighted the Rocky Mountains they raised a huzza for the *Mexican Mountains*. They camped near present-day **Pueblo** and peered up at the huge peak that had caught their eye from the prairie. They tried to climb it. Sorry, wrong mountain. They realized the peak they were seeking was even farther away, and probably couldn't be climbed by anyone. Wrong again.

The party moved west and discovered the **Royal Gorge,** which made Pike think he was near the headwaters of the Arkansas River, which he thought would lead him to the Red River, his ultimate goal. Then he blew it. He headed north, explored South Park, didn't find the Red River, but did find quite a red blush on his face when he came back through the gorge to where he had started.

Now we're talking dead of winter. The party kept going south, somehow crossed the Sangre de Cristo mountains, and landed in the **San Luis Valley** on the west side of the Rio Grande, placing them in Spanish territory.

But they thought they were on American soil, so, near the present-day town of **Sanford,** they built the first fort in Colorado, actually a fairly impressive stockade, and flew the stars and stripes. **Pike's Stockade** (which has been restored) and his flag, however, didn't impress the Spanish who, in February 1807, not so politely invited him to finish wintering in Santa Fe. Pike might have missed his mountain count, but he could count muskets and politely accepted. Convinced that Pike and his men were spies, the province's governor sent the travelers 550 miles (880 km) south to Chihuahua for more fun in the sun. The governor of that province, however, merely took Pike's notes and sent the crew off toward Texas, which they reached in July.

Pike pulled his fat out of the fire and forever etched his name in Colorado history and stone by an amazing bit of memory. Without notes, he penned the story of his trip. The public ate it up, and he reached the peak of his fame. Not only was his book a pretty good adventure story, it also gave the nation its first feel for the southwestern stretches of land west of the Mississippi that it had scored in the Louisiana Purchase of 1803.

The mountain that Pike and his men couldn't climb but could see became Pikes Peak and "Pikes Peak or Bust" became the rallying cry for the thousands who would cross the prairie in search of Colorado. Of course, they didn't end up near Pike's Peak, they were all heading for the gold and silver fields hundreds of miles away, but then again, Mr. Pike wasn't exactly a good example when it came to knowing where you are heading or where you would eventually end up.

Pike avoided putting his well-traveled foot in his mouth, a fate Colorado's other famous explorer experienced, toe, heel, and legging. But the party of **Maj. Stephen Long** did manage to climb Pike's Peak, so maybe it's a historical draw. Like Pike, Long really didn't discover much. His expedition was almost a wander in the woods compared to Pike's adventures.

In June 1820, Long's party, which included a biologist, naturalist, geologist, and other men of learning, spotted the Rockies. And spotted was about all they settled for, besides naming a peak or two, like the mountain now called **Longs Peak**, but which they called by the inspired name of **Highest Peak.** They came down the South Platte River and generally took a nice little ride down the Front Range, except for the three-day trek up Pike's Peak, and by the end of September the whole thing was over.

It was after the trip that Long and his men of learning blew it.

Long proclaimed the Great Plains to be **"The Great American Desert."** He compared them to sandy African deserts, predicted that "vegetable matter" would never grow there, and generally consigned the plains to be forever the domain of the Indians, rabbits, and buffalo. The name stuck. For decades afterwards the plains were marked "The Great American Desert" on most U.S. maps.

But the truth about the Rockies and its peaks and rivers and the plains and their fertility eventually came out. It would take the fur-trapping mountain men and prospectors—not the numerous military or government explorers who came after Pike—to really traverse the state from top to bottom, and a crop of industrious farmers and a sprinkling of water to turn "The Great American Desert" into part of "The Breadbasket of the World."

economy before the turn of the century. Over 9,000 workers toiled at the plants during the 1950s, but in the early 1980s new technology cooled the blast furnaces, costing Pueblo 3,300 jobs. Once the smoke cleared, the town decided it was time to quit waiting for corporate accountants to decide its future, dusted itself off, and went to work on itself, for itself.

Surrounding natural amenities, an entrenched blue-collar work ethic, and extra effort to spruce up the town in general (quality of life again) assured that it didn't take long for many companies to discover Pueblo was a pretty good place do business. In the early 1990s, over 6,000 new jobs softened the blows delivered by lay-offs in the steel mills.

So, even if the CF&I steel mill, which by 1990 still employed almost 2,000 Puebloans, ever gives up the ghost for good, there's a sense that such a blow will make "Steel City" just bend a bit, not break in half.

■ EXPLORING PUEBLO
Even Puebloans admit their city isn't in itself a great tourist attraction, but it does have attractive aspects.

The **Colorado State Fair,** lasting almost two weeks every August, brings thousands of people to town. This is a real state fair. Grandmothers with their preserves and peach farmers with their peaches vie for blue ribbons while eager 4-H kids wash, shave, polish, and preen their animals for judging. The fair is a reminder that from the mountains to plains, the sturdy folks relying on ranching and farming still play a key role in the state. Top-name country-western singers, carnivals, parades, and a week of professional rodeos are also on the bill of fare.

The downtown area's **Union Avenue Historic District,** made up of over 40 restored nineteenth-century buildings, is a reminder of the solid citizenry and businesses which have, through the decades, made Pueblo more than a company town. It's a real town, with real neighborhoods and a real sense of community.

Rosemount Victorian House Museum (419 W. 14th St.) is often called one of the state's finest examples of Victorian architecture. A 24,000-square-foot mansion, it contains a conglomeration of period furniture and finery. The exterior is decorated with turrets, chimneys, a sun porch, and just about every other bit of delightful, decorative, gingerbread ornamentation imaginable.

Eunice Winkless takes a dive on a dare at the Pueblo State Fair in 1905.
(Pueblo Library District)

Pueblo City Park Zoo, at Goodnight and Pueblo Boulevard, lays claim to fame as the state's largest collection of cold-blooded animals (deduct two points if the words "investment banker" came to mind).

Pueblo has successfully mixed its urban character with the outdoors in a number of ways. The **Arkansas River Greenway and Nature Center,** at 5200 Nature Center Road, is 20 miles (32 km) worth of outdoor action, from hiking to wildlife viewing to biking. On the western edge of the city limits, **Pueblo Reservoir,** which includes 60 miles (96 km) of shoreline bordered by limestone cliffs with mountain views in the background, offers anglers, boaters, and lay-abouts the chance to indulge in their particular pastimes.

The **Royal Gorge,** home to the country's highest suspension bridge—a mere 1,053 feet (316 m) above the Arkansas River—is an hour's drive from Pueblo on US 50 through Cañon City. The canyon itself is stunning, if not scary, as solid granite walls too steep to tinker with roar up at visitors on the rim. To see into the canyon, you can pay to drive across the bridge, take a tramway over the gorge, loop around the edge on an old-fashioned railroad, or just park your car and peek over for free. **Buckskin Joe Theme Park** is over-equipped with "touristy" treats like gunfights, old-time costumes, and trinkets (but kids like it).

■ URBAN OPTIMISTS ABOUND

The optimism and ability to shift economic gears that sustained the early gold and silver miners live on in today's Front Rangers. They're pretty sure that the mother lode—a diversified economy that will welcome a boom and survive a bust now and then—is within their grasp, or with just a little extra work and a new idea or two, is just around the next century, at the very least.

The Royal Gorge: a great sight if you don't have a fear of heights.

ROCKY MOUNTAINS
GOLD AND SILVER TOWNS

IT'S THE MOTHER LODE WITH A BOOMING TENT CITY with mud streets and miners turned millionaires building opera houses and stores and bars and hotels better start cutting down every tree in sight to build this town into a city for thousands by God let's just keep digging and firing smelters and shipping out the riches yippee the train is here the road is open life can only get better this is the mother lode and it ain't ever gonna end.

What?

The mines are giving out?

Those damn Eastern politicians won't buy silver?

The millionaires are going broke?

Let's get the hell out of here, this place is dead, but there's another mother lode, just over the next ridge, or maybe two mountains ranges west, come on, let's go, the mother lode is still out there, somewhere.

■ GOLDEN BEGINNINGS

From 1859 to 1893, the search for the next mother lode sent miners out from Denver into the Rocky Mountains. First they scurried through the foothills, scratching here, digging there, and panning any stream to be found. Towering mountains that don't lose their snowcaps until mid-summer didn't stop the miners' westward surge, nor did the dense stands of pine and fir trees they fought through as they kept plunging deeper into the Rockies in an arc from Steamboat Springs to Aspen to Cripple Creek. The gold seekers raced across the huge open meadows tucked in between mountain ranges because gold was in the hills and along the streambeds.

In those moments when their eyes weren't focused on gold, a few must have marveled at the pure beauty of their surroundings—steep canyons, rolling mountains, herds of deer and elk, and a deep blue sky slowly turning an orange-red at sunset or sunrise.

But what really got their attention was news of a good strike in a good location. It took transportation, smelters, and capital to make a mining town boom, so once

There's gold in them thar' hills, one way or another.

The 1872 Mining Act allows gold miners to still "dig" Aspen Mountain.

a town like Leadville or Breckenridge boomed, the miners would stream out of isolated cabins high in the Rockies and descend on the boom towns like locusts. Although prospectors' footprints covered most of the Rockies, today millions of acres of forested slopes beneath snowcapped peaks, along with wide-open meadows and their free-flowing creeks, remain relatively unscarred by the gold boom.

Mining's booms and busts are alive today in those Colorado towns that have retained their Victorian roots and enthralling mining history. The state still disgorges significant amounts of minerals from its mountainous bowels and continues to bounce in and out of the ranks of the nation's top gold- and mineral-producing states. So who knows, you might want to keep an eye on the streambed the next time you're fishing or hiking, because you might find a vein of gold as thick as your leg and stumble on the next mother lode. Mining has long been considered a reputable occupation in Colorado, even if Mark Twain did claim that a mine is "a hole in the ground owned by a liar."

■ FIBBING IN 1858

Colorado's gold rush had a rather dubious beginning when a Georgian named William Green Russell led a small party to the confluence of Cherry Creek and the

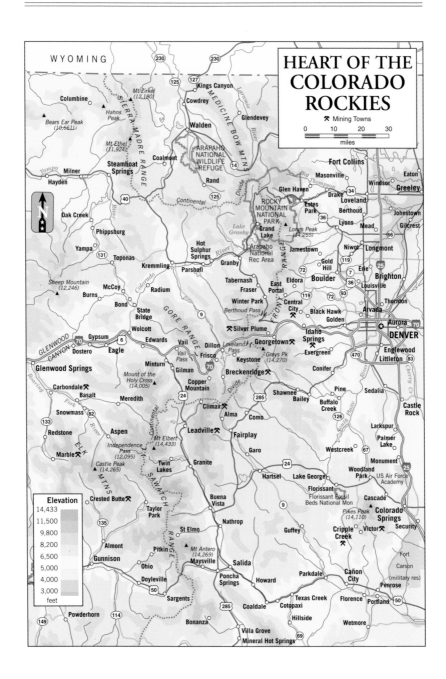

HEART OF THE COLORADO ROCKIES

⚒ Mining Towns

0   10   20   30
miles

WYOMING

Columbine
Bears Ear Peak
(10,661)
Mt. Zirkel
(12,180)
Hahns Peak
Kings Canyon
Cowdrey
Glendevey
Walden
Mt. Ethel
(11,924)
Coalmont
ARAPAHO
NATIONAL
WILDLIFE
REFUGE
Steamboat
Springs
Milner
Hayden
Rand
Fort Collins
Masonville
Windsor
Eaton
Greeley
Glen Haven
Drake
Oak Creek
Continental
Loveland
Berthoud
Johnstown
Phippsburg
Lake
Granby
Estes
Park
Lyons
Mead
Gilcrest
Yampa
Toponas
Hot
Sulphur
Springs
Grand
Lake
Longs Peak
(14,255)
Niwot
Longmont
Sheep Mountain
(12,246)
McCoy
Kremmling
Parshall
Granby
Arapaho
National
Rec Area
Jamestown
Gold
Hill
Erie
Brighton
Burns
Radium
Tabernash
Fraser
Eldora
Boulder
Louisville
Bond
State
Bridge
Winter Park
East
Portal
Central
City
Black Hawk
Thornton
Gypsum
Wolcott
Edwards
Berthoud Pass
Golden
Arvada
Aurora
DENVER
Glenwood Springs
Dostero
Eagle
Vail
Dillon
Loveland
Pass
Silver Plume
Georgetown
Idaho
Springs
Evergreen
Englewood
Littleton
Carbondale
Minturn
Gilman
Vail
Pass
Frisco
Keystone
Grays Pk
(14,270)
Conifer
Mount of the
Holy Cross
(14,005)
Copper
Mountain
Breckenridge
Basalt
Meredith
Climax
Shawnee
Bailey
Pine
Sedalia
Snowmass
Redstone
Aspen
Independence
Pass
(12,095)
Mt Elbert
(14,433)
Alma
Como
Buffalo
Creek
Castle
Rock
Marble
Leadville
Fairplay
Larkspur
Palmer
Lake
Castle Peak
(14,265)
Twin
Lakes
Granite
Garo
Westcreek
Monument
Crested Butte
Taylor
Park
Buena
Vista
Hartsel
Lake George
Woodland
Park
US Air Force
Academy
Florissant
Florissant Fossil
Beds National Mon
Cascade
St Elmo
Nathrop
Guffey
Pikes Peak
(14,110)
Colorado
Springs
Almont
Pitkin
Mt Antero
(14,269)
Maysville
Salida
Cripple
Creek
Victor
Security
Gunnison
Ohio
Doyleville
Poncha
Springs
Howard
Parkdale
Cañon
City
Fort
Carson
(military res)
Penrose
Sargents
Coaldale
Cotopaxi
Texas Creek
Florence
Portland
Powderhorn
Bonanza
Hillside
Wetmore
Villa Grove
Mineral Hot Springs

Elevation

14,433
11,500
9,800
8,200
6,500
5,000
4,000
3,000
feet

South Platte River in 1858. The party had partaken of the Georgia gold rush, and these Colorado streams looked just as peachy and golden as Georgia's. The men panned a little gold, nosed around, assumed there should be more somewhere, and decided to stay the winter and start serious prospecting in the spring.

Even in the 1850s, it was hard to keep any nugget of good gold news a secret. Word of their meager find got back to towns like Kansas City and Omaha, which had prospered supplying the forty-niners on their way to the California gold rush. Stuck in the Depression of 1857, they hated to let facts get in their way, so they declared a full-blown Colorado gold rush. Sales in the mercantiles picked up dramatically as 100,000 people headed west in the spring of 1859. Half of them never made it to Colorado. They either suffered prairie paranoia, died, got lost, or came to their senses when they arrived and saw impassable mountains, icy streams, and riverbanks lined with rocks instead of gold nuggets.

■ HEADY YEARS IN GOLD COUNTRY

The first real gold strikes were by George A. Jackson and John H. Gregory, miners who independently discovered veins on Clear Creek in 1858. Two years later, substantial discoveries were also made at Gold Hill west of Boulder. That was all it took. A boom was on. Of course, having Horace Greeley pan a little Colorado gold, a fact he loudly touted in his New York *Tribune*, didn't hurt. (Could someone the night before have dropped a little gold in the spot Horace was supposed to pan? Well . . . you never can tell about such things.)

It also became obvious that Cherry Creek, where all the hullabaloo started, contained about as much gold as the below-average bottles of whiskey being shipped by the wagon load to the gold diggers from the infant towns of Denver and Auraria, which straddled Cherry Creek and battled each other for urban supremacy. Look at a current state map and you will know who won.

Those first heady years created the myth of a lone prospector and his burro striking gold deep in the hills and coming back to town with a sack of gold nuggets that would make him a rich man. For some, that fantasy became reality. But not for many. Tugging gold out of freezing mountain streams was hard work and gold veins also put up quite a fight. As the easy gold along the river banks gave out, the gold pan was replaced by the sluice box or rockers—two-man contraptions filled with dirt that was washed away, hopefully to reveal gold.

GOLD STRIKE AT CHERRY CREEK

*T*he month of May had appeared and yet no signs of a change to the better had become manifest. The gold regions were, on the contrary, passing through the darkest days they were destined to see. The cheerless prospect exercised a depressing influence upon everything. Utter stagnation characterized material life, and hopefulness weighed heavily on the minds of all the sojourners on Cherry Creek. Everybody had the blues. Even the most sanguine became dispirited, and the idea of a general abandonment of the country was the subject of frequent discussion.

Thus affairs stood, when in the course of the afternoon of the second Sunday in May [1858], we were seated in the long-house that then represented the express office, in company with Dr. J. M. Fox, the general agent of the Express Company, and Mr. Joseph Heywood, a well known Californian, and formerly resident of Cincinnati. The trio were just discussing the unpromising aspect of things, when a short, slender, heavily bearded individual, in miner's garb, entered the room and inquired for letters. He was invited to a seat, and soon got to talking about the resources of the country. Contrary to expectation, he seemed to believe firmly in its mineral wealth. Being asked for his experience in the mountains from which he claimed to have just arrived, he stated, after a few moments of apparent hesitation, that a little more than a week ago, while following up the north fork of Clear Creek, in company with John H. Gregory and several others, he had discovered gold-bearing dirt in the vicinity of streaks of quartz rock, that ran over the mountains, in a ravine adjoining the valley of the creek. The dirt, he asserted, had yielded him as much as a dollar's worth of gold to the pan. Perceiving a manifestation of incredulity on the part of his listeners, he produced, in corroboration of his statement, a bottle containing about forty dollars' worth of flour gold, and also several fragments of a hard substance which he designated as decomposed gold-bearing quartz. Mr. Heywood stepped outdoors with one of the pieces for the purpose of examining it with a magnifying glass. He soon called out Dr. Fox, whom he told that the specimen he held in his hand was as fine quartz as he had seen in the richest quartz veins in California. Several persons having, in the meantime, entered the office and showing upon hearing the miner's tale a disposition to doubt its truthfulness, the latter grew rather excited, repeated what he had said, and asserted most emphatically that he would warrant one dollar to the pan of dirt to any number of men that would follow him to the locality in question, and added that they might bring a rope along and swing him up in case he should be found a liar.

This was the first news of the discovery of the Gregory mines that reached us. Its bearer, who had come to the Cherry Creek towns for a new supply of provisions, returned to the mountains on the following day, in company with several others, who intended to sift his story by a visit to the scene of the alleged discovery.

A few more dull days elapsed without throwing any further light on the subject, and the spark of hope kindled by the miner's apparently earnest story had nearly been lost sight of amidst the surrounding darkness, when on the fifth day a Mr. Bates, late of Dubuque, Iowa, made his appearance in Auraria with a vial full of gold, representing a value of about eighty dollars, which he claimed to have washed out of thirty-nine pans of dirt, obtained not far from the spot on which Gregory had made his discovery. Mr. Bates being known as a reliable man, his story was at once credited and he and his bottle taken from cabin to cabin. The sight of his gold forthwith produced an intense excitement, and the news of his luck spread like wild-fire and at once moved the hearts of the denizens of the two towns with gladdening sensations. Individuals could be heard every[where] on the streets shouting to each other, "We are all right now," "the stuff is here after all," "the country is safe," &c.

On the following day a universal exodus took place in the direction of North Clear Creek. Whoever could raise enough provisions for a protracted stay in the mountains sallied out without delay. Traders locked up their stores; bar-keepers disappeared with their bottles of whiskey, the few mechanics that were busy building houses, abandoned their work, the county judge and sheriff, lawyers and doctors, and even the editor of the *Rocky Mountain News,* joined in the general rush.

—Henry Villard
The Past and Present of the Pike's Peak Gold Regions, 1932

■ TECHNOLOGY AND CAPITAL

As time went on, more dirt had to be sluiced to produce less gold, leading to new and expensive technology. Coffer dams were unleashed to clean out whole stretches of streambeds. Hydraulic mining used hoses and pipes to blast away all the dirt around the stream so it could be set aside and sifted. Lode gold, or veins, quickly became the domain of mining companies that could afford to hire miners, crush tons of ore, and then ship and sell the resulting gold.

The Crystal Mill, near the ghost town of Crystal and Marble.

New technology and capital didn't stop the solitary miner and his burro. Lone prospectors still set out into unexplored territory, but if they found gold, instead of mining the claim, they would more than likely arrange a friendly corporate take-over with a well-heeled mining company, but not before securing a "golden parachute" from a percentage of earnings.

By 1865, an estimated 100 million tons of freight were being hauled to Denver by wagon. Getting as far as Denver was the easy part; hauling supplies up into the Rockies was something else again. It wasn't long before sharp-eyed and deep-pocketed men began to think about building railroads into the booming mining districts.

The lone prospector in all his "romantic" glory—Pat Lynch, 1910.
(Colorado Historical Society)

In 1867 the Union Pacific Transcontinental Railroad hit Wyoming. Three years later a Union Pacific spur reached Denver and the Kansas Pacific made a straight shot across the prairie into town. Then Gen. William Palmer created the Denver & Rio Grande Railroad and pushed its lines south to Colorado Springs, Canon City, Pueblo, and Trinidad.

Rail links still didn't make investors' eyes glow over Colorado gold. A chunk of granite and gold was a tough nut to crack, especially when the cracking was done by stamp mills that pounded the hell out of the ore to break the granite's grip on the gold. Nathaniel P. Hill, a chemist from Brown University, got the gold boom cooking in 1868 when he developed a smelter that would heat the ore, bake away the granite, and attach gold or silver to copper mattes for extraction. Forget smashing high grade ore, now you could cook low grade ore and still make money.

■ BLACK HAWK AND CENTRAL CITY

Black Hawk and Central City became "the richest square mile on earth," thanks to Hill's smelter and the arrival of William A. H. Loveland's Colorado Central Railroad in 1877.

To get there, drive due west from Denver on US 6, get off on US 119, and you'll find yourself winding through Clear Creek Canyon, where the creek banks reveal piles of rocks left by the placers and hydraulic miners. The closer you get to Black Hawk, the more mining debris, of the metal variety, there is, and when you get to town you'll see the leftovers of Hill's inventions rusting around everywhere.

Just up the road a bit is Central City, and the emphasis here is on *up*. It's hard to imagine thousands of people living in the valley of this steep little canyon. A closer look at the hills—dotted, crisscrossed, and covered with tailings piles, roads, and assorted miners' marks—makes you wonder if the miners could even swing a pick without hitting some other miner's foot or head. The town's few paved streets quickly give way to dirt roads steep enough to make a mule snort.

It's the buildings, not the roads, that enthrall. After the town burned to the ground a couple of times, a "bricks, or stone, or nothing-doing" building code was imposed. Thus, Central City probably has the state's best collection of original block, brick, and stone Victorian buildings, and they're all jammed right into a couple of easy strolling blocks. The crown jewel is the rejuvenated **Central City Opera House,** home to a summer season of opera unmatched in Colorado. Next to the

"The Richest Square Mile on Earth."

opera house is the famed **Teller House,** home to the equally famous "Face on the Barroom Floor," belonging to the lovely Madeline and painted by her jilted lover right before he died atop his masterpiece/mistresspiece. Today, at the Teller House, bartenders in tuxedos and the brass rail guarding the face detract from the room's mining camp feel, but belt down a few shots of bad whiskey, if they have any, and you can take the trip back in time in no time.

The introduction of limited-stakes gambling was supposed to bestow upon Central City and Black Hawk the long-lost taste of the wild silver camps. Riches sprouted once again from the richest square mile on earth, this time from rows of slot machines and bunches of poker tables jammed into every available building. But for the purists, the sheer number of casinos, gambling devices, and people drawn to them meant the towns' gambling cup had runneth over its former slower, more relaxed way of life.

Luckily, the best view of the new and improved Central City is from the several tiers of parking lots cut out of old gold-colored (what else) mine tailings perched above town. Several old mine tailings piles speckle the nearby hillsides and other rusted mining remnants are also visible. Jammed into every semi-level plot

"The Smelting Capital of the World."

(opposite) Silverton branch of the Denver & Rio Grande Railroad on High Line. (Denver Public Library, Western History Department)

of land in the steep canyon in which the town rests are rows of neat Victorian cottages that make up the residential sections of town. New paint has graced many a once-tattered domicile, and "No Parking" signs have sprouted like weeds. (A word to the wise: park in the lots. There isn't any other real parking, so follow the signs to the lots. Shuttle buses take you right downtown, or you can walk.)

The gambling action is centered along Main and aptly named Eureka streets. Main is shut to traffic, which allows for a leisurely stroll on alternating boardwalks and sidewalks past the casinos and gift shops. Most of the Victorian commerical buildings have had decades of paint peeled from their intricate brickwork, and had every ornate Victorian bangle or bauble accentuated with paint or bronze. Methinks the original silver boom town wasn't quite this tidy.

Part of the deal made to make gambling legal was that massive amounts of money was skimmed off the top of the casinos' take for historic preservation projects across the state. Central City didn't need the grants. Every square foot of land became a little treasure island worth its weight in gold as a prospective casino. Any building still standing with even a slight degree of structural integrity was quickly gutted, painted, and turned into a casino. (Another word to the wise: if you drive, fill your tank before you leave; there aren't any gas stations left, all having been sold and demolished in a rush of speculative frenzy.)

Perching on a wooden bench for some people-watching is one of the cheapest thrills in town. Gamblers and gawkers run the gamut from senior citizens taking a slow stroll down the streets to families searching for ice cream. The dedicated gambler is easy to spot: the glazed look in the eyes, the plastic bucket full of coins clutched close to the heart, and the quickened pace leading to the next Eldorado.

Then there's the noise. In the summer all doors are open and all manner of bells and whistles whine from slot machines which have just paid, say, $8 on a $2 bet. The incessant clanging and clanking of the machines fills the air with the promise of easy money for the lucky player. On each casino doorstep a greeter —usually overdressed in tuxedo or outlandish period costume—hails passersby with coupons, greetings, and other tricks of the carnival barker's trade.

The casinos themselves offer a range of atmospheres from the low-key Long Branch to Bullwhackers, a "new" historical mega-gambling palace, to the Teller House, which shuffled gambling into its long, significant history as the town's anchor at the corner of Eureka and Main.

Central City, primitive but pulsating in the 1860s. (Colorado Historical Society)

Black Hawk, which once was a mile down the road, but now has started to blend right into Central City, offers more of the same on a smaller scale. The historic Gilpin Hotel and Black Forest Inn maintain the memories of days past, while large new casinos have been carved into the hillsides. Gambling has accomplished one goal: Central City and Black Hawk are once again filled with treasure-seekers seeking the stroke of luck that will instantly deliver easy money into their eager hands. And pulling on a slot machine lever is much cleaner work than digging in a gold mine.

■ IDAHO SPRINGS, GEORGETOWN, AND SILVER PLUME

These three towns, which rest one after another about an hour's drive west of Denver, once swarmed with miners, and the hillsides around them were dotted with gold and silver mines.

The coming of the Colorado Central Railroad in 1877 assured the boom wouldn't die. Steep mountains blocked the line from reaching the prolific mines of **Silver Plume.** When Jay Gould bought the Colorado Central, he decided to extend the line, a decision that led to the **Georgetown Loop,** an iron train trestle which rises up 638 feet (194 m) and was considered one of the greatest engineering feats of the day. (See "Historic Railroads" in "PRACTICAL INFORMATION.")

As riders peek down from 638 feet above ground while riding "the Loop," many gasp, either in awe of the engineering, the beauty of the valley, or from a fear of heights and anxiety that those tiny little iron sticks can't really hold up a passenger-filled, steam-powered train. Atop the tressel (while in the train) is the best place to view Georgetown and the surrounding mountains, which are steep, rocky,

and still dotted with dozens of yellowish mine tailings amongst the pines.

Nestled in the valley, Georgetown's downtown (not the conglomeration of banality at the interstate off-ramp) hasn't been ruined with renovation. The back streets, and the original brick and wooden Victorian buildings downtown, evoke a comfortable, lived-in feel. This is a place where selling T-shirts isn't the only business at hand.

Silver Plume, which once contained some of the richest gold ore in the state, is interestingly Victorian once you get away from the freeway ramps, and many a mining remain is still jammed into the narrow canyon. You can relive some of the good times by taking any number of gold mine tours, the biggest being that of the huge **Argo Gold Mill** (proving there's more than one way to make money on Colorado gold).

■ CRIPPLE CREEK AND VICTOR

Latecomers to the gold rush, these towns were nevertheless comers. After an 1891 gold strike, Cripple Creek boomed. By 1900, 475 mining companies were in operation and the town's population reached 25,000. Labor troubles and falling prices beginning with the financial panic of 1907, combined with devastating fires, ended the boom almost as quickly as it started. The gold remains today, as do the miners, who now use cyanide-leech-field mining to extract the ore.

A new gold rush, based on limited-stakes gambling, descended on Cripple Creek in 1991. The earlier fires left stately brick and stone buildings along Bennett Avenue, which quickly became home to casinos large and small. The gambling halls lure those seeking easy riches to Cripple Creek, located due west of Colorado Springs but requiring a roundabout trip via highways 24 and 67. Thanks in part to Cripple Creek's stability as a year-round community, the gambling is relatively relaxed, so visitors can savor both the old and new aspects of this isolated old mining town. You can see how riches were made the old-fashioned way via a tour of the nearby **Molly Kathleen Mine,** which closed in the 1960s, or take a ride on the **Cripple Creek-Victor Narrow Gauge Railroad** to savor a true taste of turn-of-the-century life in Cripple Creek.

Gold fever still strikes in Cripple Creek.

(following pages) Albert Bierstadt's "Sunset in the Rockies," 1866. (Museum of Western Art)

■ BRECKENRIDGE

Breckenridge was a stable producer of gold until 1948. Since the town never died dead dead, many of the original buildings were torn down or modernized. Today, "modern Victorians" line the streets, and thanks to the skiing boom there isn't a very historic feel to the main drag. You have to get back into the back streets to find the town's nineteenth-century roots. (To ski Breckenridge see "SKIING.")

Large-scale hydraulic mining and dredging of the Blue River (running between the ski hill and the town) and its tributaries kept Breckenridge a gold town. It also transformed the Blue's once verdant banks into miles of piles of sterile rocks stretching like a white scar along the bottom of an otherwise green mountain valley.

The local historical society has preserved a sluicing and hydraulic operation and a dredge boat—the wooden monster that did the biggest damage. The animal sits a couple of miles out of town in a stagnant lake surrounded by bare river rock. Over 100 feet long (30 m) and about 30 feet wide (9 m), this Buckcyrus Erie model and dozens like it chewed through the Blue River and its banks like a giant cockroach through a loaf of bread.

■ SILVER BOOMS AND BUSTS

Although Nevada may have had the Comstock Lode, thanks to Leadville, Aspen, Creede, Telluride, Ouray, Lake City, Silverton, and the dozens of camps around Gunnison and Crested Butte, Colorado became the nation's Silver State, and was damn proud of it. The silver boom quickly forced Colorado into the national political spotlight because decisions made in Washington hit the Silver State right in the pocketbook.

Silver's demise came as quickly as its rise. The Coinage Act of 1873—called The "Crime of '73" by Coloradoans and fought with learned and passionate debate—put the nation on the gold standard and stopped automatic federal purchase of silver. The federal government kept buying some silver at set prices, but its policy was rudderless and dependent on the political winds in Washington. A good gust was provided by the Sherman Silver Purchase Act of 1890, which drove prices up, but silver's sails drooped when India quit coining silver in 1893, sinking a steady international customer.

The Panic of 1893 finally did the dirty deed. Wall Street money men blamed silver for the economic destruction and convinced Congress and President Grover Cleveland to repeal the Sherman Silver Purchase Act, effectively killing King Silver and the royalties that propped up once prosperous towns.

These 30 silver bars from the Black Hawk smelters fetched $45,000 before the silver crash. (Colorado Historical Society)

■ LEADVILLE: MATCHLESS AND UNSINKABLE

Leadville was Colorado's silver king. Scattered strikes were struck as early as 1870, but by 1877 it was boom time. Thousands descended on Leadville, and between 1879 and 1889, the town produced $82 million worth of silver. It seemed "Cloud City" was set to become one of the state's biggest and most prosperous towns.

All of the day's nationally known figures made sure to stop in town if they found themselves in Colorado. Feminist Susan B. Anthony gave a speech to the miners about women's suffrage which quieted Billy Nye's saloon, the biggest building in town in 1877, and raised over $100 for the cause.

Leadville residents, in a display of civic pride running nakedly amok, boasted that their red light district was the best in the nation. That debate aside, at its booming peak Leadville, with its rich mines, solid brick Victorian buildings, and magnificent opera house, was giving Denver a run for its money as *the* most important Colorado city.

The town itself rests on the first fairly flat spot available at the head of sprawling Arkansas Valley. The surrounding hillsides, stripped of all timber during the boom, are once again covered with pine trees, but they don't hide the scattered mine remains, diggings, and tailings of all sizes and shapes.

Leadville's Harrison Avenue provides a glimpse of silver promise and poverty. On the street's south end the **Tabor Opera House** hosted everyone from Harry Houdini to John Phillip Sousa. Even the long-haired, somewhat eccentric poet Oscar Wilde lectured there on the ethics of art. (Wilde's most vivid Leadville memory was not the lecture, he would later write, but a sign above the piano in Pap's saloon that read: "Please do not shoot the pianist. He is doing his best." That little pearl, according to Wilde, was art criticism at its rational best.)

Today the curious can peer at the original, time-tattered velvet seats, box seats for the silver barons, balcony for the masses, huge stage, and opulent entry. On the north end of the street the **Tabor Grand Hotel**, a massive chunk of stonework, stands empty, a monument to Tabor's grand dreams and lost fortune.

The road north of town will take you to the **Matchless Mine**, where the once-rich and beautiful "Baby Doe" Tabor (third in a notorious love triangle) died waiting for the next boom. Heading south you'll pass "string town," now a collection of innocent looking homes and businesses, but once the area set aside for the many working girls who began their shift when the miners ended theirs.

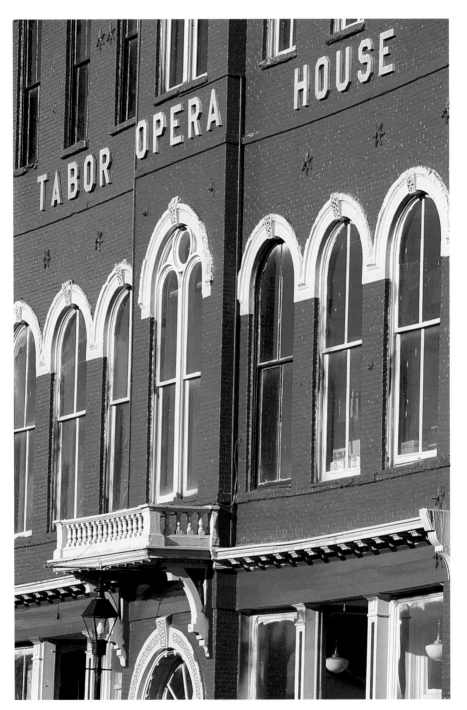

The Tabor Opera House was Leadville's cultural jewel.

The **Colorado Historical Society Healy House Museum** brings to life what it meant to be a Victorian lady or gentleman. The dainty main house was home to refined, unmarried school teachers, while the hunting cabin was where the married men congregated to drink whiskey and talk about money and women. Interspersed with original Victorian buildings are modern buildings, such as the square and boring Lake County Courthouse. The reason for the building mix is that Leadville actually never went bust.

Mining buffs will enjoy the **Mining Hall of Fame,** which has displays of mining techniques ranging from gold panning to hand-drilling and blasting up to modern twentieth century procedures and equipment.

Around the turn of the century, zinc, copper, and gold were discovered in the old Leadville silver mines, keeping Leadville alive as a mining town. The most important new find was the huge deposit of molybdenum discovered in 1918 near the top of Fremont Pass. Molybdenum hardens steel alloys ("Molly Makes Your Tool Harder"), and twentieth century America was built on steel and Climax molybdenum. The Climax Molybdenum Mine has produced 1.9 billion tons of molybdenum, and during World War II it produced about 72 percent of the world's supply.

Unfortunately, the Climax Mine has dumped billions of tons of mill tailings into what used to be Tenmile Valley, but today is a huge sludge pile completely filling the valley and making reclamation impossible. There is, however, a program underway to cover over the tailings.

■ LEADVILLE'S COLORFUL CHARACTERS

Denver may have been Colorado's biggest city in the 1880s, but it never rivaled Leadville in rags-to-riches stories, colorful characters, and pitiful demises.

Probably most familiar to Coloradoans is Charles Boettcher, who arrived in 1879 and started a booming hardware business that he parlayed into a diverse financial empire eventually based in Denver. The family's fortunes increased, and its members have played a prominent role in the city's business, philanthropic, and civic affairs ever since. The Boettcher Foundation and the Boettcher Concert Hall are just part of the legacy of a man who started selling nuts and bolts in Leadville.

A national department store chain resulted when two other Leadville merchants set up shop and got tired of the competition. Located next to the Tabor Opera House was entrepreneur David Day's Great Western Auction House and Clothing

Pits and tailings are representative of the debris leftover from Leadville's glory days.

Store, which opened its doors in 1878. Competing with Day for the town's dry goods business was a store owned by W. B. Daniels, W. G. Fisher, and Joel Smith.

The businessmen finally sat down and decided to merge their operations into a company called May D&F, the start of a nationwide dry goods kingdom that operates today as part of the May Department Store group.

Merchandising was also the beginning of the good fortune(s) of H. A. W. (Horace) Tabor and his wife Augusta, who arrived in 1860 to open stores in Leadville and surrounding mining camps. In 1877, Tabor "grubstaked" George Hook and August Rische in return for one third of whatever they found. What they found was the Little Pittsburgh Mine's 30-foot-thick (9-m) vein of silver, which made the mine a multi-million-dollar producer and Tabor a rich man. He kept investing in

mining properties, allegedly buying the Matchless Mine with about $100,000 in pocket change. The mine produced a booming $1,000,000 a year during its 14-year life.

While Tabor was becoming one of Leadville's richest men, leading lights, and civic stars (thanks to his bankrolling of the Tabor Opera House and other generous acts), he was also becoming an adulterer with the beautiful divorcée Elizabeth "Baby Doe" McCourt. A scandalous divorce from the upright Augusta (that would have delighted today's tabloids) followed, and Baby Doe became the second Mrs. Tabor.

Leadville's 1896 Ice Palace melted away, like the silver boom. (Colorado Historical Society)

The silver crash hit the Tabors hard, and although Horace did manage to become a U.S. Senator, he died virtually penniless in 1899. He told Baby Doe to never give up the Matchless because one day it would again make millions. She, with a tragic stubbornness, honored his request and for 36 years lived in a small shack at the mine. She would trudge to town for supplies, in later years her feet wrapped in burlap, and return to the mine, waiting for the silver boom that would never come. In the winter of 1935 she was found frozen to death in her little cabin.

The tragic triangle of love and money left only one person with cash and reputation intact: the staid, conservative Augusta Tabor, who got a pretty good alimony deal, and died with millions.

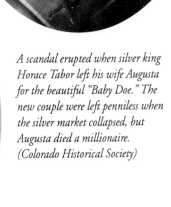

A scandal erupted when silver king Horace Tabor left his wife Augusta for the beautiful "Baby Doe." The new couple were left penniless when the silver market collapsed, but Augusta died a millionaire. (Colorado Historical Society)

REDSTONE'S IDEALIST

John Cleveland Osgood didn't just want to be an industrialist, he also wanted to be a social engineer. Believing that men worked better when they had comfortable living conditions and a stable home life, Osgood decided to engage in a unique bit of industrial/social engineering.

His experiment began in 1893 after he created the Colorado Fuel and Iron Company (CF&I). The place he picked for his novel employee/employer relations experiment was the coal mining town of **Redstone**, which rests along the banks of the Crystal River west of Aspen. The coal mines were 12 miles (19 km) away with coke ovens right outside town (the ovens are still visible at the town's entrance).

Osgood built his miners individual Victorian cottages which they decorated according to their taste, a clubhouse where they could change from gritty mining clothes before heading home or just relax, a library, theater, and a boarding house for the bachelors.

He also looked after himself by building a 42-room mansion, **Cleveholm,** that was decorated to the hilt: elephant hide covered some walls, silk and velvet were everywhere, as was every knick-knack and expensive home decoration available to a Victorian millionaire. Osgood's wife was called Lady Bountiful by the miners, in part because of general generosity, in part because at Christmastime she made sure Santa answered every Redstone child's request.

But the model industrial town lasted only a decade, thanks to those pesky Eastern captains of industry, Jay Gould and John J. Rockefeller. The slick and dastardly duo outmaneuvered Osgood in a series of stock deals and buy-out plans which gave them control of CF&I. They let Osgood's Redstone dream die a slow death.

Today, the town, resting just off Colorado 133, is still mostly made up of the original Victorian cottages. The bachelor pad has become the Historic Redstone Inn, and tours of Osgood's mansion are available.

■ ASPEN

In 1879, in the dead of winter, some intrepid souls strapped on primitive skis (called snowshoes in those days), headed due west out of Leadville, crossed the Continental Divide, and skied down into what would become Aspen. They found what they wanted: huge silver deposits, especially on Smuggler Mountain. Indeed, the largest single silver nugget ever mined, weighing over two tons, was mined in Aspen.

In no time Aspen was racing Leadville for silver and cultural supremacy. In 1883 Jerome B. Wheeler—first president of Macy's Department Store in New York— arrived, bought up mining claims, and built smelters and the stunning Wheeler Opera House.

By 1892, Aspen had 12,000 residents, making it the state's third largest city, behind Leadville and Denver, and it soon started boasting that it was surpassing Leadville in silver output. What a difference a year makes! Almost immediately after repeal of the Sherman Silver Purchase Act, most of the Aspen's mines shut down and over 2,000 minerslost their jobs. Even Jerome Wheeler, the town's high-flying knight-in-silver-armor, became a penniless stable boy with a broken shovel.

By 1930, only 700 hearty souls remained, but thanks to refinement of those original snowshoes that brought prospectors over waist-deep snow into the valley, Aspen would boom again as an international ski resort. (See "Aspen" in "SKIING.")

If you're searching for a taste of mining history today, Aspen presents pretty slim pickings. However, the **Jerome Hotel** and the **Wheeler Opera House,** both recently restored to their turn-of-the-century charm, still stand out as shining reminders of the town's silver days.

If you visit in the summer, Aspen has its allures, especially because rates for everything from a room to a hamburger drop dramatically. You couldn't ask for a more striking, scenic setting. As you enter town, Aspen Mountain starts to loom upward to become a monolith swathed with grass-covered ski trails cutting through dark green pines. A summer ride up the lifts gives you a panoramic view of the town and valley, and you don't even need a parka, although a light jacket is a good idea. In the fall, the aspens and oaks turn the mountains into a pallet of vivid color.

Snowmass Lake in the Maroon Bells/Snowmass Wilderness Area near Aspen.

Golfers can get into the swing of things on the **numerous 18-hole courses** in Aspen and Snowmass Village. More aggressive outdoor recreationists, might want to visit the Maroon Bells-Snowmass Wilderness Area and numerous hiking/biking trails just minutes from town.

Then we have the musical attractions, like the Aspen Music Festival and School (following), and intellectual exercises at the International Design Conference, the Aspen Center for Physics, and a host of other thought-provoking events at the Aspen Meadows complex, in the west end of town.

All that good stuff aside, there is also the town's "star power." You never know if, while wandering through downtown's Cooper Street Mall or dining at one of the town's dozens of outstanding restaurants, you might catch Jack Nicholson joking around, John Denver refreshing his Rocky Mountain high, The Donald playing with his latest trumpet, or Don Johnson forgetting about Miami vices and reverting to Aspen nice. The sound of automatic weapons fire may mean that gonzo journalist Hunter Thompson is making a run into town from his enclave in Woody Creek. Then there are the run-of-the-mill millionaires that come to town to hide out from the pressures such cash creates and look and play the part of casual visitor or wandering ski bum. An interesting congregation of folks and fun, in other words.

International financier Mohammed Hadid taking a dip inside his palatial Aspen home.

(opposite) The guardian of Woody Creek, author Hunter S. Thompson, at target practice.

(following pages) Ballooning is one of a myriad of sports opportunities in Colorado.

(top) Former Mayor Bill Sterling has an informal meeting with one of his constituents.
(above) Negotiating a reindeer permit, Aspen-style.
(right) Private jets are vehicles of choice for Aspen's elite visitors.

■ ASPEN'S WINTERSKOL

Because January is generally the coldest month on the slopes, Aspen decided to warm things up with a five-day celebration called Winterskol. And damn-the-weather, full-fun-ahead, is the general theme of this yearly event, which started fairly innocently as a way for the locals to catch their breath and celebrate a bit after the holiday rush. Today, Winterskol has become both one of the town's traditions, having started in 1950, and full of enough color and dazzle to attract and entertain visitors from around the world.

Did I mention dazzle and color? How's this strike you: a full-blown fireworks extravaganza fired from Aspen Mountain and visible from the whole town followed by a dramatic twisting, turning, torchlight descent down the face of Aspen Mountain. Another nighttime diversion is the famed Bartender's Drink Contest. Anything goes, and usually does, into the concoctions prepared by the towns' masters of imbibery. Daylight brings all manner of ski races to the town's ski areas; in any given year there's some mix of professional races, races to benefit charities, local and amateur races, or celebrity slides down the slopes.

You've got to love the parade, which features a cacophony of homemade contraptions expressing the eclectic intellectual interests of the locals on issues universal and mundane.

All the skiing events, fun, and dazzle mean if you've only five days to spend soaking in the Aspen experience, Winterskol week was made for you. (For more on Aspen as a ski resort, see "SKIING.")

(right and opposite) The cliché works: a winter wonderland and spectacular fireworks— the latter illuminating Aspen during Winterskol.

■ ASPEN MUSIC FESTIVAL

The faces behind the instruments of the Aspen Music Festival Orchestra are a symphony in themselves and reveal the true magic of the annual summer Aspen Music Festival and School.

During the pre-symphony preparations in the circular music tent, the veteran first-chair violinist, whose shoulder cradles his instrument, is smiling and bantering. A few chairs down, a fresh-faced student is staring intently at the sheet music, fiddling with her instrument, and looking longingly at that first chair, dreaming of the day she will be so comfortable, so relaxed before a performance. Perhaps she's dreaming of becoming the next Itzhak Perlman, or Nadja Salerno-Sonnenberg, or any of the other nationally known soloists who may be stopping in Aspen to play, teach, and refresh themselves in the relaxed splendor of an Aspen summer. When the day's symphony is complete and the crowd is applauding in earnest, the conductor takes his bows and directs the orchestra to stand for a bow of its own. As the players take their turn in the spotlight, the violinist in the first chair casts a sidelong glance, nods, and smiles at the young student farther down the row. A shy smile is returned his way and another classical dream is born.

Inside the carefully restored Wheeler Opera House.

Aspen Music Festival and School brings together some of the world's most talented young classical musicians and mixes them with established, experienced players on summer sabbatical from their usual chairs at first-rate orchestras from across the country. The combination is inspiring and explosive. The young people learn from the professionals, and the professionals, in turn, are rejuvenated and inspired by their young charges. The result fills Aspen with a finely tuned consonance of classical music. Most days the huge music tent reverberates with spirited symphonic sound, containing a unique blend of exuberance and experience. Brass and string quartets set up shop in the downtown mall, fill the mountain air with well-honed harmonies, and alternately lullaby or bombast passers-by with their combined talent and verve. The historic **Wheeler Opera House** hosts operas, ranging from the classical to the comical, in addition to a wide variety of performances which prove that the old girl's outstanding acoustics are just one of its many Victorian marvels.

Another marvel of the festival is that you don't have to own a tuxedo to attend many of the events. You're Out West, remember, so the tidy, casual look will do just fine.

■ MARBLE

Just a couple of ridges east was the next logical leap for the silver prospectors spilling out of Aspen in the early 1880s. While digging around they found some silver, and they stumbled on a huge deposit of pure white marble. But so what? No one knew how to mine it, mill it, or ship it.

Marble (the town) came alive in 1885 when a Welsh marble man opened the quarry. Those first chunks of marble were used in the Colorado State Capitol, but hauling marble with 40-mule pack trains wasn't exactly cheap or easy, so the quarry remained a nickel-and-dime operation.

That changed in 1906 when Col. Channing F. Meek came into town, bought the quarry, and incorporated the Colorado Yule Marble Company. In 1914, the quarry supplied over $1,000,000 worth of marble for the Lincoln Memorial in Washington D.C., a fact proudly touted in the firm's 1915 price list. Back then you could secure an ornamental vase ($16), fruit stand ($7), or Water Kiss Fountain ($250) made from the cuttings of the "beautiful Statuary Golden Vein Colorado-Yule Marble used in the Lincoln Memorial." In 1930, Marble received the

This is some good graz'n pardner.

contract to supply the marble for the Tomb of the Unknown Soldier in Arlington National Cemetery in Washington, D.C. It took 75 men more than a year to carve out the 124-ton block of marble (the largest single piece ever quarried), which was then squared at the mill.

These days the quiet hamlet of Marble functions primarily as an unmolested, ramshackle, summer-retreat community. Tours of the quarry are available.

■ ROCKY MOUNTAIN NATIONAL PARK

North of the mining towns of Colorado's central Rockies, and just northwest of the city of Boulder, is Rocky Mountain National Park, which preserves in all its pristine beauty the flora and fauna of the Rockies, as they were before settlers began pouring into Colorado from the east during the 1800s.

Trail Ridge Road, one of the highest paved roads in the nation, runs through the park, and will deliver a view of the top of the Rockies that cannot be matched. As you quickly climb above timberline, you'll find yourself surrounded by 18 mountain peaks over 13,000 feet (3,952 m) high. The best way to start the trip is

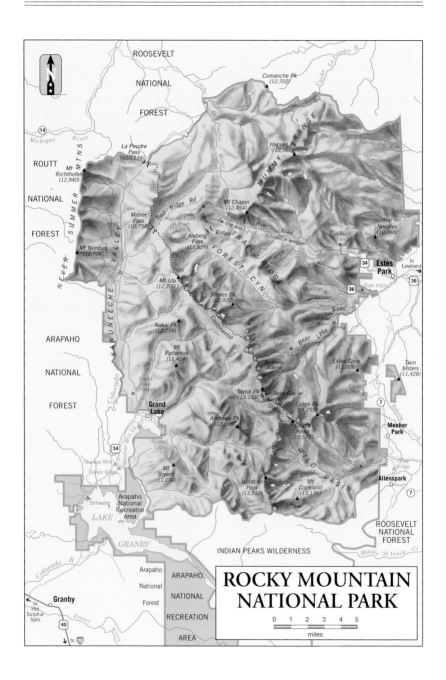

ROOSEVELT

NATIONAL

FOREST

14

Michigan River

ROUTT

Mt
Richthofen
(12,940)

NATIONAL

FOREST

Mt Nimbus
(12,706)

La Poudre
Pass
(10,194)

Milner
Pass
(10,758)

Timber
Creek

Iceberg
Pass
(11,827)

Mt Ida
(12,700)

Stones Pk
(12,922)

Onahu
Nakai Pk
(12,216)

Mt
Patterson
(11,424)

Grand
Lake
Entrance

Grand
Lake

Andrews Pk
(12,565)

Mt
Bryant
(11,034)

ARAPAHO

NATIONAL

FOREST

Shadow Mtn

Green Ridge

Stillwater

LAKE

Arapaho
National
Recreaton
Area

GRANBY

Granby

to
Hot
Sulphur
Sprs

40

to 70

34

Comanche Pk
(12,702)

Hagues Pk
(13,560)

Alpine
Visitor
Center

Mt Chapin
(12,454)

Highest Point
on Road
(12,183)

(← one way →)

Fall
River

Road
(Closed in winter)

The
Needles
(10,068)

Fall River
Entrance

34 Estes
Park

36 Park Hqtrs

Beavers
Meadows

36

to
Loveland

Ranger
Station

Bear Lake

Andrews
Glacier

Glacier
Gorge

Taylor Pk
(13,153)

Taylor Glacier

Estes Cone
(11,006)

Twin
Sisters
(11,428)

Longs Pk
(14,255)

Chiefs
Head
(13,579)

WILD BASIN

Meeker
Park

7

Isolation
Peak
(13,118)

Mt
Copeland
(13,176)

North

Ranger
Station

Olive
Ridge

Allenspark

7

ROOSEVELT
NATIONAL
FOREST

INDIAN PEAKS WILDERNESS

Middle St Vrain Cr

Arapaho

National

Forest

ARAPAHO

NATIONAL

RECREATION

AREA

ROCKY MOUNTAIN
NATIONAL PARK

0 1 2 3 4 5

miles

at the start: the headwaters of the Colorado River, which is just a trickle coming down the western side of the Continental Divide.

Granby, east of Kremmling on US 40 and north of Interstate 70, is the park's western gateway and overlooks the Colorado River. As you go north on Trail Ridge Road, you'll pass through Arapaho National Recreation Area, by Lake Granby, and Grand Lake before hitting the town of **Grand Lake.** As you might imagine, there are ample high-country camping, hiking, boating, and fishing opportunities amidst the forests, glades, and lakes in the area.

Then it's uphill as you mount a charge to the top of Trail Ridge Road. Before you sound the bugle, though, you better make sure the road is clear of snow, which sometimes doesn't occur until June. By about October, you might not get too far either, thanks to the snowy stuff, so this is definitely a summertime undertaking. That short season means you can also expect crowds, as well as possibly getting stuck behind a tour bus. But those are small prices to pay for the rewards awaiting.

The 410 square miles of park contain abundant wildlife, 700 species of wildflowers, and 150 secluded alpine lakes. Topping things off is a 13-mile (21-km) stretch far above timberline that's home to alpine tundra resembling the tundra near the Arctic Circle. A word of caution here. Don't stray from the paved paths

Alpine lakes dot Rocky Mountain National Park.

onto this fragile flora. Your footprint can do serious damage. Do, however, take some time to explore the tiny blossoms that spring out. They seem to be more vivid than any in the state.

Once you peak out and start down the eastern side of the divide, you'll witness the transformation from tundra to tree-covered mountain valleys to mellow meadows. All along the road are numerous pull-outs with informational signs describing the ecology and naming distant, snowcapped peaks. The **Alpine Visitors Center** (which includes a snack shop) and the **Moraine Park Museum** provide more information via knowledgeable park rangers. The park contains 350

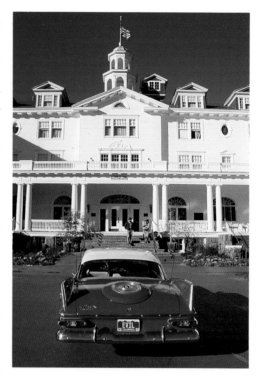

The regal Stanley Hotel in all its glory.

miles (560 km) of trails that provide access for campers, anglers, mountain bikers, and wildlife watchers.

Estes Park (which is a town, not a park) and civilization in all its glory await at the end of the 50-mile (80-km) jaunt. The town entices visitors with a melange of services and offers everything from souvenir coffee mugs to restaurants to condos.

The **Stanley Hotel** sits on a hillside above the frantic activity, secure in its glistening white facade and historic roots. Built in 1901 by F.O. Stanley, inventor of the Stanley Steamer, the hotel is a reminder of the days when touring Rock Mountain National Park was clearly a genteel undertaking.

■ GLENWOOD SPRINGS

Historically a hot spot, Glenwood Springs, almost due west of Denver and north of Aspen and Marble, didn't have any gold or silver, but it did have something that turned it into an internationally known resort. Glenwood steamed to the head of Colorado resorts thanks to **Glenwood Hot Springs Pool and Lodge** and the palatial **Hotel Colorado,** both built in the late 1880s. The Denver & Rio Grande Railroad quickly began promoting the "Spa in the Rockies," and soon everyone who was anyone, from gangsters to gunslingers to the cream of society to U.S. presidents, made Glenwood a stop on their trip through Colorado.

The town's most famous visitor was **Teddy Roosevelt,** who set up a western White House in the Hotel Colorado in 1905 and from which he went on a bear hunt in the nearby White River National Land Reserve. While he was out in the wilds he kept in touch with the White House via a telegraph line to the hotel and a messenger who rode out on his horse every day to try to find the President. (For more on this trip and the origin of "teddy bears," see "GREAT OUTDOORS.")

One of Glenwood's more infamous visitors was the gunslinger and gambler **Dr. John "Doc" Holliday,** who died and was buried in town on November 8, 1887. Holliday—a Georgian with a dental degree from Johns Hopkins University—was one of the West's most notorious gunmen, thanks to his friendship with Wyatt Earp. In 1881 Doc, Wyatt, and the rest of the Earp family were in Tombstone, Arizona, where they took part in one of the West's most famous events, "the gunfight at the OK Corral." By the time the shooting stopped, the Earps, with help from Doc's sawed-off shotgun, had summarily slaughtered the Clanton clan.

But Doc's fame and proficiency with a firearm couldn't stop the tuberculosis that was slowly killing him, or his taste for whiskey while playing cards. Unglamorous scrapes with the law involving dead men and fleeced gamblers became his calling cards. When he arrived in Glenwood Springs after such trouble in Denver and Leadville, he worked at local saloons, overseeing the faro box or playing for the house at the gaming tables. Illness forced him to retire to the hotel bed where he died at the age of 35. He was buried in Linwood Cemetery on a hill above town. In the 1960s, the town erected a monument over **Doc Holliday's Grave.** The tools of Doc's trade—six-shooters and playing cards—are etched in stone above his epitaph, "He Died in Bed."

■ GLENWOOD SPRINGS TODAY

Today, the railroad (AMTRAK in this case) still promotes Glenwood as a Rocky Mountain spa. Just outside Glenwood Springs is the world's largest natural hot springs pool, which measures over 300 feet long (91 m) with hot springs water at 89 degrees (32°C) in the big pool and a hot-tub-like 103 degrees (39°C) in the therapy pool. Vapor caves are next, actual caves full of, well, vapors, just like a natural sauna.

The city's downtown is a cluster of turn-of-the-century brick buildings, and its residential neighborhoods display an arresting mix of modern split-level homes right next to Victorian gingerbreads. The Colorado River tumbles out of the magnificent Glenwood Canyon to meet the Roaring Fork River right in town, and the White River National Forest attracts hikers, birdwatchers, and hunters.

Its strategic location between Vail, 60 miles (96 km) to the east, and Aspen, 40 miles (64 km) to the southeast, also makes Glenwood a regional shopping and supply town, where Aspenites and Vailites can come to get their car fixed for a reasonable price or buy underwear that doesn't cost as much as a new pair of shoes.

Cutting under the Continental Divide via the Eisenhower Tunnel.

This central location, plus a huge hot tub to soothe the sore, also attracts skiers who like the fact that they can buy lift tickets at the nearby ski hills without having to take out a second mortgage.

Whether you're coming or going from Glenwood Springs on Interstate 70, you will be treated to a natural wonder called Glenwood Canyon, featuring about 15 miles (24 km) worth of sheer granite walls shooting 2,000 feet (608 m) straight up and dotted with trees, cornices, startling rock formations, and on and on. Another wonder, this one man-made, is the state-of-the-art, environmentally sensitive, four-lane highway being squeezed through the narrow canyon bottom: cantilevered sections of roadway, bridges crisscrossing the river, and every other trick in the highway builder's book include easy access for rafters to the Colorado River and a bike/hike trail along the river.

(opposite and above) The "healing waters" of the Glenwood Hot Springs Pool

ALFERD [SIC] THE CANNIBAL

If you happen to be strolling along the boardwalk sidewalks in **Lake City**, and you see the following community announcement, "Annual Alferd Packer Community Dinner: MEAT PROVIDED," you've arrived at a special time. Here's the story of Alferd:

Los Pinos Indian Agency, south of Gunnison, wasn't used to many white visitors arriving at springtime on foot, especially in 1874. By all accounts that winter had been a doozie, complete with deep snows, chilling winds, few deer or elk, and general nastiness. Just walking to the Agency, about half way between Saguache and Lake City in the middle of the **San Juan Mountains**, from about anywhere was quite a feat.

That's why the Los Pinos folks were a bit suspicious when Alferd Packer arrived that April asking for whiskey, not food. In such nasty weather it would have taken him weeks, if not longer, to make it to the Agency, yet he didn't look, well, even a little bit puny. Instead, Packer looked pretty healthy, if not rosy-cheeked.

When the springtime prospecting rush arrived, suspicions about Packer's winter paunch started popping up, especially when miners on the Lake Fork of the Gunnison River a few miles below Lake San Cristobal came upon the bodies of five men. Not uncommon in those days, but these bodies were different: the flesh had been carefully carved from their bones. At Los Pinos they remembered Packer's rosy cheeks and his amazing capacity to survive a San Juan winter. Not surprisingly, the day's primitive grapevine linked the five men to Packer.

Suspicions led to questions which led to some information and then some excuses from Packer. Packer said he and five other prospectors from Utah set out in January from present-day Delta for the Los Pinos Indian Agency. Ute Chief Ouray warned them not to go.

The snow was too deep, they hadn't brought enough food, there was no game, they were starving. They started eating their boots. Then they started eating each other.

First Packer said his feet froze and the others left him behind. Then he said one man died of natural causes and was eaten by the rest, so it became a case of kill and eat or become tomorrow's cold cuts, as it were.

Packer was jailed in Saguache, but escaped and remained at large for nine years. Finally captured in Wyoming, he was brought back to Lake City in 1883 for trial. After finding Packer guilty of murder and cannibalism, Judge M. B. Gerry uttered (according to the poem by Mrs. Stella Pavich, titled "Packer the Cannibal") the following sentence and rationale thereof:

There was seven Democrats in Hinsdale County!
But you, you voracious, man-eating sonofabitch,
You ate five of them, therefore I sentence you
To be hanged by the neck, until you're dead, dead!
As a warning against reducing the Democratic population
of this State and Nation.

By the skin of his nose, Packer missed the noose. The killings had taken place on Ute land when Colorado was a territory, thus Packer was charged under territorial laws. In between the killings and the first trial, Colorado became a state, so he was tried under state laws, which was a no-no. (Lawyers, don't you love 'em?) Anyway, at his second trial, in 1886 in Gunnison, the proper legalities were observed and Packer was sentenced to 40 years in prison. Packer's case had drawn considerable attention and supporters who believed his side of the story. In 1901, the governor paroled Packer; he died in April 1907, and he's buried in Littleton.

Such a story couldn't rest in peace, though. In one of the best excuses ever conceived for taking a scientific summer field trip, a group of scientists literally dug up the Packer case in 1989. Forensic expert James Starrs gathered a gang of anthropologists, forensic experts of several stripes, and a geophysicist/engineer, and set out for a summer dig in the San Juans.

The team located the five bodies on a bluff above the Lake Fork River and found skulls that had probably been crushed when the men were asleep, signs some of the men had tried to defend themselves, and bones chipped as if they had been coolly butchered. Such "scientific" evidence proved that Judge Gerry was right to proclaim Packer a "voracious" man eater who did considerable damage to Hinsdale County's Democratic Party. That political damage has been permanent, because from statehood onward Hinsdale County has been a Republican bastion. And can you blame it?

Alferd (Alfie) Packer; not a man to
"do lunch with."
(Museum of Western Art)

SAN JUAN MOUNTAINS

THE GREAT SAN JUAN MOUNTAINS OF SOUTHERN COLORADO are not only chock full of minerals, from gold and silver to zinc and copper, but they are also rugged and isolated—so isolated they are being considered as one of the few places in the Lower 48 states appropriate for re-introduction of the grizzly bear. The region became one of the state's top mining districts right out of the chute, so to speak, and its mines are still producing. Today, there are still prospectors in the San Juans, but they use chemistry, computer-programmed geologic tracking, commodity-market hedging, and core samples instead of picks and mules, as they scour the area for the next mother lode.

■ GUNNISON

Resting at the northern edge of the San Juan mining country, Crested Butte and Gunnison are separated from the Aspen/Marble area by massive mountains that were almost completely impassable in the 1880s. They're still barely passable today via rugged roads over sheer mountain passes. Colorado 133 out of Carbondale carries you to the cutoff for Crested Butte over Kebler Pass—but only in the summer. In the winter you have to keep going, turn off at Hotchkiss on Colorado 92 and take a stunning ride around the Black Canyon of the Gunnison River before hitting US 50 and then Gunnison.

Gunnison was once the supply hub for scattered mining camps (now turned ghost towns) in the nearby mountains. Set out on the "Scenic Ghost Route," described below and you'll find them.

■ SCENIC GHOST ROUTE

Want to run over some silver miners turned ghosts and spot the houses of ill repute they frequented after a hard day's work? Head north from Gunnison on Colorado 135 until you hit the small town of **Almont**, turn right on Country Road 742, and follow the Taylor River Valley to **Taylor Reservoir**. Now, take Road 765 to our first ghostly stop, **Hillerton**, which in 1880 had 1,500 residents, a bank, and booming mines. Stay on 765 and you'll find **Abbeyville**, which was a silver

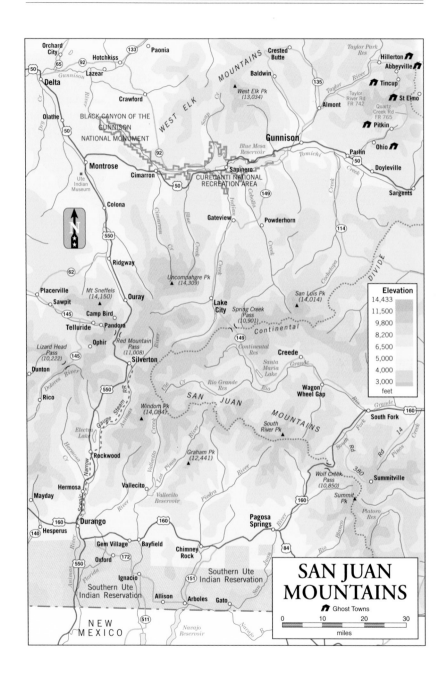

Orchard City
Hotchkiss
133 Paonia
Crested Butte
Hillerton
Abbeyville
50 65 92 Lazear
Delta
Baldwin
Tincup
Gunnison Cr
135
Taylor River Rd FR 742
St Elmo
Crawford
West Elk Pk (13,034)
Almont
Taylor River Rd FR 765
Pitkin
Olathe
WEST ELK MOUNTAINS
BLACK CANYON OF THE GUNNISON NATIONAL MONUMENT
92
Gunnison
Ohio
50
Blue Mesa Reservoir
Parlin
Doyleville
Montrose
Cimarron
Sapinero
CURECANTI NATIONAL RECREATION AREA
Tomichi Creek
50
Ute Indian Museum
Colona
149
Gateview
Powderhorn
Sargents
N
550
Ridgway
114
62
Uncompahgre Pk (14,309)
San Luis Pk (14,014)
DIVIDE
Placerville
Mt Sneffels (14,150)
Ouray
Lake City
Spring Creek Pass (10,901)
Elevation
14,433
11,500
9,800
8,200
6,500
5,000
4,000
3,000
feet
Sawpit
Camp Bird
Pandora
149
Continental
Telluride
Ophir
Red Mountain Pass (11,008)
Continental Res
Creede
145
Lizard Head Pass (10,222)
Silverton
Santa Maria Lake
Rio Grande
Dunton
Dolores River
Rio Grande Res
Wagon Wheel Gap
Grande
160
Rico
550
Windom Pk (14,094)
SAN JUAN
South Fork
14
Electra Lake
MOUNTAINS
South River Pk
South Fork Rd
Piedra
Rockwood
Graham Pk (12,441)
Wolf Creek Pass (10,850)
Summitville
Hermosa
Vallecito
Summit Pk
Platoro Res
Mayday
Vallecito Reservoir
160
Durango
160
Pagosa Springs
140 Hesperus
Gem Village
Bayfield
Chimney Rock
84
550
Oxford
172
Southern Ute Indian Reservation
Ignacio
151
Southern Ute Indian Reservation
Allison
Arboles
Gato
511
NEW MEXICO
Navajo Reservoir

SAN JUAN MOUNTAINS

🏚 Ghost Towns

0   10   20   30
miles

town in the 1880s; then from 1900 to 1912 dredges on local creeks recovered 20,000 ounces of gold.

As you proceed on 765, you'll find **Tincup**, to which by 1900 most of Hillerton's and Abbeyville buildings had been moved. (The first mobile homes in the nation? Sure, let's add that one to Colorado's list of firsts). You might run into someone besides a ghost because Tincup is alive today. Begun in 1880, by 1882 it had 20 saloons, four hotels, numerous stores, and ladies named Big Minnie, Sagebrush Annie, Santa Fe Moll, and (my personal favorite) Pass Out. Gold was mined in Tincup until 1917, then things went downhill until the town and its original buildings were revived and restored as a summer resort community.

You'll then have to lug over Cumberland Pass, a mere 12,200 feet (3,079 m), which is the highest unpaved auto road in the nation. (Yeah, we like to brag about how high our roads are here in Colorado.) At the summit you will be rewarded with views of the Bon Ton and Blistered Horn mines. Then it's on to Quartz, which started as a silver town but, because it had a rail spur from the Denver and South Park Railroad, continued to prosper as a lumbering center until 1934 when the train left town, followed quickly by everyone else.

Less fortunate was **Pitkin**, the next stop, which was the first incorporated town on the Western Slope, but only lived from 1880 to 1893. The Alpine Tunnel brought the South Park Railroad to town in 1882, but when the area's biggest silver vein played out after 75 feet (23 m) of mining things got pretty grim. However, many of the old buildings that once served the 2,500 residents remain and the old red school house contains a historical exhibit of Pitkin's fast past.

Luck was on the side of **Ohio City**, because its mines disgorged both gold and silver, so when the Silver Panic of 1893 hit, the town continued as a gold camp. The Raymond mines have been producing gold, off and on, up to today and the town has a small number of year-round residents who mix in nicely with the solitude, surrounding mountain scenery, and ghosts.

Your final stop is **Parlin**, which really isn't a ghost town, but it sure is old. It started as a stage station in 1880, and then both the Denver & Rio Grande and Denver & South Park railroads used it as a supply station and stopover. Today, it is fully functioning as a supply center for area ranchers.

As you continue down County Road 765 you'll hit US 50 and be only 12 miles (19 km) east of Gunnison, where this whole ghostly trip started.

Fall color in the remote and magnificent San Juan Mountains.

■ CREEDE

Deep in the heart of the San Juans lies the last great silver town, Creede. Its mines weren't tapped until 1889, but for the next four years it became the boomtown of boomtowns, where night and day were one and the same, millions were made, and the riff almost outnumbered the raff. Creede also hosted such sure-shooting legends as a marshall named Bat Masterson, Bob Ford (who killed Jesse James), and Calamity Jane and her pal, Poker Alice. The city never slept, turning out 80 million tons of silver during its short life.

A long slumber began with repeal of the Silver Act in 1893. Then five separate fires and some mud slides pretty much destroyed the tangible reminders of its glorious past. Today, Creede has become a regular small town buried deep in the San Juans that doesn't mind the occasional tourist, but whose real attraction is a slow, somewhat isolated lifestyle in the middle of the Colorado Rockies. If you visit, try getting tickets for a performance at the **Creede Repertory Theatre.**

■ OURAY

Ouray, on the western side of the mountains, is squeezed into a stunning canyon from which it seems there is no escape. Ouray's present mix of hot-spring spas, Victorian buildings, and modern conveniences belie its mining past. But the Camp Bird Mines and others in the surrounding mountains have produced gold on and off since 1893, when gold was found in leftover silver tailings. Visitors today should ask for directions to the spectacular **Box Canyon Falls.** This involves a short walk up Box Canyon, until it becomes very, very narrow, then a quick step back to avoid being given a massive shower bath by the falls.

■ SILVERTON

This little Victorian hamlet is set on top of the San Juan mining town pile. It's in a magnificent, isolated valley which enjoys, oh, about 80 days of summer and summer tourists a year. It's also home to the Sunnyside Mine, which produces gold and other minerals. From Silverton you can only go down, but it's a great ride regardless of which side you decide to descend.

Exploring an ice cave in Box Canyon, one of the San Juan's treasures.

■ DURANGO

If you drop off the hill south of Silverton, this is where you end up. You can take the trek by car on US 550 and wind through the rusted remains of many an old mine and mill, as well as the *unrusted* **Purgatory Ski Area;** or you can settle in on the restored **Durango and Silverton Narrow Gauge Railroad,** an authentic steam-powered locomotive that makes daily runs during the summer. A towering plume of steam will tip you off to the train's whereabouts. (See "Historic Railroads" in "PRACTICAL INFORMATION.")

Durango is an interesting old town that keeps itself new. Because of its location, it became the supply center for the San Juan mining camps, and the surrounding Indian reservations, as well as the area's farms and ranches. With **Mesa Verde National Park** about an hour's drive to the west on Colorado 160 and all the old silver mining towns, camps, and roads to the north, Durango is a good spot to set up camp during a San Juan stay.

As you stroll down to the historic **Strater Hotel** to catch a little honky-tonk piano or a melodrama, you'll pass blue-collar bars where you can rub elbows with real cowboys and Indians, scope out a broad selection of restaurants or ice cream shops catering to both visitors and locals, and find a funky postcard or curio shop or two, too.

(above) This ain't no "dime-store cowboy."
(opposite) The Durango and Silverton Narrow Gauge Railroad clears the tracks.

RACING RAILS AND ROADS TO SILVER

When silver began to outpace gold as king of Colorado's mineral court, silver mines and mining camps started popping up throughout the state quicker than they could be marked on a map. Unlike the gold country, which was relatively close to Denver and the Front Range, silver strikes were made in generally inaccessible high country in the central and southwest Rockies. The coming of a railroad or even a wagon road could thus turn a simple silver mining camp into a booming city and the road builders into millionaires. Thus, conditions were ripe for more than one high-stakes railroad race and several extraordinary displays of high-country road building.

Leadville was the first jewel lusted after by more than one railroader. Coming from the south, both the Rio Grande and the Santa Fe laid tracks right up to the mouth of the narrow Royal Gorge. Before rail crews decided with fist and sledge which track would be the only one to fit through the canyon, a deal was struck. The Rio Grande paid for the privilege to build into Leadville, and reached town in 1880. One railroad wasn't enough to serve Leadville, however, so the Denver and South Park line kept plugging away and reached town four years later.

The Rio Grande was involved in two other races, and won both. It was the first to hit **Gunnison** in 1881 and beat the Colorado Midland to Aspen in 1887. The Colorado Midland, though, was a gutsy little line. Starting in Colorado Springs, it ran through South Park and topped the 11,500-foot (3,496-m) Hagerman Pass (which was replaced in 1890 by the Busk Ivanhoe Tunnel) on the way to Aspen.

While most attention focused on Leadville and Aspen, **Otto Mears** attacked the rugged **San Juan Mountains**, whose gold and silver would be no more than piles of shiny curiosities if they couldn't be shipped out of the isolated valleys. The jagged peaks didn't deter Mears, an immigrant Russian Jew, who set out to connect the isolated mining camps with a series of toll roads. In all, Mears built over 300 miles of toll roads in the San Juans, linking the area to the outside world and earning the sobriquet "The Pathfinder of the Southwest." Many of Mears' original roads later became rail lines and his work is still evident today. His road from **Ouray** to **Silverton** is now part of the famed "Million Dollar Highway."

But the days of home-owned railroads were doomed by one man—eastern financier **Jay Gould.** Gould was insatiable. He already held significant interests in the Missouri Pacific, the Rio Grande, the Union Pacific, and the Denver Pacific, and he had operating agreements with the Santa Fe and Rock Island lines. He also bought the Denver and South Park, the Kansas and Pacific, and the Colorado Central. Thus, not only did faceless corporations come to dominate Colorado mining, but Gould, one of the slickest and most ruthless operators in capitalism's heyday, came to control most of the state's railroads, which were its lifelines. The result was predictable. When the once booming silver towns went silent, the screech of the steam whistle, the clackety-clack of iron wheels on iron rails, and the steady chugging of a steam locomotive also receded into silence, all victims of a bust that would have to wait for the intervening decades to provide the historical perspective that supplied the incentive and willingness to fire up the engine, blow the whistle, and let the steel wheels roll once again. (See "Historic Railroads" in "PRACTICAL INFORMATION" for a list of the state's historic steam-powered train rides.)

Toll station on Otto Mear's Bear Creek Road from Ouray to Silverton.
(Colorado Historical Society)

■ TELLURIDE

The problem here wasn't good gold, of which the area had plenty, but that it occupied the bottom of a sheer box canyon with just a rough road in or out. Thus, it languished until Rio Grande Southern Railroad chugged to town in 1890, touching off gold boom days.

Bad labor relations and isolation combined to stifle Telluride by 1930, but "To-Hell-You-Ride" was brought back to life in 1953 when the Idarado Mining Company bought old gold mining claims and began mining gold, zinc, and silver—which it did until 1978. The price was a huge, somewhat toxic pile of mine tailings right in the middle of this now exclusive resort community.

It still takes a bit to get to Telluride, even though it looks like it's just an inch west of Ouray on the map. Don't be fooled. It's a rough inch.

The classic **New Sheridan Hotel** is the centerpiece of the neat line of Victorian buildings along Telluride's main drag today. **Bridal Veil Falls** at the head of the canyon is a dramatic sight, as are the almost automatic rainbows that appear to reach from one mountaintop to the other at any hint of moisture. These falls were utilized to create the first practical method of air conditioning. Furthermore, Telluride was the first electrified town in the world.

(above) Telluride tucked into its sheer box canyon.
(opposite) Bridal Veil Falls cascades from the canyon wall east of Telluride.

Most summer weekends you'll find something going on, more specifically film, dance, and music festivals, the latter ranging from folk music, to bluegrass to jazz. (See "Events" in "PRACTICAL INFORMATION" for details.)

■ MILLION DOLLAR HIGHWAY

For a spectacular drive through the San Juans, take US 550, a loop from Ouray through Durango, Cortez, and Telluride. If you're refilling your stash of cold ones in **Ouray,** you might not want to glance up Red Mountain. If you do, you might think there is no way in the world to drive to the top of that hill without cardiac or carburetor arrest. Calm your beating heart. It's just an 11,000-foot (3,353-m) mountain pass that was born over 100 years ago when Otto Mears cut and carved a wagon road up the same hill. Not too many travelers have fallen off it since.

Mear's gutsy road-building feat laid the base for US 550, more commonly referred to as the **Million Dollar Highway,** which is just the beginning of the **San Juan Skyway,** a loop of state roads that takes you to almost every delight southwest Colorado has to offer. If you really want to take advantage of this trip you're going to have to take a couple of days, but once you get rolling you'll see taking a day or two on "the most beautiful drive in the nation" will more than make up for missing the tour at New Mexico's White Sands Missile Range.

Several peaks within the rugged San Juan Mountain Range top 14,000 feet.

Don't be alarmed if your car doesn't exactly roar up Red Mountain Pass; this is one steep puppy, so just take your time. There's plenty to look at anyway. Once you peak out, you'll drop, slightly, into the Victorian mining town of **Silverton.**

As you head south toward Durango the roadside is littered with ghost towns, old silver mine buildings and tailings. Still, you'll be traveling through Colorado high country at its finest, and topping two mountains passes over 10,000 feet (3,040 m) before reaching **Durango.** This historic town mixes turn-of-the-century charm with doses of progress, making for a real town that also happens to host tourists.

Now, turn west on Colorado 160, into Indian country, both past and present. To the south is the Southern Ute Mountain Indian Reservation and just past Mancos is the entrance to **Mesa Verde National Park.** Scanning the seemingly endless mesa you'll understand why it took so long for white men to discover the park's magnificent cliff dwellings and other archaeological wonders. (See "SOUTH-ERN COLORADO" for more information.) Farther west, you hit **Cortez,** the largest town in the region and the center of today's Indian culture and politics. Straight north on Colorado 145, then four miles (six km) north of **Dolores** is the **Anasazi Heritage Center,** a trove of ancient Indian artifacts and information about the Es-calante-Dominguez Expedition of 1776. Over Lizard Head Pass is **Telluride.** Nes-tled in a box canyon with ski hills on the right, towering mountains on the left, and bridal veil falls in front, you can't find a more picturesque mountain town.

Moonlit night in Silverton.

You're actually due south of Ouray right now, but to get there you'll have to take Colorado 145 to Placerville, then hit Colorado 62 to Ridgeway, which is where actor Dennis Weaver has built a house out of old tires and other refuse to draw attention to the nation's energy and conservation issues. Right past town is US 550, which will take you back to **Ouray**. Congratulate yourself. You have traveled 236 miles (378 km) and had the chance to view five million acres of national forest land. Oh, one final tip. If you do take the entire loop, stop in Ouray when you're finished and spend some time in one of the town's natural hot springs pools or spas.

■ SUMMITVILLE

The ghosts going bump in the night in the once-booming gold-rush town of Summitville don't have to rely on the same old ghost stories to entertain themselves these days. Instead, they can gather together and peer up South Mountain and watch Colorado's biggest gold-producing operation continue to pull the precious metal from the earth.

Summitville, due south of Del Norte and just east of Wolf Creek Pass at over 10,850 feet (3,298 m), experienced its first boom from 1872 to 1874, but the area's gold didn't pick up and leave like the prospectors, so the town has experienced a number of gold-driven rebirths that has kept the ghosts hopping in and out of the old miners' cabins.

In the early days, Summitville's mines made it the state's third largest gold-producing area. Eventually, about 50 mines on South Mountain disgorged 257,000 ounces of the shiny stuff.

Pretty impressive, until you consider 245,000 ounces of gold have been produced since the spring of 1986 when a Canadian firm started mining again. That made the mine the state's largest gold producer by the early 1990s, and made Colorado one of the nation's top gold producers.

But gone are yesteryear's gold pan, pick and shovel, sluice box, or hydraulic hoses. Also gone are the nuggets or flakes of gold easily spotted by the naked eye. Today's miners search for microscopic flecks of gold. At Summitville, tiny bits of gold are recovered from an open-pit mine 1,000 feet by 2,500 feet (304 m by 760 m), from which 24 million tons of dirt have been removed by trucks that can haul 50 tons of dirt each. Instead of crushing or smelting gold ore, the mine sorts the

Just a leisurely stroll in the San Juans.

microscopic gold from the dirt using a weak mix of cyanide and water held in large processing ponds called leeching fields.

Like the miners of old, the Summitville operation is making hay while it can. The company estimates that, at best and under optimal operating conditions, the mine's profitable reserves will only last a few more years. Then the huge earth-moving equipment and the computerized control panel will leave South Mountain in peace.

And the ghosts roaming the tattered, weather-beaten old buildings in Summitville will chuckle a bit, find another form of entertainment, and generally have the place to themselves once again.

Summitville's solitary inhabitant, George Popovich, still prospects for the mother lode.

WESTERN SLOPE
FROM DINOSAUR BONES TO PEACHES

IT WAS A HOMEMADE T-SHIRT, BUT ITS MESSAGE CAME THROUGH loud and clear. The design featured the red international "NO" symbol—a red circle with a slash through it. Inside the circle were a carton of milk and toast popping out of a toaster. Around the edge of the circle were the words, "U.S. National Hang Gliding Championships Dinosaur, Colorado," an event, at least as far as the T-shirt wearer was concerned, which automatically disqualified the milque toast crowd.

The T-shirt man was in Dinosaur's B&B Cafe fueling up for his flight and regaling his compatriots with excited predictions. He must have filled his tanks to overflowing because instead of merely strolling out of the rather anachronistic little eatery, he did a tap-dance hoochie-coo to the strains of the twanging, honkytonk, country-western song blaring out of the juke box.

Dinosaur, a tiny town with two motels, two cafés, a drive-in, and a city hall, is an unlikely place for over 100 hard-core hang-gliders to descend. The streets cut and jut in random order. Fresh paint and street signs don't overwhelm a visitor, so you have to feel your way around, but it's a short feel.

Dinosaur's isolation and steady winds were why the hang-gliding confab was being held there. The gliders could expect to hop off Cliff Ridge and ride the wind for up to 100 miles (160 km) in any direction, knowing chances were slim they'd land in a shopping mall parking lot or atop a suburban home.

But if a hang glider hit one hell of an updraft that sent him circling around northwest Colorado, he would be treated to a variety of sights far more interesting than shopping malls or suburbia. Floating north out of Dinosaur, he could gaze into the gorges made by the Green and Yampha rivers as they cut through Dinosaur National Monument. As he headed west, he would peer down on mile after mile of untouched brown-hued hillsides splattered with sage and piñon.

Then, abruptly, around Craig, the pine and spruce-covered western flank of the Rocky Mountains would rise up in greeting. Continuing south, he would cruise over the densely forested, dark green White River National Forest southeast of Meeker. Cutting back to the west he would zip over the Piceance Basin, where the land alternates between blocks of green, irrigated hay fields, and gray-dry chunks of land waiting for water. Amid the rolling hills of spruce and piñon he might spot

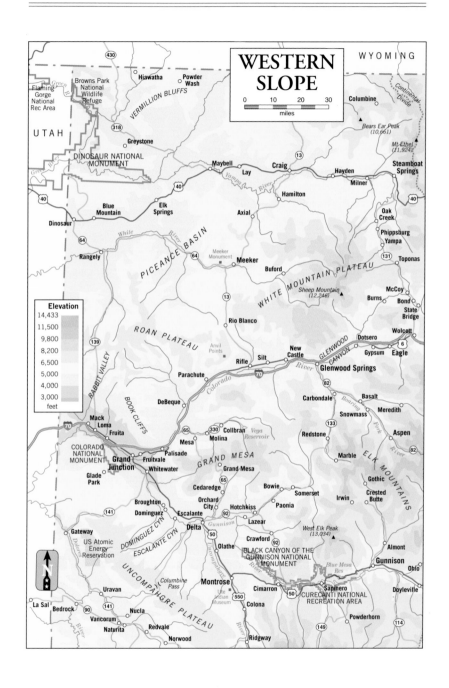

WESTERN SLOPE

0   10   20   30
miles

WYOMING

UTAH

Elevation

14,433
11,500
9,800
8,200
6,500
5,000
4,000
3,000
feet

hundreds, if not thousands, of the deer and elk that make the basin one of the finest places in the state to view wildlife.

Swooping back northward along the Utah border toward Dinosaur and the desolate desert, again a mottled mixture of red, grays, and browns will lay underneath until, with his head spinning with images ranging from desert to forest to mountain to pasture, our hang glider once again reaches the isolated burg of Dinosaur.

Here's a clue as to how isolated and desolate the area around Dinosaur once was: 100 years ago Butch Cassidy and his famous Wild Bunch used to hide out here after bank robberies or other "indiscretions."

The current residents are somewhat proud of that legacy and of the rough-hewn spirit necessary to survive in this unforgiving land. Indeed, you won't find a wimpy polo player on the menfolk's sport shirts, nor do they go for slacks, silk socks, or loafers with cute little tassels.

Dinosaur is the far northwest outpost of Colorado's Western Slope, which can be broken into two distinct regions. The northwest, generally referred to as the Piceance (PEE-aunce) Basin, contains one of the nation's largest storehouses of valuable minerals. This chunk of mostly federally controlled real estate faces Utah on the west, Wyoming on the north, the Rocky Mountains on the east, and bottoms out along Interstate 70 on the south. South of Interstate 70 the mountains still loom to the east with Utah to the west before you head into the San Juan Mountains and southern Colorado.

The basin's natural resources have created a diverse legacy: extensive ranching and farming plus development of oil, coal, uranium, and natural gas, on the one hand; the birth of the wilderness area idea, and two national monuments and a national recreation area on the other; and endless debate over who and what should come first—the miner/oil driller/rancher or the hiker/hunter/camper. Since huge chunks of the basin are federally controlled, most decisions affecting in the region aren't made by the people who happen to live there.

■ DINOSAUR NATIONAL MONUMENT

Whether you head toward Dinosaur National Monument from Steamboat Springs, Meeker, or Grand Junction, it takes hours of two-lane driving to get there. As you meander through this somewhat desolate landscape of red, tan, and white rock, it's hard to imagine that this was once a tropical landscape where giant vegetarian dinosaurs roamed through clumps of conifers, ferns, mosses, and cycads.

The sight of today's huge winged creatures—hang gliders—cruising and cutting into the up and down drafts above the Piceance Basin sky isn't entirely unprecedented. About 140 million years ago a winged dinosaur called the *Rhamphorhynchus* sailed the skies during the Jurassic Period and peered down on the huge walking dinosaurs which have captured the imagination of children and curiosity of scientists ever since. The *Rhamphorhynchus, Brontosaurus,* and herds of other dinos once called the region home, and their fossilized remains are scattered throughout northwest Colorado.

A bonafide race was on after the first dinosaur fossil discoveries were made around 1900, and tourists and paleontologists began to pick up bones and lug them away. The bone boom got going full bore in 1909 when a Carnegie Museum paleontologist arrived and was stunned to see eight tail bones of a *Brontosaurus* sticking out of the ground. Carnegie cash assured that many a museum would become a dinosaur depository. Fifteen years after the first discoveries, over 350 tons of dinosaur bones were dug up and shipped to museums across the country.

The wholesale "grave robbing" came to an end in 1915 when 80 acres of the diggings were designated as Dinosaur National Monument. In 1938 another 326 acres were added.

Therein lies the town of Dinosaur's real claim to fame: it's the gateway to Dinosaur National Monument. (Sort of. Rangely, about 18 miles [29 km] south of Dinosaur also claims the title, and since it has a community college, a downtown, and it resembles a town, it's hard to argue the point.) Actually, the gateway and the original portion of the current monument is over 20 miles (32 km) to the west in, egads, Utah, and features the much publicized **Visitors Center** where real paleontologists chip real bones out of a real dino dig.

■ GREEN AND YAMPA RIVER VALLEYS

Between 1950 and 1955, the nation's eyes focused on Dinosaur National Monument. Those eyes weren't peering in awe at 200-pound (91-kg) dinosaur bones, they were glaring at proposal to dam the Green and Yampa rivers where they meet just outside the original monument's boundaries.

Thanks to some serious shenanigans that set the tone for the "mainstream" environmental movement from then onward, the dam wasn't built and the Green

COLORADO'S AGE OF DINOSAURS

Dinosaur National Monument provides us with a grand view of the Jurassic landscape of 145 million years ago, when the earth's continents were joined together in a single land mass now referred to as "Pangaea." As you look about you at the subtle greys and browns of the desert, try to imagine the brilliant green ferns, conifers, and mosses which once grew here, and the behemoth dinosaurs that wandered among them. One of these was *Apatosaurus* (a.k.a., *Brontosaurus*), a long-necked and long-tailed vegetarian—measuring over 70 feet in length and tipping the scales at 35 tons. Because *Apatosaurus's* brain was smaller than ours, though given the job of directing a body as big as 18 station wagons, some people assumed it was dull-witted and spent most of its time sloshing around in swamps. Yet, now we know from studying rock strata in such places as Dinosaur National Monument that *Apatosaurus* galloped around in herds, probably with its young in the middle, kicking up dust and trampling trees. The smell must have been awful, but they may have been fairly smart. After all, *Apatosaurus* belongs to one of the most successful groups of animals ever to live on the earth.

Other smaller dinosaurs shared Jurassic Park with these monsters, among them the comely *Stegosaurus* ("roofed reptile"), known for the bony knobs and bumps all over its body, the upright plates on its back and its tail spikes. These animals grew to 20 feet in length and weighed about one-and-a-half tons. Early researchers thought that the back plates served as a defensive weapon, but more recently scientists have suggested that they served as solar panels and radiators regulating *Stegosaurus's* body temperature.

Roaming around with these oversized vegetarians were meat-eating carnosaurs, who packed their weight behind large heads, powerful necks, stout hind limbs, and small forearms. These included *Allosaurus* ("strange reptile") and *Ceratosaurus* ("horned reptile"). Adult *Allosaurus* was close to 40 feet long with a skull that reached nearly three feet in length; it had sharp, recurved daggers for teeth—serrated on both sides—lining its jaws. Possibly, it sped around Jurassic Park on its long, powerful hind limbs and grabbed its prey in the claws on its small, muscular forelimbs. *Allosaurus* probably fed on whip-tailed *Apatosaurus*.

As you climb into your two-ton station wagon to leave Dinosaur National Monument, you may feel vaguely relieved to return to the twentieth century, where the descendants of *Allosaurus* (birds) prey on insects and worms.

—Mark Goodwin, scientist at the U.C. Berkeley Museum of Paleontology

(following pages) Rudolph Zallinger's famous mural of the Jurassic Period gives an imaginative view of a world dominated by dinosaurs. (Peabody Museum, Yale University)

and Yampa River canyons were preserved. The canyons are located due north of the town of Dinosaur, through juniper and piñion country that contains nary a dinosaur bone, but remains indelibly etched in the memory of environmentalists and Coloradoans who watched "outsiders," like congressmen from Iowa or Sierra Clubbers, spouting off about what should be done with Western Colorado's natural resources.

Yep, the polo shirt and tassel-shoe crowd had arrived, and they struck the compromise: in return for construction of the Glen Canyon Dam, the Green and Yampa canyons were saved by being added to Dinosaur National Monument.

These two staggeringly abrupt cracks in the earth make you feel fragile in the face of the forces that created them out of windswept desert, especially when you are standing at the edge of the Yampa River Canyon, surrounded by miles of unmolested desert, or are taking a trail that lets you wander the rim and peer into the deep canyon to watch the snake-like Yampa River slowly and silently twist its way through the bottom. The same feeling of insignificance invades if you are rafting or fishing the Green River and peering up, in between bursts of whitewater, at its towering canyon walls.

On the northern edge of the monument is the **Brown's Hole Wildlife Refuge**, where Butch Cassidy and many other notorious outlaws hung out. These days it's a place to see nature and its creatures as they have been for centuries. (See the "GREAT OUTDOORS" for more information.)

■ WILDLIFE IN THE PICEANCE BASIN

The best way to get a feel for the Piceance Basin is to drive Colorado 64 between Rangely and Meeker. Thousands of animals feel quite comfortable ambling across the land and picking their way through stands of sagebrush, cedar, piñon-juniper, and Douglas fir. Towns and motels are non-existent, so if you'd like to spend the night along the way, bring a tent and sleeping bag.

There aren't any towns in the middle of the basin because in the 1880s the first white men didn't think the place was worth a damn. There wasn't gold and silver for the taking like there was in Central City or Leadville. Thus, many original mining claims were quickly abandoned and of the basin's 804,500 acres, about 675,000 acres eventually landed in the lap of the Bureau of Land Management

A wild horse stands alone in a Piceance Basin blizzard.

(BLM). But centuries ago people lived a pleasant life here, as evidenced by the **Dutch Creek Wickiup Village,** a prehistoric site listed on the National Register of Historic Places. Some 35 other sites may be eligible for the same honor.

As you travel the two-lane road, you'll see timber-covered mountains and rolling hills from which tumble small streams. The streams have been channeled and tamed into irrigation works that created 82,000 acres of farmland and another 400,000 acres of open range. Ranches dot the landscape, as do herds of cattle and sheep. The forested hills are also harvested, in the form of thousands of cords of piñon and juniper firewood and hundreds of thousands of board-feet of Douglas fir for local lumber yards.

It's almost impossible *not* to see wildlife either on the ground or in the sky. The area contains one of the largest migratory mule deer herds in North America—numbering over 25,000 head—along with over 1,200 head of elk (see "GREAT OUTDOORS"). In all, there are over 350 species of wildlife in the basin, including 22 species of raptors, ranging from owls to eagles, and, for good measure, a wild horse herd. Underneath it all are oil, gas, asphalt, nacholite, oil shale, and possibly gold.

SCAMS, BOOMS, AND BUSTS

The first brilliant idea for plundering the Piceance Basin took all the gall of scam artists Philip Arnold and John Slack. In 1872, they walked into a San Francisco bank with a bag of northwestern Colorado diamonds. Word got around, the men pocketed $600,000 for their own company, and other diamond companies sprouted overnight.

Thumbs down for Exxon; thumb out for a fresh start.

Reality reared its ugly head, however, when a U.S. government geologist discovered the diamond claims had been "salted," meaning diamonds had been literally planted a bit below the ground. The investors went bust, but Arnold and Slack had a booming time; they pocketed their cash and got off scot free.

Ten years later, as legend has it, settler Mike Callahan arrived on the basin, built a cabin, and fired up the fireplace. Within minutes the fireplace was burning and so was his cabin. He had built his fireplace from oil shale.

After watching cowboys build a shale fire, Goldie Manker's father-in-law Ed decided to stake a shale claim based on the Mining Law of 1872. The family kept the claim alive through the years, but as the 1990s began, Goldie was still waiting to cash in.

She's got a lot of company.

New technology kept old fields producing, and new oil fields always kept oil shale "just around the corner."

Rifle and **Parachute** were sure the 1980s were the right time for the real shale boom, and they were in the right place. Located 15 miles (24 km) apart from each other on Interstate 70, both towns were ready to belly up to the shale trough and start slopping it up. The oil shocks from 1973 to early 1980s prompted years of uncertainty and sent oil prices and shale dreams soaring. The big boys were playing —Unocal, Occidental, Exxon—and their playground was going to be the Piceance Basin.

Then it happened. During a Sunday night meeting in a New York boardroom, Exxon decided to kill its proposed $1 million-a-day shale project. Black Monday, May 2, 1982, arrived, and so did pink slips for about 2,200 shale workers. Overnight the boom busted. Then the exodus began. There wasn't a U-Haul trailer to be had from Vernal, Utah, to Denver, Colorado. "Mothballed until more favorable economic conditions" became shale's new motto.

Craig and Hayden, located along the basin's northeastern edge, were happy campers when their deep, rich veins of clean-burning, low-sulfur coal (the basin contains over 400 million tons of coal) started getting more attention than shale. Over half a dozen small (100,000 tons a year) and large (over two million tons a year) coal mines are roadside attractions in the area around Colorado 13 and 40 and bumper stickers proclaim, "Coal Miners Do It Deeper," and "Environmentalists Can Freeze in the Dark."

Both towns, however, also know that national and international energy markets can send their economy up and down as fast as pumping units.

When you consider that range of resources, it's hard to follow all the bouncing balls around the Piceance Basin and the dozens of special interests which want their particular ball to slip through federal fingers and fall to the ground in the most profitable manner possible. For them first, that is, and then the public, of course.

■ MEEKER: WHERE WILDERNESS WAS BORN

In 1919, a federal employee in Meeker, looking at the pristine beauty of the forests east of the mineral-laden Piceance Basin, decided there should be a way to assure that the public interest come first, foremost, and forever. That radical idea would eventually rock the Western Slope, rattle Colorado, and reshape the nation's public lands.

The man, Arthur Carhart, a Forest Service landscape architect working in the White River National Forest east of Meeker, was upset. The tranquil beauty of Trappers Lake was being threatened by plans for summer homes, guest ranches, and "civilization" in general. Carhart's radical idea was that certain places should forever be preserved as wilderness, untouched by man.

Carhart's idea of wilderness areas where homes, roads, mines, farms, and men's other "civilizing" tendencies would be banned was picked up and pushed ahead by nationally known conservationists of the day such as Gifford Pinchot, Bob Marshall, and Aldo Leopold. Thus, just west of one of the state's largest mineral storehouses was launched the idea that vast sections of public land should be set aside for those who wanted to merely look at wild land or tread without trace through it, instead of overwhelming it with technology, stripping off its trees, or tearing into its bowels to search for its hidden riches.

As Aldo Leopold wrote: "We abuse land because we regard it as a commodity belonging to us. When we see land as a community to which we belong, we may begin to use it with love and respect."

In 1964, Carhart's radical idea was codified as the U.S. Wilderness Act, which was fought tooth and nail by most Colorado politicians. Today, although wilderness areas attract a steady stream of tourists, creating more wilderness is still a hot topic because old ideas and old ways die hard, especially in ranching country.

Meeker, which rests between Rifle and Craig on Colorado 13, is a small ranching community which gets some mineral-based glory and grief but is sustained by the surrounding cattle ranchers and sheepmen ("Eat Lamb, 100,000 Coyotes Can't Be Wrong"). Driving through Meeker, with its old brick downtown buildings, mellow, small-town ambiance, and quiet well-kept residences, it's easy to believe the town spawned the idea of tranquil wilderness. Meeker is also home to the **International Sheep Dog Trials,** and therein rests a clue why it's in the middle of the newest public land debate.

In the fall of 1990, Meeker was in the spotlight over public land policy when five black bears were found dead near a poisoned, partially eaten lamb. The poisonings highlighted what could be the next "tooth-and-nail" national federal lands battle: a concerted effort to ban all sheep and cattle grazing on federal land. But federal grazing rights are sacrosanct to ranchers who have used them for generations. The problems today, according to grazing opponents, are that cows and sheep destroy the range, fees are too low, no one looks after the land, and the whole program is a federal subsidy that fattens ranchers' wallets more than their animals.

Sheepmen and environmentalists immediately decried the Meeker poisoning as an "inhumane and disgusting act." Radical environmental groups thought a sheepman just wanted to get rid of some pests, recalling decades of complaints about sheep eaten by bears, mountain lions, and, of course, coyotes. Sheep ranchers immediately proclaimed their innocence. Sheepmen proposed the idea that "eco-terrorism" could be a ploy to help build public support to drive all livestock from public lands.

If poisoned bears and hot rhetoric are any indication, Meeker's, and the nation's, next big environmental battle could involve a lot more than political shenanigans and gentlemanly compromises; it could get downright nasty.

Meeker was originally named after **Nathan C. Meeker** who arrived in the area in 1878 to head the White River Indian Agency, and change the Ute Indians from hunters and horse racers to solid Protestant farmers. For more about this disastrous enterprise read the "Utes" sidebar in "SOUTHERN COLORADO" (where the Utes now live.) Today, a simple farm implement is prominently displayed at the **White River Museum** outside of Meeker. It's *the plow.* The plow Nathan Meeker planned to use to turn the Utes' horse track into a corn field. Two miles (3 km) west of Meeker on Colorado 64 is a plain wooden sign and stone monument that pinpoints the **White River Ute Indian Agency.**

Behind the sign you can see the broad valley that the Utes used to call home and that has been tamed into pasture and farmland. But turning to the east, you can see the hidden valleys, hot springs, and peaceful retreats that the Utes will always remember as "the land of shining mountains."

■ GRAND JUNCTION: PEACHIEST TOWN AROUND

As soon as they were fairly certain the Utes would be removed from the Western Slope, land speculators and farmers went right to work. It is not stretching the truth to say that fruit trees and crops were being planted, mining claims staked, and hot springs turned into spas before the Utes' footprints had disappeared.

Grand Junction was the apt name speedy speculators chose for a grand town to replace the Ute camps at the confluence of the Grand (Colorado) and Gunnison rivers. Nestled between desert plateaus on the west and mountainous, pine covered mountains to the southeast, and with water readily available, Grand Junction was able to take advantage of every leg upon which the Western Slope economy rests.

Today, this city is the Western Slope's largest town, supplying the region with everything from transmissions to tricycles.

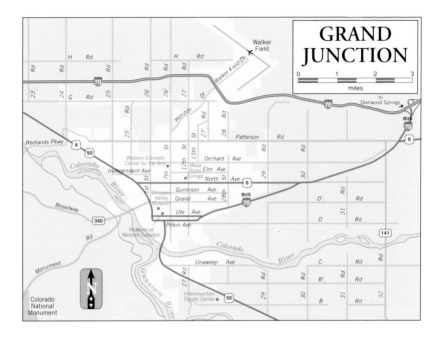

Grand Junction itself is an interesting mix of what's old, brick, and stable, and what's new, gleaming, and hopeful. Coming off Interstate 70, you'll be greeted by the gleam in the form of a strip of new motels, office buildings, and commercial space sparked by nearby Walker Field Airport. The airport's modern glass and polished chrome design is a solid benefit of the 1980's shale boom, since the oil companies were soaked for most of the bill.

Traveling from the airport strip to town on 12th Avenue gives you a taste of suburban solidarity, broken by the sprawl of Mesa State College, on the corner of 12th and North Avenue. North Avenue, if you use your imagination, could become famed Route 66. This was *the strip,* complete with funky motels and eateries, before the Interstate arrived. The hotels and restaurants have been updated, and North Avenue still hums with the sound of kids cruising on summer nights, and later in the evening, the roar of two "hot" cars screaming side by side is not unknown.

One sight does jolt the eye: the Far East restaurant, a veritable Chinese palace towering above the middle of Middle America.

Downtown—with its trees and flowers, serpentine lanes, pedestrian-friendly stoplights and crosswalks, and solid brick stability—looks new, but that's because it's been working on renewing itself for a long time. In 1962 Grand Junction became the second city in the nation to take a chance on reviving its downtown by creating a more relaxing, "shopper-oriented" atmosphere featuring ample parking, unique, locally owned shops (not chain stores), and an air of general pleasantry. It worked. Good speculators in this neck of the woods, it seems.

Of particular interest downtown is the **Dinosaur Valley Museum,** a special exhibition of the Museum of Western Colorado, whose other exhibits include a great gun collection—from muzzleloaders on up—and loads of other Western Slope lore. Dinosaur Valley features half-size replicas of several dinosaurs which move, stomp, and roar, a working paleontology lab, and other educational exhibits.

Since Grand Junction sits astride Interstate 70, making it easy to find and get to, regardless of the weather, it's a good launching pad from which to set out on targeted trips to the region's attractions.

Colorado National Monument at sunset.

■ GRAND MESA

The nation's highest flat topped mountain, Grand Mesa is just to the east of Grand Junction. Hunters, fishermen, campers, and nature lovers stream to the forest and its hundreds of streams and over 300 lakes via Colorado 65, plus county and four-wheel-drive roads. (See "GREAT OUTDOORS.") **Colorado National Monument,** which can be reached off Interstate 70 from either Fruita or Grand Junction, is a dramatic dose of desert wind carving, jolting color juxtapositions, and unanticipated arches.

A good introduction to the monument is the 23-mile (37-km) Rim Rock Drive. The road's tunnels are punched through the same red sandstone the wind has carved into arches and gentle curving formations. The red of the rock is accentuated by stands of bright green juniper and piñon trees, some seeming to grow right out of the rock. Lonely sandstone spires stand sentinel atop steep canyons dropping 2,000 feet (608 m) that afford a quick view of the Colorado River valley below as the road twists and turns back around and upon itself.

■ RABBIT VALLEY DINOSAUR DIGS

You don't have to take a long drive through uninhabited country to Dinosaur National Monument to satisfy your children's fascination with dinosaurs (or yours— come on, admit it). Today, right off Interstate 70 near Grand Junction where the Western Slope's northern and southern halves meet, you can avail yourself of guided tours and supervised digs just minutes from civilization.

Just ask Valerie Wolny.

Valerie was eight years old when she started touring, searching, and digging for dinosaur bones in the Rabbit Valley with crews from the Museum of Western Colorado.

Located 24 miles (38 km) west of Grand Junction in the middle of dusty desert-like landscape, Rabbit Valley gives you a chance to take an unsupervised stroll or guided tour through actual, scientific dino digs. Also along the trail are some partially uncovered fossils and other chunks and pieces that the "pros" think they know all about.

Then Valerie arrived on the scene.

In the summer of 1990, 14-year-old Valerie hit the mother lode when she discovered what may prove to be one of the biggest dinosaur bones ever found in the area: a vertebra which may be from a newly identified species, the *Apatosaurus*. That got the pros' attention and, since one bone usually leads to another in this line of work, all the animal's fossilized parts may eventually be excavated.

So if you take the guided tour through Rabbit Valley, keep your eyes peeled.

Also of interest to dinosaur buffs are the self-guided tours through **Riggs Hill** and **Dinosaur Hill** near the town of **Fruita**. Fruita is on the brink of breaking into dino-land big time with the planned development of **Devil's Canyon Learning Center**. The 26,000-square-foot "Disney does Dinos" features full-scale dinosaur exhibits, as well as a number of other ecological, geographical, and educational exhibits.

■ DELTA AND MONTROSE

Driving south of Grand Junction on US 50, you may get the feeling you're lost in the middle of the desert. If you dote on the desert and have some extra time, turn west on Colorado 141 at Whitewater to get a taste of the type of slickrock desert country that appeals to mountain bikers, dirt bikers, or backpackers seeking desert solitaire. The highway eventually runs into and follows the **Dolores River,** which is fed by a number of small streams pouring out of an isolated chunk of the Uncompahgre National Forest to the east. Desert, river, and forest all in one bundle, in other words.

Eventually, 141 takes you to the old uranium towns of **Nulca** and **Naturita,** where you can choose to head east to the San Juan Mountains, and if your desert thirst hasn't been quenched, continue south along the Utah border all the way to Cortez.

For those who think a desert is as exciting as a kitty box and choose to stay on US 50 out of Grand Junction, that particular stretch of desert will quickly give way to some of the state's most productive farmland. The key to its productivity is the **Gunnison River,** which you wouldn't know existed except for the roadside markers pointing out its beautiful canyons. Among the most magnificent are **Escalante and Dominquez canyons,** named after Franciscan priests who tromped through western Colorado in 1776 and claimed the whole place for God and Spain. (See "SOUTHERN COLORADO.")

KEEPING THE COLD WAR HOT

When the Ute Indians created war paint from a yellowish rock found throughout Colorado's Western Slope they could not have imagined what the white men who displaced them would create from that same rock. The rocks that supplied the Utes with yellow pigment was a form of uranium ore, and the atomic bombs that destroyed Hiroshima and Nagasaki owed their existence, in part, to Colorado uranium.

Between the Utes, the atomic bomb, and the uranium boom, Colorado can claim another atomic link. In the middle of the Rockies along the banks of the Colorado River is a little town named Radium. It was here that famed French chemist Madame Marie Curie came before the turn of the century to collect uranium samples for her pioneering radiation experiments. Her work allowed physicists to create the theories upon which the atomic bomb was based.

As World War II raged and the Manhattan Project sped toward creation of atomic bombs, attention focused on Colorado's uranium country. The area's mill tailings were reworked for their uranium, and over 70 percent of the Manhattan Project's domestic uranium came from Uravan and neighboring Vancorum.

After the shooting war stopped, the Cold War really heated up the uranium business. Prospectors were everywhere and so was uranium. Over 100 uranium companies set up shop in Grand Junction and the boom was on. By 1955, Colorado led the nation in uranium and vanadium production, with over 400 mines feeding over a dozen processing plants.

While uranium towns like Uravan prospered, workers took no special precautions against radiation exposure because little was known of its long-term effects. Mill tailings—which everyone assumed didn't contain enough uranium to be a problem—were blown about by the wind and used as fill dirt and in concrete in hundreds of Western Slope buildings.

The residents of Uravan, like thousands of other Coloradoans who had worked the uranium mines and mills, had an unwelcome surprise coming. First, the uranium and vanadium market slowly shrank, forcing many plant and mine closures. Vanadium was still processed at several mills into the 1980s. Then, it became clear that uranium exposure could cause cancers and other deadly side effects. In addition, it turned out that even slight amounts of uranium, such as those in the tailings piles, emitted radon gas, which could cause lung cancer. By the 1990s, the federal government agreed to compensate workers whose health had been affected by job-related uranium exposure.

That's why the uranium boom and bust is not going to reach the ghost town stage. The federal government is going to cover up, seal off, destroy, or hide all traces of the uranium industry. The health problems associated with the processing sites in the state prompted a $366 million, multi-year effort to tear down the old processing mills and haul off or stabilize the 25 million cubic yards of radioactive waste generated by those plants. The clean-up effort was a final radioactive irony because it created one last, but very final, uranium boom on the Western Slope.

Of course, the Spaniards didn't tell the Ute Indians that their home wasn't theirs anymore. It took settlers from the east another 100 years to accomplish that task. Being forced to leave the mountains they had roamed for generations brought the Utes bitterness, anger, shame, and pain. Many of the newer settlers couldn't have cared less or were delighted to be rid of the natives.

Occasionally, time heals emotional voids and provides perspective. Today, Delta and Montrose have asked the Utes back, honored them with a museum, and preserved some of their more powerful symbols.

Delta, located at the junction of the Gunnison and Uncompagre rivers about 40 miles (64 km) south of Grand Junction on US 50, is a casual farming community that also delivers a real taste of Ute tradition.

A small sign near the entrance to Delta points travelers toward the **Ute Council Tree,** a Colorado historic landmark. Because of its central location, this huge cottonwood (85 feet tall and seven feet in diameter [26 m by 2 m]) was a meeting place for several Ute bands whose leaders would gather to discuss common affairs. As time passed, these centered more and more on the pros and cons of staying to fight the whites, or ceding territory in return for peace and promises that some part of the Western Slope would remain theirs. Today the stately tree sits in between two houses at the end of a small lane lined by homes.

So much for the promises.

In the town of Delta, one sign points the way between a McDonalds and a Kentucky Fried Chicken to "Fort Uncompagre." The fort provides a summer setting for colorful Ute culture during summertime productions of "Thunder Mountain Lives Tonight!" Ute Indian dancers in full regalia bring back to life their tribe's ceremonial and traditional dances.

Delta also proudly proclaims itself "the city of murals." A quick trip down Main Street, with its comfortable lived-in look and its drugstore with a real soda fountain, provides evidence the claim is more fact than fiction. And, as one local noted, not one of the detailed murals has been despoiled by graffiti or other acts of juvenile hooliganism. "That kind of lets you know what sort of town this is."

There is one special mural, though, that graphically describes what sort of town Delta is and what kind of region surrounds it. The muralist canvassed almost every aspect of the region's historical roots and natural wonders while updating the agricultural bounty now pouring forth from the surrounding lands and towns they support.

A big, brown, snarling grizzly bear, surrounded by some very meek but tasty-looking fruit, arrests the eye as a symbol of the Growers and Traders Company of Hotchkiss. The logo for Skyland Apple Juice, made from Colorado apples, rests amidst a scene of towering, snow-capped peaks, lush valleys, and dense forests. The same postcard delights also form the backdrop for a group of mammoth, bright-yellow, Paonia pears at the peak of perfection.

A towering rock monolith etched with ancient Indian petroglyphs is the apt symbol for Indian Rock Colorado Peaches from Bridgeport. A colorful Navaho

Ute Indian scouts crossing the Los Piños River. (photo by H. S. Poley courtesy Denver Public Library, Western History Department)

Ute Chief Ouray stressed negotiations, not battle. Neither saved his people's independence. (Denver Public Library, Western History Department)

blanket serves as another apt symbol, this time as the trademark for Blanket Brand Paonia cherries.

The serene Plains Indian in full buckskin regalia, feathered war bonnet, and grasping a waist-high tom-tom informs viewers about Tom-Tom Colorado Apples, of Delta. Another Plains Indian in full costume is a fairly placid pitchman for Tomahawk apples from Eckert. (How pleased modern-day Indians are to see themselves identified with apples remains unclear.)

You can see the inspiration for the mural everywhere you look. To the east is the massive Grand Mesa with its blanket of dark timber. Turning west, you can imagine the desert just beyond the horizon. In every direction are the orchards and farms that make up the region's economic backbone and create a resilient population whose pride in their accomplishments can't be dampened by gyrating commodities markets or broken by an occasional killer frost.

The trip to **Montrose,** 20 miles (32 km) south of Delta, continues through a region of abundant fertility. Stretching to the mountains on the east and stepping up gentle plateaus on the west are fields of rich soil that, with water, can grow anything from onions to sweet corn to broccoli. That fertility continues south until the San Juan Mountains start to loom in upon you, and you enter another realm, southern Colorado.

A comprehensive view of Ute life is available in the Colorado Historical Society's **Ute Indian Museum,** located two miles (three km) south of Montrose. The museum

Henry Farney evokes the Indians' nomadic life in this 1902 oil on canvas.

occupies the former farm of famous Ute Chief Ouray, and his equally famous wife Chipeta, who is buried there. On display in the museum are Ute beadwork, ceremonial objects, feather bonnets, and other clothing, as well as extensive photos of tribal members dating from the 1880s and an explanation of Ute religious and ceremonial life.

■ BLACK CANYON OF THE GUNNISON AND BLUE MESA RESERVOIR

The **Black Canyon of the Gunnison National Monument** and **Blue Mesa Reservoir** stretch almost the full length of US 50 from Montrose to Gunnison. The canyon's black, jagged, granite walls towering thousands of feet above the Gunnison River make the Black Canyon both spectacularly beautiful and almost inaccessible from the rim, but a great place to raft or fish. Here, the river is deeper for its width than any other river in North America—almost one half mile straight down. The canyon is the also the highest vertical climbing face in Colorado. Look up and you may see climbers on it. But that wild canyon and fish-filled river is just part of the fun. Blue Mesa Reservoir, the largest puddle in Colorado, also offers great boating and fishing. (For more specific information, see "GREAT OUTDOORS.")

The huge reservoir ending abruptly at an awesome wild canyon captures in a nutshell the great water questions that have been debated since the attempt to dam the Green and Yampha rivers near Dinosaur: "We've got to store water for irrigation, growth, and hydroelectric power, and the lakes will be great recreation places for the average outdoor lover—not elite whitewater rafters, rock climbers, and backpackers."

Versus: "All rivers weren't created to be dammed. The 'elite' spend money too, and even more people will be attracted to a natural place carved and niched by nature, water, and wind over centuries instead of built by man in a decade."

Agriculture has sustained the area from day one and won't go away. Logging is another mainstay, and there always seems to be another plan cropping up about increasing the "harvest" from surrounding national forests to feed sawmills and fireplaces.

The final question still being debated is: How do you accommodate and generate wealth from everyone, be they farmers, lumberjacks, and miners, or hunters, fishermen, and campers?

■ EDUCATIONAL WESTERN SLOPE LUNCHES

Down the road was a simple-looking café and lounge, the parking lot was full of pickups, the tables full of older, clean-shaven men wearing jeans (not slacks), cowboy hats, and cowboy boots. On the formica counter was mustard without a French name on it. It was plain old French's mustard.

The beans were in; the onions weren't. The waitress was a Denver Bronco fanatic. The men casually recalled how to sneak around a now-closed BLM road leading to a stand of top-dollar cedar. The older men, who looked past retirement age, paid their bills and headed back for an afternoon of work, leaving the local paper for a lunch companion.

The back page had a homecoming photo spread showing local football players and cheerleaders, and, yes, the local boys won.

The editorial page was hot. A "timber advocate" noted that the National Wildlife Society, Audubon Society, Natural Resources Defense Council, and the Environmental Defense Fund had a combined yearly budget of over $151 million. The directors of those groups (the guys with silk socks and tasseled loafers) were paid a yearly total of $562,000. That seemed like quite a bit of money in a town where a full-blown cheeseburger deluxe cost $2.45.

Next to a letter linking planning, zoning, and communism was one by the president of Colorado Women in Timber, who wrote that more wilderness areas would just lock up more forest and be an outright attack on the timber industry.

The motel restaurant nearby didn't have counter service, but did have carpet. A local landowner and his city friend were putting catsup on their burgers. They wore high-tech hiking boots and were getting ready for a fishing trip and muttering about wildlife-threatening timbering and the latest water diversion irrigation/hydropower scheme which would deliver to the fish and waterfowl the short and messy end of the stick.

Their chit-chat was familiar: the relative fatness of farmers' wallets, Eastern companies making most of the money, federal subsidies, federal bureaucrats, and the locals getting leftovers.

Those at the motel restaurant and the café up the road had one thing in common. They had made almost exactly the same remarks about how much money "outside" groups were spending in the region, and the unfortunate results being achieved.

■ BOUND TOGETHER

There are two threads that bind together all those who live on the Western Slope or love it. One is the land and its natural wonders, ranging from towering mountains and rippling streams to veins of coal and pools of gas. The other is the effort it takes to live there: the necessity of doing without civilization's "improvements" and the spunk required to scratch a living out of, or to preserve the land.

So the hardscrabble coal miner, gritty drilling-rig hand, commercial river-runner, dusty cowboy, suntanned farmer, and conservationists should all get a copy of that Dinosaur hang glider's T-shirt, because the milque toast crowd just ain't gonna cut it out here.

Close quarters in the early mining days called for compromise, a term still being defined on today's Western Slope. (Colorado Historical Society)

SOUTHERN COLORADO
INDIAN / SPANISH / HISPANIC

IN SOME FLASH OF UNINTENDED INTELLIGENCE OR semi-conscious consistency, the U.S. Congress made the right move when it created a single congressional district including the Western Slope and southern Colorado.

Both areas have much in common: a dependence on natural resources, stunning scenery, and isolated communities that don't take much of a hankering to outsiders telling them what to do. Once you drop south out of the San Juan Mountains or head west from Salida, a change starts to take place that sets southern Colorado apart.

Around Cortez and the Four Corners region the desert starts to take on the bone-dry, reddish, windswept look and feel found in Utah and New Mexico. Farther east are forested mesas and very few towns. If enough water is available, green hay fields thrive and feed the area's cattle and sheep. Where there's no water, the land is gritty and covered with sagebrush. The triangular San Luis Valley, of south-central Colorado, is one of the largest level basins in the state's mountainous regions. Ringed by mountains, its streams keep the area lush by Colorado standards.

In a bizarre twist of nature, at the northeast end of the valley is **Great Sand Dunes National Monument,** a veritable white ski hill made of sand and tucked between the green fields of the valley and the towering peaks the **Sangre de Cristo Mountains,** maybe even more inspiring than anything up north.

But it's more than the scenery that sets southern Colorado apart. It's also the history: ancient Anasazi cultures and cliff dwellings, the Spanish conquest, and the arrival of traders and settlers in the 1800s who came by horse and covered wagon. In today's southern Colorado there's also a unique ambience. It's a slower pace, an old-fashioned grace, and the pleasure one feels in visiting an area steeped in time, rather than racing furiously toward the future. If anything, southern Colorado tends to look south to Santa Fe for inspiration, rather than north to Denver, and since the **Ute Indian Reservations** straddle and dip into New Mexico, perhaps the whole area's in the wrong state. Certainly, the area retains and heartily embraces its Indian, Mexican, and Spanish roots.

Four Corners: a desolate dot where four state boundaries meet.

■ FOUR CORNERS, CORTEZ, AND THE ANASAZI

No one knows if it is a map-maker's joke, a fluke, or just something that happened, but barely a mile off US 160 is the only place in the nation where **the borders of four states meet.** Once only a circular bronze plaque set in concrete informed you that, if you got down on all fours, you could be in Colorado, Utah, New Mexico, and Arizona all at the same time. Today the plaque is circled by plywood booths filled with Ute, Navaho, Apache, and other Native American artwork, crafts, artifacts, and rugs. If you are traveling west into Colorado, it's worth a stop to touch all the states and to see what real Indian arts and crafts made by real Indians look like, and cost.

Looking into Colorado, past the surrounding desert, you can see the outline of the San Juan Mountains. As you continue into Colorado on 160 toward those mountains, you enter the **Ute Mountain Indian Reservation. Towaoc,** nestled

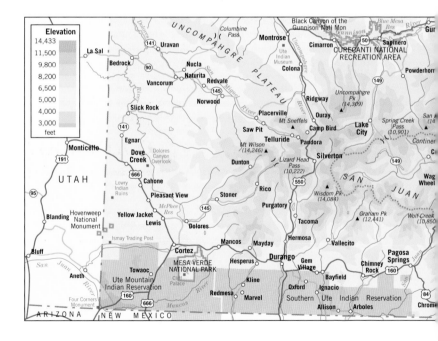

against the hills off US 160, is the only substantial town on the reservation. Towaoc's **Ute Mountain Tribal Park** features a pottery showroom, visits to ancient Anasazi dwellings, and guided hikes into the backcountry.

A certain question starts to crop in your mind as you start to leave the reservation. For miles previously, the land has been barren, desert-like, with just a sprinkling of native shrubs and bushes. But as you leave the reservation, verdant hay fields, pastures, and ranch land spring to life. The reason for this has to do with the availability of water.

Cortez, the largest town in the region, is also a depository of current Southwest Indian art and culture, thanks to its many art and craft galleries featuring work from Ute, Navajo, Apache, and other Native American artisans. The town and surrounding area are excellent places to get a feel for Anasazi culture. The **Anasazi Heritage Center,** located nine miles (14 km) north of Cortez in **Dolores,** houses educational and participatory exhibits on the Anasazi. It is also the storehouse for

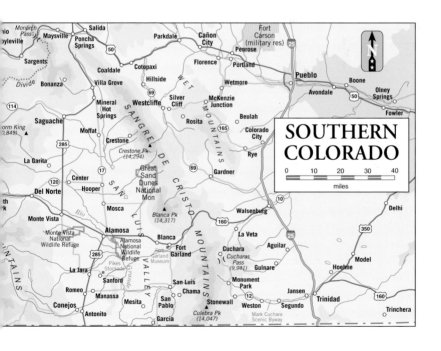

two million artifacts that would have, without some arm-twisting, been drowned by the McPhee Reservoir, farther north.

The University of Colorado operates the **Cortez Center,** which specializes in lectures and tours of current diggings. The **Crow Canyon Archaeological Center** stresses "do-it-yourself" archaeology by showing and telling amateur diggers where and how to dig for artifacts.

Just west of Cortez , through desert country reminiscent of dozens of generic car commercials, is **Hovenweep National Monument** (Hovenweep is Ute for "Deserted Valley") where tall towers still guard some of the deserted ruins. The ruins were saved from savaging thanks in part to their inaccessibility (even today, you can only drive to one set of ruins) and partly because it was designated a national monument in 1923. The **Lowry Pueblo,** built around A.D. 1000 and uncovered in 1928, features the largest ceremonial room, or *kiva,* discovered to date and is more accessible, thanks to its 1965 restoration and designation as a national historic landmark in 1967. (The Visitors Center is just across the border in Utah.)

A hard-core Anasazi buff would need several days to hit all these sights, and Cortez is accommodating to such folks. It hasn't been glamorized and offers a relaxing small-town atmosphere for visitors.

■ MESA VERDE

The entrance to Mesa Verde is just ten miles (16 km) east of Cortez on US 160; then you've got miles of park to explore and, in the Cliff Palace, some of the most enthralling ruins of an ancient civilization to be seen anywhere in the world. The National Park Service **Visitors Center** provides background information and directions, and is the only food stop on the way—so pack a lunch or pack your wallet if you want to eat.

After the Visitors Center, it's an uninterrupted drive through piñon-covered hills and mesas where long ago (and almost unbelievably) corn, beans, and squash were once grown. No streams are now visible, nor are there any remnants of irrigation works. In the mesa area, you will see numerous half-ruined pit houses and other structures that belonged to ancestors of the later cliff-dwelling Anasazi, whose dwellings you're on your way to see.

After driving those miles, most people seem to come to the conclusion that the Anasazi chose this spot to live in for purposes of defense or because it was easy to hide in. It would have taken some serious seeking to find these folks just to make a little war and plunder their pottery.

■ ANASAZI HISTORY

A rudimentary Anasazi culture first got underway about the time the Western World went from B.C. to A.D. This first Anasazi group is now called the "Basket-makers" and for about 450 years they eked out a meager existence, foraging for desert plants, hunting with spears, and making baskets. Eventually this culture evolved into what is now called the "Modified Basketmaker Period" (450 to 750), identified by the use of the bow and arrow, pottery, beans, corn, and underground pit houses. Then came the houses and communal buildings erected from stone and adobe built from 750 to 1100.

Which is another way of saying that the people who moved into the cliffs didn't just pop from behind some sagebrush with all their spiritual and cultural refinement. Rather, they were taking advantage of centuries of history and experience. And they used every shard of it in such monuments to their culture and skill as the Cliff Palace.

■ CLIFF PALACE

When the Ute Indians first migrated into this area, they looked at the Anasazi ruins, decided they were haunted, and afterwards avoided them. Indian tribes farther south in New Mexico also had seen evidence of the vanished culture as they'd migrated through southern Colorado into New Mexico. They were the ones who first referred to these ancient people as "Anasazi," or "enemy ancestors."

No one thought much about the ruins at Mesa Verde after that for a long, long time, not until the winter of 1888 when two cowboys out looking for stray cows way the hell in the middle of nowhere suddenly stopped in their tracks in a state of shock. What Richard Wetherill and Charlie Mason had caught sight of was an intact, abandoned stone city fit for 400 folks. It's not recorded if they found the cows, but the world quickly learned what they did find—the **Cliff Palace**—a complex of about 200 individual homes, 23 underground ceremonial *kivas,* and towers rising as high as four stories.

The world came to see what the cowboys found, and every clod in a pith helmet came away with something, be it a stone or pottery shard, from the surrounding area's estimated 800 cliff dwellings. Congress got off its duff in 1906 to stop

(following pages) The stunning Cliff Palace at Mesa Verde National Park remains an architectural triumph and retains an air of mystery.

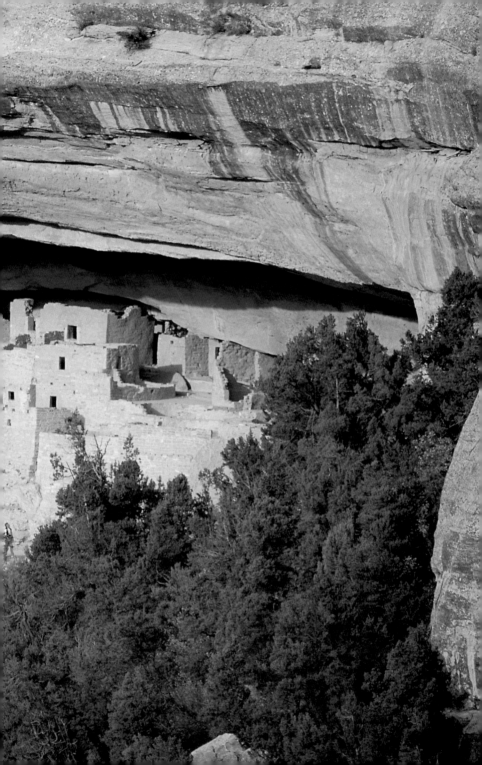

the random looting and created **Mesa Verde National Park,** the first national park designed to preserve archaeological treasures.

Tucked underneath huge overhangs, built from A.D. 1100 to 1300, then abandoned almost as soon as they were completed, the cliff-dwellings still stun and mystify. Some of the stone-crafted dwellings, such as the Cliff Palace, could accommodate up to 400 people. The masonry walls were not just rocks and mortar slapped together, but were crafted with care, plastered, and in some cases decorated. The fact that many of these buildings are still standing 700 years later is testimony to the masons' skill.

The mystery of Mesa Verde seems to resolve itself into two basic questions: Why did these people come here, and why, after barely 100 years, did they start to leave the Club Med of the day? Every Southwestern archaeologist in khaki shorts tries to answer those questions, and most visitors arrive at their own conclusions after a tour.

The pros speculate the dwellers departed for one or more of these reasons: drought, over-intensive farming which ruined the land, or in order to flee from nomadic raiders.

Same goes for the move to the cliffs: fear of attack, trying to protect the water feeding the state's first irrigation systems, or just stumbling on the caves' natural protection and building from there.

■ SPANISH EXPLORERS

The Catholic kingdom of Spain entered the New World to reap both riches and souls. By 1521, with the aid of guns, horses, and armor, Mexico had become a Spanish colony, and its silver and gold mines began their prodigious production, via the natives' slave labor. But like every gold- or silver-crazed prospector, the Spaniards lusted after the big bonanza, the quick strike somewhere over the next ridge or just north of the next river where gold was resting in piles for the taking. In their case they thought that bonanza was the legendary "Seven Cities of Gold," or "Cibola." Throughout the 1600s and 1700s, expeditions—some going as far north as Colorado—set out from Spanish territory to find cities built of gold.

The most famous Spanish explorers to reach Colorado were two Franciscan priests, Silvestre Escalante and Francisco Dominquez. In 1776, when the newly formed United States of America began its battle for independence, the Franciscans

KIVAS, CROSS, AND CRESTONE

There's a voice in the wilderness crying,
A call from the ways untrod:
Prepare in the desert a highway,
A highway for our God!
The valleys shall be exalted,
the lofty hills brought low;
Make straight all the crooked places,
Where the Lord our God may go!
—Isaiah 40:1-11

From *kivas* to Catholicism to Crestone, southern Colorado has witnessed and been a testimony to an unrelenting faith in powers greater than what mere mortals possess.

For centuries the Pueblo peoples turned to their *kivas*, to seek in solitude the power of their gods and spirts. Starting as a rude hole in the ground, the *kiva* evolved into a standardized, circular pit that provided symbolic structure to honor nature's four elements—wind, water, fire, earth—or other supernatural elements in the ceremonial life.

The *kivas* are silent now, but a sensitive traveler can descend into one *kiva* at **Mesa Verde**, for instance, and still get just a tingle, a tremor of feeling that something special, unexplainable, but still powerful can occur when people slow their hurried pace and listen to the earth around them, the earth that still sustains them, the earth that they will eventually be buried under.

The Spanish conquerors who brought the Catholic faith and its churches to southern Colorado also brought a unique off-shoot of Catholicism: the **Penitentes**. Begun in the thirteenth century to honor St. Francis of Assisi, the Penitente societies, which died out everywhere in Europe except in Spain, met in *moradas*, or lodges, and practiced self-torture as part of their devotions. From the early 1800s on, these exclusively male societies filled a void in the isolated towns of northern New Mexico and southern Colorado, many of which had no priests or others willing to undertake charitable work and maintain a sense of spiritual community.

Penitentes obeyed the tenants of the Catholic Church except during Holy Week. Then, dressed in black hoods and white breechclothes, they would publicly perform a painfully honest re-enactment of Christ's capture, trial, and crucifixion.

The re-enactment included self-flagellation with whips or cactus, carrying a heavy wooden cross, and actually having one member tied to the cross until he fainted.

The societies and their grisly ceremonies were eventually banned by the Church, but that just made the Penitentes secret societies instead of open ones. Hundreds of Penitentes continued their unique devotions well into the 1900s, and some portions of the groups' ritual self-torture are still practiced today. Also, many of their *moradas* remain scattered throughout southern Colorado.

In **Crestone**, located at the top of the San Luis Valley on the edge of the San Isabel National Forest, earthly calls of another nature beckon to those of a new age and to the spirit of a new breed of believer. This little summer hide-away has become the focus of many New Age spiritualists.

The area, allegedly sacred to the Indians, is supposed to be the center of some cosmic earth wart where all manner and variety of earthly, unearthly, spiritual, and transcendental planes, energy sources, and general action converge, coagulate, reincarnate, cross-mutate, and co-mingle. Doubters dub it a reincarnation of the Age of Aquarius; skeptics wait for the new spirituality of Crestone to start enduring the test of time. Believers come to rest, refresh themselves in the natural surroundings, listen to the vibrations from earth, wind, and trees, and soak in powers unknown but felt all the same. (Some also buy real estate, but that's another story.)

The cliff-dwellers went into underground kivas for ritual ceremonies.

No one knows why this southern Colorado has been and still is home to such a sustained sprouting of spiritual outburst. The He/She/It who provokes such shows of faith isn't saying. Maybe if you climb into a *kiva*, feel the passion of a Penitente, or commune with a Crestoner you will receive a glimmer of the grace that fuels such faithful fire.

Theories abound as to why the cliff-dwellers abandoned their cities.

set out on a trek that would make winter at Valley Forge seem like a Boy Scout weenie roast, complete with hot chocolate.

Embarking from Santa Fe, they headed northwest, hit and bounced around the San Juan Mountains until they came to the Dolores River, followed it to the Gunnison River, then onward to the White River, stopping here and there to pray a bit and officially claim all they tromped over for God and Spain. They then headed due west into Utah in an effort to find a trail to California, until heavy snows and inhospitable desert forced them back to Santa Fe.

What the desert-dwelling Native Americans thought about being "discovered" by Spanish explorers is unrecorded, but they may have thought they'd just discovered something: a new breed of pale and pretty peculiar men. What kind of fool would come to the desert wearing heavy clothing, a helmet on his head, and armor over his clothes that turned him into a miniature sweat-drenched pottery kiln?

The new breed's "big dogs" and "booming sticks," however, did get the natives' attention, and although they themselves became expert horsemen and riflemen, a combination of warfare with Europeans and exposure to their diseases would cause the ultimate destruction of their culture and genocide of their people.

By the late 1700s, southern Colorado was just a hop, stagger, and donkey ride from Santa Fe, in relative terms, and was claimed and settled quickly in the Spanish era, thanks to land grants direct from the King of Spain himself. Thus, the area retains some of Colorado's deepest Spanish/Mexican roots and an identification with New Mexico and Mexico, which in turn made it the final link in a chain that started hundreds of years earlier when the Spanish "discovered" the New World.

■ SOUTHERN UTE INDIAN RESERVATION

As you travel along US 160 you can see the mineral-laden mountains to the north that the Spaniards didn't explore thoroughly, but which white prospectors swarmed all over. Their persistence led to huge mineral discoveries around Durango, Silverton, and Lake City and also prompted the removal of Ute Indians from those mountains.

South of US 160 as it makes it way from Durango to Pagosa Springs is the **Southern Ute Indian Reservation.** The tribe is headquartered in **Ignacio,** about 20 miles (32 km) southeast of Durango. Amid rolling hills and ranch land is the

Piño Nuche Pu-ra-sa Tourist and Community Center, which features a motel, restaurant, arts and crafts shop, museum, and guided trips into Ute country during the summer and hunting season.

It would seem, what with all the Ute cultural centers, the national park, and historic sites and preservation actions taking place from Cortez to Ignacio, that the federal government was right on top of things in southern Colorado.

Nice try.

Through the years it always seemed the same white men who gloried in the myth of the rugged individualist always got the government goodies first, with the leftovers blowing south to the reservations that, in the 1880s, the whites thought consisted of worthless land. After a century of reservation life, broken promises, and patience, members of the Ute Mountain and Southern Ute tribes are still fighting a two-front battle.

First is the fight for respect; second, the struggle for the right to help mold their own destiny by shaping decisions about how and when to develop the natural resources—water, coal, natural gas—modern prospectors found in abundance on the "worthless" land.

As for respect, the following story gives the general picture.

The painting was a melodramatic 1880's effort depicting a "bloodthirsty savage" scalping a hapless white man. No one knew where it came from, why it was chosen, or how long it had actually been hanging in the Bureau of Indian Affairs' "Treaty Room," in Washington D.C.; but after a "suggestion" that it be removed, by then congressman (and Native American) from Colorado Ben Nighthorse Campbell, the offensive painting was replaced with other art.

Campbell, now a U.S. senator, is proof it doesn't hurt to have a Native American from a Colorado reservation stomping around Washington in cowboy boots and bolo tie reminding his colleagues about places like Towaoc, and that when treaty-makers talk about "as long as the sun shall shine and the grasses grow," that's a very long time.

When it comes to having some say in their own destiny, the Utes are still trying to hold the government to one of its oldest promises. This promise was made in 1902 when the government decided to build the Animas-La Plata dam and diversion project to provide water for (among others) Utes. But as of the end of 1990, not one shovel full of dirt for Animas-La Plata had been moved.

UTES: EXIT FROM THE LAND OF SHINING MOUNTAINS

The Ute Indians who roamed Colorado could always rely on one thing: safe haven in the mountains and valleys they called "the land of shining mountains." Ute bands roamed from the Great Plains into Utah and on the borders of present-day Arizona, New Mexico, and southern Colorado. Whether seeking refuge from other raiders or a quick escape after a raid of their own, the mobile Utes could lose their pursuers in the mountains they knew so well.

Before the Spanish brought horses into North America, the Utes scratched out a living much like the Paiutes, Navaho, and Apaches, with whom they shared their far-ranging domain. They relied on small-game hunting and gathering desert and mountain plants for subsistence.

Physically, the Utes were a stocky, powerfully built people with dark, bronze-colored skin. They would move their camps into the high country for summer hunting, but retreat to gentler climes to wait out winters. Their women's bead-work was, and still is, intricate, colorful, and refined into art itself.

The Utes also developed a rich ceremonial and spiritual life. They "knew" the bear and how to coax him from hibernation with the Bear Dance that signalled the beginning of spring. The Sun Dance, initiated in the middle of summer, was to ensure good hunting.

The Utes were also a playful people, and many of their dances—the Circle Dance, Coyote Dance, Tea Dance—were strictly social in nature. Social, but more serious, were the melodies from handmade flutes that a man used to attract his true love. All sorts of games occupied idle time, including stick dice, archery, ring spearing, juggling, wrestling, and foot races. Horse racing was without question the most popular sport and, unfortunately, contributed to the ultimate removal of the Utes from Colorado.

Spaniards spotted the Utes as early as the 1600s, and eventually arrived at an uneasy peace with them. The Spanish also provided the Utes with the horse, although that certainly wasn't their intention. The Utes became one of the first tribes with extensive herds, thus greatly increasing their mobility and heightening the respect given them by other tribes.

The Utes had few squabbles with the mountain men who arrived from the east in the 1830s. Many married Ute women and appreciated the Utes' knowledge of the land and how to live off it. But things changed when gold was discovered in the

1860s. The gold and silver seekers wanted control of the land, and the farmers who followed saw potentially productive land being "wasted." As Colorado became first a territory and then a state, the drive to drive the Utes off their land intensified.

That drive was accomplished with a series of treaties. The Utes ceded the San Luis Valley (in southern Colorado) in 1863, were moved west of the Continental Divide in 1868, and gave up their claim to other mineral-rich land in 1873. Thus, west-central and northwest Colorado became their home. Its advantages were plentiful game, natural mineral hot springs with their spiritual and healing powers and, for a while, lax federal supervision.

That paternalistic neglect, however, came to an end in 1878 when Nathan C. Meeker arrived to head the White River Ute Indian Agency. Meeker had worked for Horace "Go West Young Man" Greeley, before coming Colorado to lead the utopian Union Colony on the eastern plains. Unfortunately, things got a little more "western" than Meeker probably had in mind.

He quickly decided hunting, fishing, racing ponies, and generally enjoying life just wouldn't do for Utes. In modern jargon, he had no respect for the Ute's unique cultural or belief systems. Instead of free-roaming Indians, he wanted sedentary, Christian farmers. The culture clash made conflict inevitable.

When he suggested a good place to start the "civilizing" process was to forget about racing ponies and plow up the race track, the Indians refused in a manner Meeker thought a little surly. He called for some troops. To the Utes, troops equalled massacre, so they ambushed the troops, killed and mutilated Meeker and all the men at the agency, kidnapped Meeker's wife and daughters, held them for a week, and then released them unharmed.

The politicians and public were outraged; the newspapers went nuts and soon the women's kidnapping became a lurid tail of horror at the hands of the redman.

"*The Utes must go,*" became the cry of the day.

And go they did, under Army escort, burning forests as they went, to reservations in Utah and southern Colorado on a trek they called the "Trip of Sorrow."

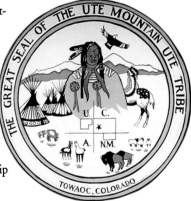

The Utes, who long ago lost their faith in the government experts, are now bringing their own lawyers, accountants, environmental experts, and congressman to the table and could forge a compromise allowing dirt to move on the project before the 100th birthday of the federal promise.

The Ute's accountants and lawyers are also matching wits with the terrible two-some of the federal government and the oil companies. Just because much of the Four Corners region looks barren, there's no reason to think it is underneath; in fact, it's loaded with coal (which could be developed with Animas La-Plata water) and natural gas.

Flute playing was an important Ute courting ritual. (Center of Southwest Studies, Fort Lewis College, Durango, Colorado)

■ SAN LUIS VALLEY

As you keep driving east on US 160, climb over the Continental Divide, and loop around the Rio Grande National Forest, you drop into another mysterious section of southern Colorado: the San Luis Valley. With its northern outpost of Saguache, the triangular valley stretches out 50 miles (80 km) in width and runs all the way to the border of New Mexico, making it one of the world's largest valley basins. The northwest border is formed by the San Juan, La Garita, and Conjeos-Brazos mountains, from which the Rio Grande River has its humble beginnings. The water from the Rio Grande and other mountain streams, along with centuries-old Spanish land grants and immigrants, created the conditions for a farming culture that has a long and deep taproot. With sufficient water to feed the valley's hay and potato farms and generations of farming families working the land, the valley has long been a green little emerald encircled by mountains. On the southeast side, the inspiring Sangre de Cristo Mountains put an abrupt end to the flat valley floor. At sunrise or sunset, the sky turns a vibrant red against and around the range's peaks, making it easy to understand why "blood of Christ" became the obvious choice when it came time to name the range.

In the valley itself, the small, isolated towns that have been influenced by the Indian, Spaniard, and white man are not only steeped in history, but radiate a friendliness and open-mindedness unequaled anywhere else in the state. The scenery is breathtaking as well, and the forests provide many nature-oriented diversions. The **Cumbres and Toltec Scenic Railway**, running from Antonito to Chama, New Mexico, provides as authentic a narrow-gauge railroad trip as any in the state and the mountain scenery is unbeatable all along the route. Just the train ride makes it worth a trip through the area. (See "Historic Railraods" in "PRACTICAL INFORMATION.")

Alamosa, the largest town in the valley, is home to Adams State College and the gateway to the **Great Sand Dunes National Monument**, 30 miles (48 km) to the north. This huge pile of sand sandwiched between flat farmland and mountain splendor is a geological wonder and quite a playground—you can even ski on it.

The town of **Manassa**, off Interstate 285 on 142 south of Alamosa, might be worth a visit for boxing aficionados, as it has a small museum dedicated to the great boxer, Jack Dempsey, also known as the "Manassa Mauler." East of Manassa lies the town of **San Luis** which, in 1851, became Colorado's first "officially" incorporated town. It also has the second oldest "common"—land open for use by all residents —in the U.S., with Boston's puny little square being the first. Residents are now engaged in building a religious shrine for special Holy Week celebrations. (See "Religious Tradition," following.)

The San Luis Valley's abundant natural hot springs are as soothing as the famous springs in Glenwood, Ouray, or Steamboat, but they remain, for the most part, under-promoted and basically undeveloped. The surrounding mountains get hundreds of inches of pure Colorado champagne powder perfect for skiing, and do contain small ski areas, but no mega-resorts typical of the central mountains.

Kit Carson

■ SAN LUIS HISTORY
After the Mexican War of 1846, the United States gained the territory of New Mexico, which included the San Luis Valley, its people, ranches, communities, and a culture which had been doing quite nicely all by itself for decades, thank you. But trouble with raiding Indians forced the government to pay attention, and in 1852 puny Fort Massachusetts was built in the hills above the San Luis Valley. It was abandoned six years later because it was too vulnerable to Indian attack.

That logic set well with the Utes, but not with the valley's white settlers. **Fort Garland** was built in 1858, and its strategic location at the head of the San Luis

Valley and accommodations for over 100 soldiers provided a bit stronger sense of security. Assigning legendary frontiersman **Kit Carson** to command the fort in 1866 helped morale a bit, too. The fort is now restored to its past glory as a living museum.

■ RELIGIOUS TRADITION

The San Luis Valley did not draw its strength or morale from muskets and men alone. For centuries the area's strength has also come from its common culture, a mixture of Spanish and Mexican, which took root long before the United States, New Mexico, or Colorado existed. Faith in the time-tested credos of Catholicism also became a cornerstone upon which much of south-central Colorado was built and that continues to infuse new life into the people of the area.

The Spanish explorers brought Catholic priests on their expeditions in an effort to at least lay claim to any lost souls they might encounter. For 300 years those priests found northern New Mexi-

Life springs eternal, even on the Great Dunes of the San Luis Valley

co and southern Colorado a fertile ground for soul searching (even if the Indians didn't think much of it). The San Luis Valley was no exception. It is home to the state's oldest Catholic church, **Our Lady of Guadalupe**, located in **Conejos**, and officially dedicated by the bishop of Santa Fe in 1863.

The church was the centerpiece of life in small, isolated towns. Priests and sisters cared for the sick, taught the children, and sheltered the poor and homeless. If priests or nuns weren't available, the Penitentes, who were more widely known for their self-flagellation ceremonies during Holy Week, would step in to fill the void.

Today, the town of **San Luis** is hoping that a unique, newly created path through the Holy Week observances will not only be a spiritual experience for all Christians, but a positive economic experience for the small town.

On a nearby mesa, the town's 800 residents have carved a 1.4-mile (2.2-km) gravel trail that twists through the trees and cuts through the rocks. The trail will be lined with 15 bronze sculptures representing the **Stations of the Cross.** The two-thirds of life-size sculptures make the whole project look more like a shrine than a piece of religious art.

The shrine/artwork will serve several purposes. It will provide the area's devoted residents a unique Holy Week celebration. The scale of the effort is also sure to bring pilgrims, the curious, and those seeking a little different Holy Week experience or spiritual renewal than can be had in an urban pew.

Those pilgrims and visitors should prove a boon for the small, isolated town and its artists and merchants. Although any such economic spin-offs will be gladly accepted, the oldest town in Colorado will endure regardless, since it seems to have learned another lesson quite well:

By your endurance you will gain your lives.
—Luke 21:19

An early Catholic church and mission. (Colorado Historical Society)

■ THE PROBLEM WITH GOLD

Recently, the area's sense of community has been sorely tested, as it has had to battle corporations and bureaucrats far from Alamosa or San Luis.

One reason is gold. The first wave of gold and silver booms and busts didn't pass the area by; indeed, the south-central district was a leading gold producer in the good old days. But new mining techniques have made the area a top producer again, and there is a catch to today's high-tech gold mining. Huge open pit mines are now in operation, where millions of tons of ore are dug up and dumped into pools filled with a weak cyanide solution that leeches out microscopic specks of gold. Not exactly an environmentally benign undertaking, so to speak.

A gold mine is now planned four miles (six km) southwest of San Luis, and the mining company has been granted permission to water its cyanide leeching ponds by sucking up groundwater from its nearby ranchland. Bitter, almost unanimous local opposition in San Luis was overruled when it came to groundwater, environmental impacts, and the possibility that the mine could harm the area's main irrigation water supply. Hopefully, however, the law which now requires that these excavations and pools be returned to their original state after the operation is completed will be strictly enforced.

■ TRINIDAD: WAR IN THE MINES

The beginning of the twentieth century saw unions and miners in the gold and coal mines agitating about hours, conditions, wages, scabs, use of the state militia, and union representation. Violence was common on both sides. The Western Federation of Miners (WFM) won recognition in Telluride in 1901, but that success was hard to repeat. In 1903, Cripple Creek became a battlefield and when a WFM agitator blew up a trainload of scabs, killing 13, the public turned against the union. By 1904, the strike was over, the public anti-union, and the miners still complaining statewide.

But the biggest collision between the workers and their corporate bosses, and one that retains a place in union history, took place in 1914. It pitted coal miners and the United Mine Workers (UMW) against coal mine owners and Rockefeller's CF&I. The miners wanted an eight-hour day, better wages and safety controls, and the ability to choose their own housing. The miners were urged on by a personal visit by Mary Harris, better known as the famous socialist organizer, "Mother Jones."

The strike in the Trinidad coal fields became official in September 1913. The owners tried to keep the mines open with non-union workers; the strikers tried to keep the strikebreakers out. Union men and their families set up tent cities near the mines and lived off union strike funds. Tension heightened through the winter. The mine operators called for the state militia, which was promptly dispatched.

A scuffle between the militia and miners on April 20, 1914, was the spark that touched off the explosion at Ludlow Station, 18 miles south of Trinidad. The militia tried to move the 900 miners and their families from their tent city, killing five miners and one militiaman. Afterward the bodies of two women and 11 children were found in the burned remains of the tent city, thus the action became known as the "**Ludlow Massacre**" (which is marked with a monument about 15 miles [24 km] north of Trinidad off US 25).

WILLA CATHER'S COLORADO

*I*n Mexican Town lived all the humbler citizens, the people who voted but did not run for office. The houses were little story-and-a-half cottages, with none of the fussy architectural efforts that marked those on Sylvester Street. They nestled modestly behind their cottonwoods and Virginia creeper; their occupants had no social pretensions to keep up. There were no half-glass front doors with doorbells, or formidable parlors behind closed shutters. Here the old women washed in the back yard, and the men sat in the front doorway and smoked their pipes. The people on Sylvester Street scarcely knew that this part of the town existed. Thea liked to explore these quiet, shady streets, where the people never tried to have lawns or to grow elms and pine trees, but let the native timber have its way and spread in luxuriance. She had many friends there, old women who gave her yellow rose or a spray of trumpet vine.

Dr. Archie took up a black leather case, put on his hat, and they went down to the dark stairs into the street. The summer moon hung full in the sky. For the time being, it was the great fact in the world. Beyond the edge of the town the plain was

Ten days of outright war erupted and was only quelled when President Woodrow Wilson dispatched the U.S. Army to the area. That settled the violence, and negotiations ended the strike in December 1914. It was only a partial victory for the union, since the UMW wasn't recognized as the miners' future representative. Instead, a "company union" was created that was supposed to represent the working man. That plan was applauded at the time as a great compromise, but such "company unions" are one reason that even today in Colorado coal country you're likely to see a baseball cap that states, "Guns, God, and Guts Made the UMW."

Visitors to Trinidad today will find a quiet town, with many, well-kept nineteenth century buildings, and lovely parks. In the center of town is **Kit Carson Park** where a larger than life bronze statue of Kit and his horse ride forever toward the Mountain Branch of the Santa Fe Trail. Downtown at 300 E. Main Street is the home of the Colorado Historical Society which includes the 1870, two-story **Baca House** and the 1882 brick **Bloom House**. Behind them is the fascinating Historical Museum.

---

so white that every clump of sage stood out distinct from the sand, and the dunes looked like a shining lake. The doctor took off his straw hat and carried it in his hand as they walked toward Mexican Town across the sand.

North of Pueblo, Mexican settlements were rare in Colorado then. This one had come about accidentally. Spanish Johnny was the first Mexican who came to Moonstone. He was a painter and decorator, and had been working in Trinidad, when Ray Kennedy told him there was a "boom" on in Moonstone, and a good many new buildings were going up. A year after Johnny settled in Moonstone, his cousin, Famos Serreños, came to work in the brickyard; then Serreños' cousins came to help him. During the strike, the master mechanic put a gang of Mexicans to work in the roundhouse. The Mexicans had arrived so quietly, with their blankets and musical instruments, that before Moonstone was awake to the fact, there was a Mexican quarter; a dozen families or more.

As Thea and the doctor approached the 'dobe houses, they heard a guitar, and a rich barytone voice—that of Famos Serreños—singing "La Golandrina." All the Mexican houses had neat little yards, with tamarisk hedges and flowers, and walks bordered with shells or whitewashed stones. Johnny's house was dark. His wife, Mrs. Tellamantez, was sitting on the doorstep, combing her long, blue-black hair.

continued on following page

(Mexican women are like the Spartans; when they are in trouble, in love, under stress of any kind, they comb and comb their hair.) She rose without embarrassment or apology, comb in hand, and greeted the doctor.

"Good-evening; will you go in?" she asked in a low, musical voice. "He is in the back room. I will make a light." She followed them indoors, lit a candle and handed it to the doctor, pointing toward the bedroom. Then she went back and sat down on her doorstep.

Dr. Archie and Thea went into the bedroom, which was dark and quiet. There was a bed in the corner, and a man was lying on the clean sheets. On the table beside him was a glass pitcher, half-full of water. Spanish Johnny looked younger than his wife, and when he was in health he was very handsome: slender, gold-colored, with wavy black hair, a round, smooth throat, white teeth, and burning black eyes. His profile was strong and severe, like an Indian's. What was termed his "wildness" showed itself only in his feverish eyes and in the color that burned on his tawny cheeks. That night he was a coppery green, and his eyes were like black holes. He opened them when the doctor held the candle before his face.

"*Mi testa!*" he muttered, "*mi testa*, doctor. *La fiebre!*" Seeing the doctor's companion

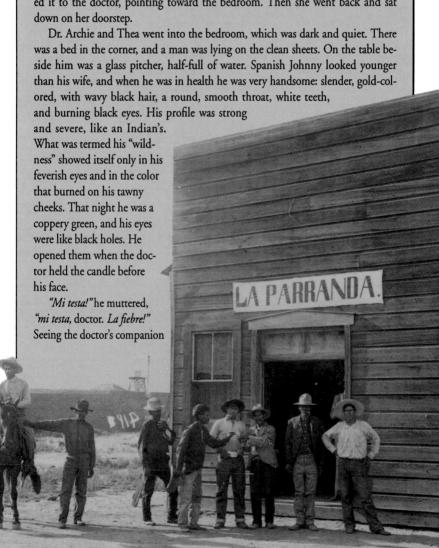

at the foot of the bed, he attempted a smile. *"Muchacha!"* he exclaimed deprecatingly.

Dr. Archie stuck a thermometer into his mouth. "Now, Thea, you can run outside and wait for me."

Thea slipped noiselessly through the dark house and joined Mrs. Tellamantez. The somber Mexican woman did not seem inclined to talk, but her nod was friendly. Thea sat down on the warm sand, her back to the moon, facing Mrs. Tellamantez on her doorstep, and began to count the moonflowers on the vine that ran over the house. Mrs. Tellamantez was always considered a very homely woman. Her face was of a strongly marked type not sympathetic to Americans. Such long, oval faces, with a full chin, a large, mobile mouth, a high nose, are not uncommon in Spain. Mrs. Tellamantez could not write her name, and could read but little. Her strong nature lived upon itself. She was chiefly known in Moonstone for her forbearance with her incorrigible husband.

Nobody knew exactly what was the matter with Johnny, and everybody liked him. His popularity would have been unusual for a white man, for a Mexican it was unprecedented. His talents were his undoing. He had a high, uncertain tenor voice, and he played the mandolin with exceptional skill. Periodically he went crazy. There was no other way to explain his behavior. He was a clever workman, and, when he worked, as regular and faithful as a burro. Then some night he would fall in with a crowd at the saloon and begin to sing. He would go on until he had no voice left, until he wheezed and rasped. Then he would play his mandolin furiously, and drink until his eyes sank back into his head. At last, when he was put out of the saloon at closing time, and could get nobody to listen to him, he would run away—along the railroad track, straight across the desert. He always managed to get aboard a freight somewhere. Once beyond Denver, he played his way southward from saloon to saloon until he got across the border. He never wrote to his wife; but she would soon begin to get newspapers from La Junta, Albuquerque, Chihuahua, with marked paragraphs announcing that Juan Tellamantez and his wonderful mandolin could be heard at the Jack Rabbit Grill, or the Pearl of Cadiz Saloon. Mrs. Tellamantez waited and wept and combed her hair. When he was completely wrung out and burned up,—all but destroyed,—her Juan always came back to her to be taken care of,—once with an ugly knife wound in the neck, once with a finger missing from his right hand,—but he played just as well with three fingers as he had with four.

—Willa Sibert Cather
The Song of the Lark, 1915

(opposite) From stirrups to sombreros, Spanish and Mexican influences came north from Santa Fe into southern Colorado (Colorado Historical Society)

■ CUCHARA SCENIC BYWAY

If you've come into the San Luis Valley from the south, arriving at Trinidad on Interstate 25, take the Cuchara Scenic Byway (Colorado 12) on a drive through desert, mountain, and plain. Beginning at Trinidad, it loops around to the west through the towns of Segundo, and Monument Park, over Cucharas Pass to Cuchara in the San Isabel National Forest, then on to La Veta before arriving at Walsenburg further north on Interstate 25. (Needless to say, the drive is equally delightful if you're driving from Walsenburg south to Trinidad.)

GREAT OUTDOORS

COLORADO'S EXPANSIVE WILDLANDS, FROM DESERT to mountain to plain, offer almost too much to do, to see, to hear:

- The splash of color as a pheasant bursts from a row of yellow-dead corn and shoots into the sky like a miniature helicopter.

- The solitude of an untouched mountain valley in full summer bloom where the only sounds are the faint rattle of aspen leaves, feet crunching on the narrow path, and barely audible mumbles about finally finding God's country left the way He designed it.

- The crackling and small pops of a campfire and its glowing coals which send a small circle of light just a little way into the surrounding wall of pine trees, beyond which is nothing but quiet darkness.

- The grunts and gulps of thin air needed to create a conquering yelp at the top of a 14,000-foot (4,256-m) peak.

- The slight swish of fishing line as it slices the air and lands with a gentle plop in the middle of a rippling mountain trout stream as the wind whisks through the neighboring willows.

- The sensation of softly treading through fall foliage in search of elusive deer and elk.

- The gentle lapping of a seemingly gentle river against raft and paddles that suddenly have to battle a torrent of tossing turns and shouted instructions as the water turns as white as the knuckles on the paddles.

- The sweet sweat from mountain bikers or cross-country skiers as they muscle their way over trails through forest and desert.

■ FISHING AND BOATING

Every sizable Colorado stream or lake with ready access is stocked with fish. The Division of Wildlife (DOW), thanks to its huge hatcheries, sees to that. That means it's not whether you're going to catch a fish on your trip, but what kind of fish you want to catch and how you want to catch it.

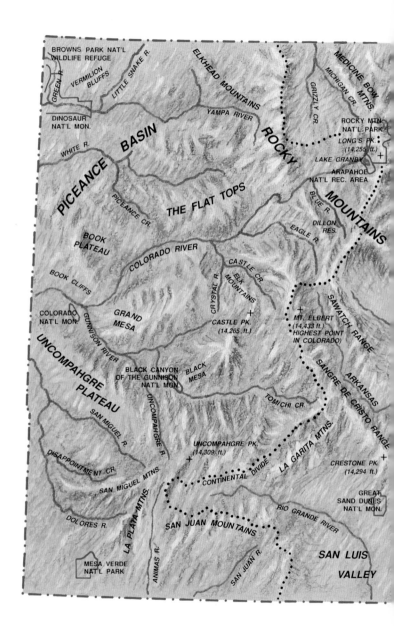

BROWNS PARK NAT'L
WILDLIFE REFUGE

MEDICINE BOW
MTNS.

GREEN R.

VERMILION
BLUFFS

LITTLE SNAKE R.

ELKHEAD MOUNTAINS

MICHIGAN CR.

GRIZZLY CR.

YAMPA RIVER

DINOSAUR
NAT'L MON.

ROCKY MTN
NAT'L PARK
LONG'S PK.
(14,255 ft.)

WHITE R.

PICEANCE

BASIN

ROCKY

LAKE GRANBY

ARAPAHOE
NAT'L REC. AREA

PICEANCE CR.

THE FLAT TOPS

BLUE R.

MOUNTAINS

BOOK
PLATEAU

DILLON
RES.

EAGLE R.

COLORADO RIVER

BOOK CLIFFS

CASTLE CR.

ELK
MOUNTAINS

CRYSTAL R.

COLORADO
NAT'L MON.

GRAND
MESA

CASTLE PK.
(14,265 ft.)

MT. ELBERT
(14,433 ft.)
HIGHEST POINT
IN COLORADO)

SAWATCH RANGE

GUNNISON RIVER

UNCOMPAHGRE

PLATEAU

BLACK CANYON
OF THE GUNNISON
NAT'L MON.

BLACK
MESA

ARKANSAS

SANGRE DE CRISTO RANGE

UNCOMPAHGRE R.

TOMICHI CR.

SAN MIGUEL R.

DISAPPOINTMENT CR.

UNCOMPAHGRE PK.
(14,309 ft.)

LA GARITA MTNS.

CRESTONE PK.
(14,294 ft.)

SAN MIGUEL MTNS.

CONTINENTAL DIVIDE

GREAT
SAND DUNES
NAT'L MON.

DOLORES R.

LA PLATA MTNS.

SAN JUAN MOUNTAINS

RIO GRANDE RIVER

MESA VERDE
NAT'L PARK

ANIMAS R.

SAN JUAN R.

SAN LUIS

VALLEY

NATURAL FEATURES

THE

GREAT

PLAINS

Lake fishing has its followers, and it's easy to see why. Just bring your gear, a camp chair, and a cooler of beer, then cast your line, settle down, reel 'em in, go back to camp and start lying.

On the Western Slope, good places to undertake such strenuous activity include Vallecito Reservoir, a good-sized pond surrounded by pines and San Juan scenery west of Durango; the dozens of lakes spotting the Grand Mesa just west of Grand Junction; Steamboat Lake, nestled up north right under Hahns Peak, and Lake Granby, at the edge of Rocky Mountain National Park.

Urban fishing forays are even easier endeavors. Pueblo has it the easiest, with Pueblo Reservoir almost in the city limits. A couple hours of beautiful mountain driving time to Hartsel from either Cañon City or Colorado Springs will deliver you to the middle of Middle Park and Spinney Mountain Reservoir, which yields some of the biggest fish in the state with appalling consistency. Lurking just west of Fort Collins is Horsetooth Reservoir, with miles of shoreline and mountain views that might make you want to leave your camp chair and cooler. Well . . . on second thought. And you can also think about John Martin Reservoir, on the plains bordering US 50 outside Las Animas, when it comes to a long shoreline for cooler placement.

All those lakes can accommodate some sort of floating craft from which to ply rod and reel, but there are two monster reservoirs that give you a chance to run your motor out of gas. Dillon Reservoir, saddled between Dillon and Frisco on Interstate 70, offers all manner of motor- and sail-propelled boating. Blue Mesa Reservoir, east of Gunnison, is the biggest body of water in the state and, thanks to icebox-like winters, also becomes the biggest ice cube in the state. As with the other lakes mentioned, those with the proper gear (some say lack of intelligence being the most important) can brave the below-zero temperatures, dig holes in the ice, set up a camp chair or ice fishing shack, uncork the thermos of hot chocolate or other anti-freeze, reel 'em in, then go back home, and start lying.

Stream fishing brings out anglers of a different cast, so to speak. These folks actually prowl up and down a riverbank, fighting through cottonwood stands, willows, and oak brush to find the right ripple, the gentle swell, the slow rolling flat spot that could harbor the rainbow or brown trout they seek.

Again, the DOW stocks most streams, so your choice rests in how you want to go about luring a wily trout onto your hook and reeling it into your creel. Bait fishing —worms, salmon eggs, marshmallows, cheese, leftover hors d'oeuvres, or whatever is handy—will work just fine.

Gold-medal trout streams, on the other hand, were set aside for those who eschew such feeding frenzies and prefer the craft involved in tempting trout with merely a fly or lure, and the respect for your prey integral to the catch-and-release concept, which places the fish fight above the fish fry. Portions of ten rivers in the state have received the gold medal designation, and they are scattered all over the place; this is a regional sampling of gold medal goodies.

Before it becomes a wide slug of water, the **Colorado River** starts out as a pretty innocuous creek in Grand County, and about nine miles (14 km) of that Colorado River is golden between **Kremmling** and **Hot Sulphur Springs** along US 40.

You can hook two gold medal streams in one day by visiting the **Frying Pan River,** golden from Ruedi Reservoir downstream through a narrow, red-rock canyon until it hits **Basalt** and the **Roaring Fork River,** which gets gold as it comes out of Aspen along Colorado 82 and continues onward to Glenwood Springs.

The **Gunnison River** tumbles out of Black Canyon to shift gears into a gold medal fishing playground, rolling and twisting its way down to the **North Fork of the Gunnison.**

The Western Slope doesn't have a monopoly on gold medal fishing, though. The **North Platte River,** just west of **Walden** and accessible by Colorado 14 from east or west, runs golden all the way to Wyoming. Down south a bit, a number of stretches of the **South Platte** are gold medal material as the river makes its way from reservoir to reservoir. This is a favorite with Front Range urbanites because within an hour or so you can go from being in a traffic jam to being knee-deep in great fishing. In the San Luis Valley, the

Three golden trout that didn't get away.

■ WATCHABLE WILDLIFE

A full range of Rocky Mountain wildlife can be seen throughout Colorado. Although most species hide from humans by inhabiting the state's millions of acres of national forests and parks, there are a number of places where if you get out of your car, look in the right direction, and open your eyes, you have a pretty fair chance of seeing wildlife. Below are some of the most accessible areas for watching wildlife.

■ GEORGETOWN

Rocky Mountain sheep, the state animal, prance and parade among the rocky cliffs and crags directly above Interstate 70 near Georgetown, about 50 miles west of Denver. The Bighorn Viewing Site (exit 228) is equipped with high-powered telescopes and information about these nimble cliff-dwellers. A herd of about 200 animals can usually be seen all year.

■ JENSEN STATE WILDLIFE AREA

Located between Meeker and Craig in northwest Colorado, this wildlife area is home to elk, deer, blue grouse, red-tailed hawks, rabbits, coyotes, grouse, and pheasant, depending on the season. For more information, call (303) 878-4493.

■ ROCKY FLATS

For decades the U.S. Army manufactured the most noxious of nerve gases and other high-potency killing devices on a small portion of this huge federal reserve, located west of Westminster between state highways 72 and 93. In 1992, all the land that wasn't part of the munitions manufacturing became a wildlife refuge. The area boasts hundreds of species including deer, bald eagles and other birds, and dozens of other small animals.

■ SAN LUIS VALLEY

Approximately 20,000 sandhill cranes invade the Monte Vista National Wildlife Refuge during their spring migration through the San Luis Valley. A number of endangered whooping cranes usually accompany them. Bus tours and other events mark the event, which usually takes place in February and March. Call (800) 835-7245 for more information.

■ SEVERENCE

This town of just over 100 people located about ten miles north of Fort Collins hosts as many as 50,000 snow and Canada geese for the winter. It's pretty easy to spot birds in the adjoining fields and farmlands.

Rio Grande is designated gold medal from where the South Fork hits to a couple of miles beyond.

What all these rivers have in common, and most other gold medal waters do, too, is that less restrictive fishing is nearby, meaning you can drop the fly-fishing fans off, go a couple of miles, break out the marshmallows and camp chairs, and partake of regular river regulations. Thus, all types of fishing fans can hook up and figure out a way to wade into the type of water that suits them without having to break up families, end long-standing friendships, and otherwise turn the bait bunch against the fly and lure lovers.

■ BIGHORN SHEEP

It's the quintessential Colorado wildlife scene, and one not soon forgotten by those fortunate enough to see it: hundreds of feet above a canyon floor a group of Rocky Mountain bighorn sheep in single-file delicately pick their way up the barren, canyon wall. As the rams, ewes, and lambs scale a nearly vertical granite face, they alternate between gentle, precisely placed steps and adventurous, high-energy bounds, which send loose rocks clattering into the canyon below. The bighorns' climb looks impossible because the human eye cannot detect the tiny toe-holds and miniscule ledges which form their uphill trail. When the group tops out, a mature ram happens to stand still for a moment, his sturdy figure and curled horns appearing in silhouette against the skyline.

Such a scene delights every variety of wildlife enthusiast, from hunters to photographers, but few would have the opportunity to see it today if not for man's "meddling" with nature.

Originally plentiful, bighorns, like deer and elk, were decimated by the 1880s, thanks to the influx of hungry miners in every nook and mountainous cranny. By the turn of the century there were no sport-game hunting seasons in the state, and only one surviving bighorn herd, located near Tarryall west of Colorado Springs.

The effort to re-establish bighorns throughout Colorado, begun in 1945, has involved trapping and moving about 1,800 of the Tarryall bighorns to new areas in the state. By 1953, thanks to transplants from the Tarryall herd, the state's bighorn population had risen to about 3,000 animals scattered in enough regions to allow for the first bighorn hunting season since 1887. By 1990, transplants,

Campers in Colorado's Weminuche Wilderness.

disease control, and other management techniques enabled the bighorn population to top the 6,000 mark.

There are currently nearly 80 different bighorn herds scattered throughout Colorado's high country. These herds range in size from the 20-head group in Waterton Canyon outside Denver to the 300 bighorns roaming the Collegiate Range. Bighorns have also been reintroduced to Rocky Mountain National Park, Dinosaur National Park, Mesa Verde, and the Colorado National Monument.

As the number of bighorns has grown, so has the sale of bighorn hunting licenses, and fees go to support the transplant program.

As with most big-game animals, habitat loss and increasing development pressure are serious threats to Colorado's bighorns. Since the animals usually roam above timberline in generally inaccessible terrain during the summer, man's activities haven't had a significant impact on their summer range. Winter range in the lower elevations, however, is a different story. For example, there once was a herd of bighorns that wintered on the cliffs and amongst the apple orchards of the Vail Valley. As can be expected, as soon as ski runs and condos started going up, most of the bighorns left.

The bighorns' tight-knit social structure also makes them susceptible to devastating outbreaks of disease, such as lungworm and other bacterial infections. One such outbreak decimated the Tarryall herd, which fell from 3,000 animals to 150. Despite the various threats to Colorado's bighorn sheep, a combination of the transplant program, limited hunting, and consistent disease control should allow the state's bighorns to flourish.

■ HUNTING

Due to modern wildlife management, deer and elk thrive once again in Colorado —after having been brought to the point of extinction by early miners and settlers. The variety and volume of game animals in Colorado have earned the state a reputation as a hunters' heaven, so whether it's a black bear or a bunny rabbit you want to blast, Colorado will give you a good shot. Most species of big game, small game, varmints, and about anything else not on an endangered species list are fair game during the dozens of Colorado hunting seasons.

A mule deer buck with felt-covered, summertime antlers.

Big game animals—deer, elk, antelope—draw the most attention from those who want to pin a set of trophy antlers on the wall or fill the freezer with organic meat. Hunters have all sorts of options when it comes to bagging a buck or bull.

All the national forests and wilderness areas have some deer or elk hiding amongst the trees, and farther north when things start to look more like Wyoming, antelope start to appear. However, there are a couple of hot spots where the big game hunting is consistently good, if not consistently trophy-class.

The San Juan Mountains, in the south and southwest corner from Durango north into the Rio Grande and San Juan national forests, grow 'em big and nasty. Indeed, one look at the record books proves that if you're tough enough to tackle the terrain, you could come home with quite a lot of meat. Oh, did I mention tough? Come equipped to this neck of the woods—it's not a good spot to just wander into. Also, the weather can turn nasty, as in knee-deep snow arriving overnight, as early as September, so hunt the early seasons.

The **Blaze Orange Corridor** is next, running roughly from Gunnison through Glenwood Springs, Rifle, Parachute, and up through Meeker, Craig, and Steamboat. Right in the middle of the corridor are the **Gunnison** and **White River national forests** and, in the northwest corner, the **Piceance Basin**, home to one of the nation's largest migratory deer herds.

The area attracts hunters because there is plenty of game. But it also offers some pretty civilized hunting, meaning, if you don't want to, you don't have to freeze your neck in this neck of the woods. Many a hunter has partaken of a comfortable sleep in a Meeker motel, bolted from bed in the dark of morning, bagged a buck or bull, and hit Rifle in time for drinks and dinner.

The area's numerous wilderness areas, on the other hand, attract solitude-seeking types who like their hunting wild, accommodations primitive, travel tough, and animals worth all the work it takes to track, kill, and pack them out.

All of these towns go whole hog for hunters. Blaze orange is the color of the season, welcome banners greet anyone with a firearm or four-wheel-drive, information tents sprout up everywhere.

Small game hunting, trapping, and hawking are alive and well in Colorado. You can become a knight errant and take your hawk out on a hunt. One reminder. If you use a European ferret with your hunting hawk, you must get a permit and the ferret must be dyed, neutered, and tattooed. Hey, look it up.

TEDDY TO FIGHT BEARS WITH KNIFE

GLENWOOD SPRINGS—President Roosevelt is planning to eclipse his previous reputation for daring and will try to kill every bear he gets in Colorado on his coming trip with a hunting knife, instead of a rifle.

While the story has not been generally credited . . .

Front Page, Denver Post, April 2, 1905

As it turned out, President Theodore Roosevelt did kill some black bears during his 1905 Colorado trip, but not with a hunting knife. His love of big-game hunting was not the only reason for his visit. The forests through which Roosevelt trekked were at that time part of the White River National Land Reserve, created by President Benjamin Harrison in 1891, and Roosevelt wanted to include it in the system of national forests, which remain one of the most appreciated legacies of his presidency.

As the President readied for the hunt, his staff saw to the installation of phone and telegraph lines, turning Glenwood's elegant Hotel Colorado into the "Little White House of the United States."

The President, meanwhile, picked out a nondescript Cayuse pony named Possum, climbed on a well-worn saddle, and said "well, okay" to letting a scruffy hunting terrier named Skip follow along side. Before long he was headed toward a tent camp pitched at 9,000 feet (2736 m) in the forest south of Silt.

One member of Roosevelt's staff was then assigned the task of climbing on a horse every day at the Hotel Colorado, tracking down the President, and keeping him up-to-date on national and international affairs. On May 5, Roosevelt came out of the backcountry for a brief stay in the Hotel Colorado that, thanks to a ragtag cloth bear, became almost as important as his hunting trip.

There are a couple of versions of the teddy bear myth. One has it that Teddy's daughter Alice was admiring the bears brought back by the hunters and decided to name one Teddy. A second version claims that the maids at the Hotel Colorado stitched together a crude little stuffed bear named Teddy and presented it to the president. Anyhow, a little marketing and hype later, the teddy bear was enthroned as an indispensable children's toy, a position it still holds.

When he was finished, Roosevelt took back to Washington the scruffy little dog, Skip, he'd grown fond of on the trip, as well as tales of how he shot his first bear two days into the trip, and how 10 black bear and three lynx were bagged by the rest of his entourage.

Nulca and **Naturita**, about 50 miles (80 km) west of **Telluride,** have become the controversial capital of varmit shooting, thanks to the **Top Gun Prairie Dog Shoot.** Hundreds of sure shots descend on the little towns to shoot prairie dogs by the hundreds. That's put the towns in the cross-hairs of animal rights activists, who view the shoot as simply killing for pleasure.

Waterfowl flock over Colorado and splash and dash in wet spots from the plains' irrigation canals to the Western Slope's mountain streams. This provides ample opportunity for enjoying bird watching. Geese, ducks, mergansers, and coots visit the state via both the **Central Flyway,** east of the Continental Divide, along the **Arkansas Valley** and its adjoining reservoirs, and the **Pacific Flyway,** west of the divide, in the Montrose-Gunnison area, for instance.

Numerous state and federal regulations, seven special seasons, special permit areas, dozens of exceptions in certain areas, and scattershot lead shot decrees make waterfowl hunting a complicated game where change rules the rules. The best approach, again, iscontacting the DOW and getting up-to-date information. That's about the only way to keep from going into your blind blind to the latest conditions and exemptions.

Blaze-orange hunters ready to blaze away.

Game birds are a easier to figure out, even if they are a bit harder to hit once you've figured and flushed them out. Rails, quails, grouse, ptarmigan, pheasants, and the like are confirmed vegetarians. That means where there's wheat and corn, and maybe a bit of barley, you've got a shot at these elusive birds.

On the Western Slope, the fertile farmland around Delta, Olathe, Montrose, and Paonia has traditionally been good bird country. Plenty of corn and other grain crops provide food; irrigation ditches and gullies provide water and good cover. For the most part, this is private property you're going through, so don't be a jerk. It is absolutely against the law to just hop a fence and start blasting away on someone else's land. Ask permission first. Besides, those farmers have lots of practice with a shotgun full of rock salt. "Butt out" could be painful, in other words.

In the far northeastern corner of the state, around Fort Morgan and Sterling along Interstate 76, you can try a double: pheasant and quail. This is rolling country at best, flat-out flat otherwise. Once again, irrigation ditches, ground cover, and good cropland make the area good grazing ground for our flying friends. Once again, we're talking private property, so ask permission.

A cute, furry, little marmot.

Now There's Some Good Eat'n'

It's the most often told and most often denied hunting story in Colorado. Every wildlife official says it absolutely cannot be true, but the story persists, despite the official denials, or maybe because of them.

Here's the story:

Back in the 1960s (or was that the 1950s or it could have even been the 1940s), a game warden was quietly going about his work at one of the many check stations set up on Colorado highways during deer and elk season. The warden was checking for illegal kills, be they of the wrong sex, from the wrong area, or taken by a hunter with an improper license.

Things were normal that day until a pickup truck with out-of-state plates pulled up. (The state name is optional and usually reflects the opinion the teller of the tale holds for the state used.) A very proud hunter hopped out of the vehicle, ready to display the impressive animal he had bagged and tagged, all legal and proper.

The warden, who wasn't used to such enthusiasm and general cooperation during such burdensome checks, gladly walked around the back of the truck and helped the hunter pull back a tarp.

And there it was. The biggest mule he had ever seen.

No, not mule deer.

We're talking regular mule, as in long-eared, ornery, standard issue, plow-pulling farm animal.

The hunter proudly pointed out the care with which he had dressed the animal and showed the warden the cow elk license, filled out to perfection, attached to one of the mule's legs.

A bit stunned and almost speechless, the warden pondered the situation. Then he made his decision. He patted the hunter on the back, congratulated him on a successful hunt, thanked him for his cooperation, bade him a safe trip home, and added, "Hope you get some great steaks out of that one. She's a dandy."

Off went the out-of-state hunter, a happy man envisioning a freezer full of fine Colorado elk meat that would provide many a tasty feast.

End of story.

■ WHITEWATER RAFTING

Any river that runs high enough to float a good-sized log will probably also be hosting some sort of raft, kayak, or canoe. All the rivers mentioned under "Fishing and Boating" are regularly rafted and generally floated (and fished while floating, too) by individuals or by rafting companies that provide the raft, guide (complete with bad jokes), paddles, or any combination thereof. The following three rivers go beyond just a quiet little float. They combine either wet and wild whitewater rapids or serene scenery which makes them a gorgeous trip.

Way up north, the **Green River** offers a great view of Dinosaur National Monument from the bottom up. It's hard to believe there is a runnable river anywhere near this high desert country. Once you get onto the river and peer up the surrounding sheer dusty canyon walls, you forget the mesas and sink deep into the feeling of being surrounded by an amazing act of nature. You will have to go through federal floating permit hassles, but the trip is worth it.

For most of its run through Colorado, the **Colorado River** is pretty docile, if not downright mellow. There is one section, though, that gives you a good splash and stuns with startling scenery: where the Colorado follows Interstate 70 and cuts through Glenwood Canyon, a granite-lined, tree-sparkled slash in the earth that reaches about 2,000 feet (610 m) above the river, with a surprise—possibly a Rocky Mountain bighorn sheep or startling peak view—around every twisting bend.

You need to trust your guide or be a serious river rat to run the **Gunnison River** through the **Black Canyon National Monument.** Yes, the towering canyon walls are black granite, and yes, you can lose yourself, your boat, and your booties as the river crashes down one of the steeper drops in the state. This is not a rookie's river. You can only get down to it or up out of it at a few points. Again, federal regulations rule, but getting the right to float is the easy part, getting it floated is the challenge.

■ WHEELS IN THE HILLS

There are all kinds of ways to get into the backcountry. Some are as easy as driving to work, some require a little more effort than shoveling snow off the sidewalk, and some are downright difficult. Let's start with the easy stuff.

Rafting many of Colorado's rivers can be thrilling enough, and kayaking can be downright exciting.

Thanks to ranching, logging, and mining, four-wheel-drive and off-road vehicle roads lace, traverse, and loop through almost every national forest in Colorado. Here comes the broken record again. Since it's not like these roads get regular road-grader service, go to the local Forest Service or BLM office, get a map, find out which are still passable, and get going. During the winter, these same thoroughfares become great **snowmobile** or **cross-country skiing routes** as well.

The best time of year for vehicle sightseeing has to be fall when the aspen turn golden, the oak brush become copper, and the cottonwoods convert into canopies of color, all set off by the dark green of the interspersed stands of evergreens or red rock mountainsides.

Another tip about off-road access concerns the state's 21 designated wilderness areas. You can't drive a motorized vehicle or mountain bike into a wilderness area, but in many cases you can cruise right up to the edge of the wilds and at least look in from the comfort of your rig, or maybe even open the door and take a few steps in.

National parks and monuments also offer some easy driving/hiking duty. Most have trails that allow you to get out of the car for a couple of hours and tramp around. You can either just get a glimpse of the scenery (**Dinosaur**) or take a stroll with an educational bent (**Mesa Verde, Rocky Mountain**).

■ MOUNTAIN BIKES

Mountain bike riders also enjoy the state's trails: if you can drive it, horse it, or hike it, you can probably bike it. Anticipating the mountain bike boom, Colorado pedaled into the craze ahead of the crowd. Volunteers and donations helped create two unique mountain bike trail systems.

Kokopelli's Trail starts out with a taste of the best sandy desert biking experience and, for dessert, lands you in the alpine high country. The original trail was a 128-mile (206-km) trek from Loma, near Grand Junction on the Western Slope, to Moab, Utah. Success spawned offshoots, more volunteers, and opportunities to tie into half a dozen other existing trails. The next few years could see far western Colorado and eastern Utah become home to over 1,000 miles (1,600 km) of trails ready for knobby tires and tireless peddlers.

The Colorado Trail, on the other hand, will take you through the middle of the Rocky Mountains from Durango to Denver. You'll have to skirt some wilderness areas, and some sections are definitely not for amateurs, but with a map you can figure out how to take advantage of the trail for a quick ride or an all-out enduro.

■ FOOT, HORSEBACK, OR SKIS

Wilderness areas are the domain of the backpacker, horse camper, angler, and cross-country skier. You don't have to undertake a five-day outdoor expedition to enjoy a little wilderness wonderment, either. You can travel for an hour or so and watch all traces of civilization vanish with each step in some of the state's lesser-known and less-traveled wildernesses. Or you can partake of the pedestrian-mall wilderness experience, for instance, in the Maroon Bells/Snowmass Wilderness Area outside Aspen. Generally, the closer the wilderness to resorts or towns, the heavier the traffic, so if it's solitude you seek, head for a wilderness area you've never heard of or hasn't been recommended by dozens of guidebooks and outdoor magazines. The unheralded places—**Mt. Bierstadt** (14,060 feet/4,274 m) is a good example. Go to **Georgetown** on Interstate 70, drive past town to Guanella **Pass**, park the car, hop on the trail, and after two hours, three miles (five km), and a 2,500-foot/760-m) altitude gain, you are atop a 14'er. "In-shape" and "experienced" are the key words here when tackling such summits, so don't go wandering up any mountain with just a peanut butter and jelly sandwich in your pocket. Get a map, bring food and water, don't go alone, and dress appropriately.

You shouldn't get the impression that finding a good hike is rougher than the hike itself. Winter or summer, we're talking easy duty when it comes to finding a trail. The national forests are laced with hiking trails. Almost without exception, every resort town has created or is creating some sort of hiking/pedestrian "experience" within a stone's throw or quick drive from your motel room.

Cross-country ski trails are the logical result when snow covers all the state's hiking trails and forest roads and trails. Most of the state's ski areas also offer cross-country trails to break the monotony of lift lines and to stretch downhill muscles (See "SKIING").

Any mention of cross-country duty has to include the **Tenth Mountain Hut and Trail System**. Developed by members of the famed Tenth Mountain Division (of World War II), the trail and huts (actually comfy cabins) stretch from Aspen, through the Leadville area—the division's old stomping grounds—onto Vail, offering a number of multi-day treks through some of the most scenic mountains in the state. If you use the huts, you can ski for a day, then relax with a gourmet meal eaten next to a warm wood stove, sleep in a real bed, and get up raring to go again the next day.

THE BOBCAT WAS A BIRD DOG

Jake was an odd person, neighborly as they come, shyly polite with Mother, and full of fantastic stories. Jake had a liking for the bizarre, the shocking, and he told his stories with a sly humor. He had known, or said he had known, more fantastic people than the manager of a freak-show. He knew a man once, he said, who heard an uproar in his chicken house one night and went out to find a bobcat there. He caught the bobcat with his bare hands, choked it into submission, put a collar on it and tethered it for the night. The next day he began taming it. It took quite a while, but this was a very patient man. He tamed the beast and taught it to hunt with him. Taught it to point, like a bird dog, in fact. It would point quail, standing with one paw raised and not a quiver except its bobtail, which signaled the man what kind of birds were there and how many. If it wagged its tail sideways, that meant quail. If it bobbed its tail up and down, that meant prairie chickens. And the number of twitches the tail made indicated the number of birds.

Things went fine and the man lived high for the better part of a year. He happened to be a bachelor, living all alone. Then the bobcat began to point redbirds instead of quail. This made the man mad. He cussed that bobcat till he was blue in the face. By then, of course, the cat understood human language, and he didn't like the names the man called him. He spat and growled and snapped and snarled, and one night the two of them had a fearful fight. Folks a mile away heard the uproar. The next morning they went to see what was going on.

They got to the house and there wasn't a sign of the man. The bobcat was there, asleep in the man's favorite chair. The man's shoes were on the floor, but not another sign of him. The folks who came to investigate didn't care for bobcats, so they shot him. After they'd skinned him out they opened his stomach to see if they could find any clue to what had happened. Inside that bobcat's stomach they found just two metal pants buttons, not another thing. And the coroner issued a death certificate: "Dead of unknown causes, probably et by a bobcat." And they buried the two pants buttons and put up a gravestone over them.

—Hal Borland
High, Wide and Lonesome, 1956

(following pages) A dusting of snow highlights the autumn gold of aspen trees.

S K I I N G

HERE'S A SURE BET. AFTER A DAY ON THE SLOPES, walk (or limp if it was a real rough day) into the nearest bar. Settle down next to some likely looking locals and ask what contributions their particular ski town made to ski history. Then watch it fly, and I don't mean snow. Ten to one you will be snowed under with colorful tales, bits of truth, a little exaggeration, or downright lies about how this place, or the ridge just down the road, is where it all started.

Out will come stories of miners and their "snowshoes" racing down a slope with a long pole behind them serving as a rudder. Also presented will be a long list of people's names who "really" had the idea first that Colorado's towering mountains were the perfect ski hills. Technologically speaking, there will be reminders of how an ingenious rope/pulley system was used to lug people up an infant ski hill, or how early ski lift towers were built by muscle and guts, or how someone tore the engine out of a Buick and jury-rigged it to primitive cable lifts to create the first modern ski lift.

Listen intently, nod your head a lot, laugh now and then, maybe say you heard some other town claimed a particular first, agree wholeheartedly with the locals about what a load of baloney that is, and you might end up drinking for free all night.

■ EARLY DAYS

So who's telling the truth about the beginning of Colorado's huge, internationally famous ski industry?

Well, almost everyone, actually.

Let's start with God.

Or a messenger of His named Father John Dyer, who strapped on a pair of skis and figured out how to operate them well enough to avoid meeting his maker. By 1864 the Methodist minister delivered the Word and the mail to the hardscrabble mining camps in South Park and the soon-to-be-boomtown of Leadville.

It's hard to refute any story about half-drunk gold or silver miners strapping barrel staves to their feet and scooting across the snow. It was probably more fun than dancing to the pounding of a pickled pianist with the few well-worn women

in town. Many of Colorado's mining camps and towns created ski clubs in the late 1800s.

Primitive skis also came in handy to cowboys, miners, or mail carriers who couldn't let snow deter them from their rounds, even in the late 1800s. Thus, anywhere snow measured belly deep to a tall mule, skis were part of the Colorado gold and silver scene. From then on, though, things get a little harder to nail down because the definition of "developing skiing" takes on meanings ranging from skiing with fellow miners to a vague idea about cutting down a few trees whose bark had been damaged by impact from early skiers, to actually designating entire mountains just for skiing and developing the machinery to get skiers on snow.

So, the following is a cursory glance at the start of recreational skiing in Colorado, but remember, it's not comprehensive enough to base a bar brawl on. Just keep smiling and nodding your head.

The first star of Colorado skiing was Norseman Carl Howelsen, a champion ski jumper who eventually landed in Steamboat Springs. In 1914, Howelsen organized a winter festival (which survives to this day), constructed a ski jump on Howelson Hill, and demonstrated his talents to the awed locals.

About the same time the scene shifted to an unlikely ski town—Denver—and an unusual ski hill—Genesee Mountain. A number of ski clubs decided any trip very far into the mountains was as risky as actually skiing, so they brought the skiing closer to home on Genesee Mountain, just west of town. They cut a skinny little ski run from the trees, built a jump for the adventuresome, and *violá*, Denver became a ski pioneer. Throughout the first twenty years of this century, ski clubs in Boulder and Colorado Springs also trekked to the nearest snow-covered hill and plowed down the thing.

Ironically, the Depression was when skiing really went commercial. Hey, during the Depression spending a Rocky Mountain winter day with sticks strapped to your feet, being dragged up a mountain by a rope, reaching the top—complete with frozen butt—and then heading downhill so you could fall face-first into the snow would be one hell of a good time. Or at least that's what people thought in Aspen, Breckenridge, Steamboat, Wolf Creek Pass, Monarch Pass, Glenwood Springs, Estes Park, Allenspark, Grand Lake, Creede, Cumbres Pass, Berthoud Pass (which featured the state's first rope tow in 1937), Hot Sulphur Springs, and Glen Cove, since they all had some sort of rudimentary ski area operating before World War II.

THE FIRST SKIERS

So far as anyone can find out, skiing came into being in Norway. A cave drawing from about 2000 B.C., near the Arctic Circle in that land, shows a man skiing down hill on twelve-foot skis with a balance pole, knees slightly bent. The oldest surviving pieces of skis are 4,500 years old. The pragmatic purpose of the ski, obviously, was to enable people to move efficiently and quickly through snow-covered country impassable, or nearly so, to the unaided human foot. Skis allowed snow-bound country folk to visit neighbors in the dead of winter or to go to the nearest village for company, supplies, a mug of brew, the latest news or, maybe, some romancing with a lusty town wench (women's lib was late coming to the harsh winter climates of Scandinavia). And, more important, skis endowed the wintertime hunter with a mobility as magical as jet airplanes to modern man, a potentially as lethal as the horse to footbound soldiers. However, though people in several parts of our world have been using skis for transportation, sport and, alas, war for more than a hundred years, the human beast is a fun-loving creature who eventually discovered how to turn a cheap, simple tool into an expensive, complex toy.

Skiing emigrated to both Europe and American about 1850, but around 1960 its expansion took off with a rush, changing this sporting activity into a social event with economic and political implications as far removed from moving efficiently through snow as snow is from smog.

—Dick Dorworth
"The Ski. The Tool," *Mountain Gazette,* 1978

Miners, cabin fever, and "snowshoes" got Colorado skiing going downhill. (Colorado Historical Society)

But those efforts all paled in comparison to what was happening at Winter Park, which was destined to become the state's first truly commercial ski area.

When the Moffatt Tunnel was completed in 1927, the Denver & Rio Grande Railroad ran right past some very enticing ski hills. In 1938, the city of Denver annexed the area and developed the unnamed trails into the Winter Park Ski Area. Using donations, city and federal funds, and volunteers and laborers from Depression-era government agencies, work went quickly. The new T-bar lift was a quantum leap over the old rope tows or boats. By 1941 runs, lifts, buildings, and skiers were all over the place, thanks in part to the famous "ski trains" that delivered skiers right to the slopes. (The ski train is still operating today; see "PRACTICAL INFORMATION.")

Skiers in the late 1940s disembark from the ski train at Winter Park. (Colorado Historical Society)
(opposite) Over 200 inches of snow falls annually in the Colorado Rockies.

■ CHOOSING A SKI RESORT

Skiers today can sample three distinct skiing experiences in Colorado: **mega-resorts**, **historic hideaways**, and **hometown hills**. They can also decide, by their choice of resort, whether chicken cordon bleu or chicken salad is more to their taste.

Proximity to the urbanites along the Front Range and Denver made the eastern slope of the Rockies the logical place to build mega-resorts. These resorts run the gamut from full-scale, planned, resort complexes that can accommodate a destination skier flying in from Tulsa, to just a great ski hill and parking lot to accommodate the Denver accountant who moved from Tulsa to be within an hour's drive of great skiing.

Scattered deeper throughout the Rockies and farther from Denver are the historic hideaways, ski resorts that mix their mining heritage with champagne powder to entice destination skiers. Flung far and wide, north to south, and every place in between are the hometown hills. These unpretentious ski areas, usually miles from the nearest town, feel like Mom and Pop operations compared to the big resorts, but once you find them you might fall in love with their simplicity, friendliness, and miles of uncrowded ski runs that give most people a skiing day just as challenging, diverse, and delightful as you'd find anywhere else.

Probably the best way to start planning your ski vacation is with a copy of the *Colorado Ski Country USA* ski guide. The group is a nonprofit skiing promotional outfit and the guide will provide an avalanche of good information about all the ski areas and amenities they offer. Write Colorado Ski Country USA, 1560 Broadway, Suite 1440, Denver, CO 80202; (303) 837-0793. Ticket price ranges are listed in this book as:

Inexpensive = under $30; Moderate = $30-$40; Expensive = over $40.

■ VAIL: THE ULTIMATE MEGA-RESORT

Irish Baron Lord Gore's hunting party probably peeked into the Vail Valley in the 1850s. All they saw were deer, elk, and buffalo, which they killed in prodigious numbers and left to rot. It would take more discerning eyes and about 110 years to see the valley's potential as not merely a baron of Colorado skiing, but the king of the "planned unit development" approach to ski areas.

The eyes belonged to Earl Eaton, a uranium prospector, and Pete Seibert, a former Tenth Mountain vet, who needed only one peek at the valley's mountains to envision a great ski area. By the late 1950s and early 1960s, ski areas were cropping almost as fast as the gold camps of a century earlier, so the two got crafty. Instead of shouting to the rooftops about this mother lode, they quietly applied for a forest area ski permit, formed the innocent-sounding Trans Montane Rod and Gun Club, and started buying land.

There was nothing at the base of the mountain, so Vail planned and created a historic aura. With Victorian mining towns a dime a dozen, the architects went further back into history and drew up tidy plans based on European resorts: a huge Tyrolean Hause to house skiers.

With plans locating every tree, park bench, and ski rack, the entire resort was built in one year. Vail opened in 1962, with the usual lack of snow that God or someone seems to love to ordain new ski resorts with. Never fear. A Ute medicine man was called, arrived, did his dance, chants, and gyrations, and *voilà*, the snow came. Strange but true.

Vail then set out to become the Rockies' most famous resort, using a mega-promotional campaign that, by some estimates, cost more than the construction of the resort itself. It worked. Then came the clincher: the resignation of President Richard Nixon. Vailites forgot politics and jumped for joy: one of their part-time own, Gerald Ford, was now President. As a Congressman, Ford had vacationed in Vail for years (who cared). Now he was the big cheese and Vail was "Gerry's" Western White House. Basking in the glow didn't describe Vail's reaction. Sending the whole town into a tanning booth and hitting broil is closer.

Vail's success drew corporate attention. Ralston, Quaker Oats, Federated Stores, Sears Roebuck, Gillette Holdings (the owner at the beginning of 1991) and other corporate giants have all owned a piece of Vail, which always made it part of corporate skullduggery somewhere else than Vail. Familiar story, different Colorado setting, in other words.

Corporate cash covered every inch of the valley with golf courses, condos, West Vail, East Vail, and made Vail a year-round resort replete with a summertime full of enticing events in a town surrounded by millions of acres of national forest. Repeating such successes is **Beaver Creek,** the exclusive ski mountain and development just down the road. Again, every shrub and condo was placed by design (except for the trailer court you pass on the way to the slopes. Oh well, reality has to rear its ugly head every once in a while, even in Ski-ra-la).

A bit of reality arrived in the late 1980s when the town of Vail discovered a glaring omission: no cemetery, presumably because the planners didn't plan on people preferring permanent plantation in a town with no roots. The roots have grown. The town of Vail, not Vail, Inc., is plotting cemetery placement and who should be planted there, as in only long-time residents or also mere condo owners seeking eternal rest under the snow they loved.

■ VAIL TODAY

You can't miss Vail if you're driving Interstate 70 because the town, with its original Tyrolean-style core, has been supplemented by bigger and newer hotels and commercial areas. The ski runs are right off the road. Indeed, the hardest part of a Vail vacation just may be the two-hour drive from Denver and getting off the highway. Once off, the town and its businesses take over. Park your car in the parking garages and prepare to be shuttled to and fro, from and around. You can ride from motel to ski lift to restaurant to shopping areas and back again day and night.

The place works. The snow gets plowed. The trash gets dumped. The shuttles run on time. It's clean. The lifts are fast and plentiful. The people are friendly.

Then there's the snow: standard issue Colorado white gold, especially in the back bowls, which covers more runs than you can cover in a three-day weekend. Vail/Beaver Creek remains the first, and still probably one of the best, of the planned ski resorts.

Vail/Beaver Creek, Box 7, Vail, CO 81658; (800) 525-2257 or (303) 476-5750 reservations; (303) 476-5601 general information; (303) 476-4888 snow report.

Vail Mountain

Terrain: 120 trails on 3,834 acres: Front side: 32% beginner, 36% intermediate, 32% advanced; Backside bowls: intermediate and expert *only.*

Lifts: one gondola, seven high-speed quad chairs, two fixed-grip quad chairs, two triple chairs, six double chairs, two surface lifts.

Snowmaking: 332 acres.

Vertical drop: 3,250 feet (991 m).

Ticket prices: Expensive.

Rental equipment and lessons; child care; disabled skiing, call (303) 476-3229.

Dining: 14 restaurants ranging from full service to delis to hot dog shacks strewn across the mountain and at base facilities.

Olympic medalist Billy Kidd plows through powder at Steamboat Springs.

Accommodations: Vail central reservations, (800) 525-2257

Cross-country skiing: 30 kilometers of groomed trails.Ticket prices vary.

Beaver Creek, Box 915, Beaver Creek, CO 81620; (800) 525-2257 or (303) 476-5750 reservations; (303) 476-4888 snow report.

Terrain: 59 trails on 940 acres; 23% beginner, 43% intermediate, 34% advanced.

Lifts: two high-speed quads, five triple chairs, four double chairs.

Snowmaking: 361 acres.

Vertical drop: 3,340 feet (1,018 m).

Ticket prices: Expensive.

Rental equipment and lessons; child care; snowcat excursions.

Dining: five restaurants, ranging from cafeteria to gourmet, on the mountain and at base lodges.

Accommodations: see Vail.

Cross-country skiing: 30 kilometers of groomed trails on Beaver Creek Mountain. Ticket prices vary.

■ ASPEN

In 1938 Elizabeth Paepke visited Aspen and fell in love with the charming, if somewhat dilapidated, old buildings that survived the silver boom. People were being hauled up Ajax Mountain in a boat tow. Famed Swiss mountaineer Andre Roche had designed "the Roche," a 3,000-foot (914-m) tow on the face of Ajax Mountain. It hosted a number of regional and national ski races in the late 1930s and early 1940s.

The war put everything on hold, but in 1945 Elizabeth brought her husband Walter to Aspen. He looked at the ski hill and Victorian town and decided this was the place for a world-class resort. Unlike other skiing visionaries, Paepke had the money, education, and drive to make it happen. He started buying land, gave away paint to spruce up the town, and tapped Pfeifer and Herbert Bayer, to turn his plans into reality.

Thanks to his Container Corporation of America—which revolutionized the cardboard box business—Paepke was a wealthy man. But he still needed some investors, and they came gladly. Others soon signed on: motel man Conrad Hilton,

Paul Nitze—Paepke's brother-in-law and later Secretary of the Navy—and D. R. C. (Darcy) Brown—a local who retained extensive family holdings in the area. The Forest Service quickly finished the paperwork, two lifts were built, Ajax was renamed Aspen Mountain, and in 1946 the locals held the first Roche Cup on their new ski hill.

The January 11, 1947, grand opening included the U.S. Army Band, the governor, the Tenth Mountain Division Color Guard, dozens of notables, and no snow in Aspen. Luckily, at 11,300 feet (3,444 m) where the lifts topped out, there was plenty of snow and the celebration was a success.

In 1950, Aspen claimed its place among the world's best ski hills when it hosted the Federation Internationale de Ski biennial world championships. The world's best ski racers descended on Aspen for the event and proclaimed Aspen Mountain one helluva ride. Aspen the ski town was on its way.

But Paepke, with his classical education at Chicago's Latin School and Yale, wanted more than a ski resort. The Athenian ideal of a fit body and cultivated mind was the ultimate goal. Skiing pretty much took care of the body, and in 1949 Paepke went to work on the mind. That year was the 200th birthday of the German poet, philosopher, and statesman, Wolfgang Goethe, and Paepcke planned to celebrate that birthday in Aspen. He invited the world's foremost philosophers and thinkers to town for "contemplation of the noblest works of man," in Paepke's words. He convinced Albert Schweitzer to attend, along with Arthur Rubenstein, Dorothy Maynor, Mortimer Adler, and Dimitri Metropoulos and his Minneapolis Symphony. The event was stimulating, to say the least, and put Aspen on the world's cultural map.

Ski developments and the town kept pace with the intellectual rampage. New runs and lifts were added on Ajax, making it one of, if not the, most challenging ski hills in the nation. The once-deserted streets started to fill, the nineteenth century miners' cottages were restored, businesses and motels opened up, and Aspen's second boom started.

But a mountain that challenges international racers can also scare beginners or casual skiers, so Friedl Pfeifer turned to **Buttermilk Mountain** in the 1960s to create a teaching hill for beginners and those seeking a more casual skiing experience.

Fred Iselin then built **Aspen Highlands**, which took on the aura of an unpretentious, home-town, ski hill. Finally, the Aspen Ski Corp. made the big jump to Snowmass Valley south of town and built a brand new ski area with modern lifts, challenging runs, and a complete ski village that existed only to serve the skier.

Danny Sullivan, Chris Evert, her Olympian husband Andy Mill, with Billy Kidd, and Jill St. John at an All-Star lunch on Aspen Mountain.

Even though many of the state's ski areas have tried to duplicate the Aspen example, there still remains just one Aspen, because no other ski area has all the Aspen elements—a Victorian mining town history, pioneering ski efforts, fantastic ski terrain, a hometown hill, a learning hill, a completely planned ski area and town built just for skiing, and a heady dose of culture, philosophy, and music to stimulate the mind.

■ SKIING ASPEN

Today, get off Interstate 70 at Glenwood and start up Colorado 82's four lanes which turn to two not-so-safe lanes just past Carbondale to reach Aspen. The road is called "Killer 82" because of so many car/car wrecks and car/deer wrecks. Go slow, enjoy the scenery—basically wide-open ranchland squeezed between mountains on both sides—and don't pass; you'll get there soon enough.

Woody Creek, on the left across from the Snowmass Ski Area is interesting. Stuck in the middle of a trailer park full of Aspenites who actually work is the

Woody Creek Tavern, the earthy and infamous hang-out of gonzo journalist Hunter S. Thompson, who has a spread farther up the road so his target practice with all manner of weapons—from typewriters to submachine guns—won't disturb the neighbors.

You can see the runs on Snowmass Mountain from the highway, with The Burn, a powder-hound, tree-bashing delight on the far left. Past the airport rests Buttermilk Mountain and then, when you're on the edge of town, comes a glimpse of Highlands Ski Area.

Your first choice as you hit town is a Y. Bear left to find Intellectual Alley, properly named the Aspen Meadows—home to the Aspen Institute for Humanistic Studies, the International Design Conference, the Aspen Center for Physics, and the Aspen Music Festival, where students ("Practice or Perish") from around the world come for a summer of instruction. This is also the famed West End, full of huge, generally empty, usually lavish, second homes of movie stars, moguls, and idly rich who "need" a home in Aspen. The same breed has covered Red Mountain with similar homes.

Take a right at the Y and then a big bending left and you're on Main Street. This is still Colorado 82, which will eventually lead you over Independence Pass in the summer, but is closed in the winter. The funky old Aspen fades the closer you get to the middle of town—Mill and Main, a corner occupied by the **Hotel Jerome.** Aspen Mountain's famous runs are visible anytime you look up. As you head toward the hill, salons, restaurants and bars, boutiques, and "shoppes," some in nineteenth century buildings, a few in 1960–1970 style leftovers, and some in brand new efforts, are the order of the day, a mix also apparent in the pedestrian mall two blocks from the ski lifts.

If you're staying for a few days or fly in, forget about a car. Bus service is reliable and will deliver you all over town and to all the ski hills. And it's the cheapest ticket you'll buy during your stay, to boot.

Aspen Mountain

Aspen Skiing Company, Box 1248, Aspen, CO 81612; (800) 262-7736 or
   (303) 925-1220; (303) 925-1221 snow report.
Terrain: 76 trails on 625 acres: 70% intermediate, 30% advanced.
Snowmaking: 210 acres.
Lifts: one high-speed six-passenger gondola, one quad superchair, two quad
   chairs, four double lifts.

Vertical drop: 3,267 feet (996 m).

Ticket prices: Expensive.

Rental equipment and lessons. Disabled skiing, call (303) 925-2086 for those
with physical handicaps, (303) 923-4873 with visual handicaps.

Dining: Three on-mountain restaurants, one at the top, bottom, and middle.

Accommodations: Aspen central reservations, (303) 925-9000 or the Chamber
Resort Association (800) 262-7736.

Cross-country skiing: There are miles of cross-country trails, both heading into
the backcountry or quick loops in and around the Aspen vicinity. Contact
Snowmass Touring Center (303) 923-5600 or Aspen Touring Center (303)
925-7625.

No snowboarding.

Buttermilk Mountain/Tiehack Mountain

Aspen Skiing Company (see address and phone numbers above).

Terrain: 45 trails on 410 acres: 35% beginner, 65% intermediate.

Snowmaking: 108 acres.

Lifts: six double chairs.

Vertical drop: 2,030 feet (619 m).

Ticket prices: Expensive.

Rental equipment and lessons; child care; Fort Frog for children; activities for
the disabled.

Dining: two on-mountain restaurants and one in the base lodge.

Accommodations: see above.

Cross-country skiing: see Aspen Mountain. above.

Snowboarding allowed.

Snowmass

Aspen Skiing Company (see address and phone numbers above).

Terrain: 113 trails on 2,099 acres; 9% beginner; 69% intermediate; 22% expert.

Snowmaking: 55 acres.

Lifts: three quad SuperChairs, two triple chairs, nine double chairs, two platter-
pulls.

Vertical drop: 3,615 feet (1,102 m).

Ticket prices: Expensive.

Rental equipment, lessons; child care; disabled skiing (one of the best: call
(303) 923-4873).

Dining: four on-mountain restaurants.

Accommodations: in Aspen call the Aspen central reservations (303) 925-9000, in Snowmass Village (800) 332-3245.

Cross-country skiing: see Aspen Mountain.

Snowboarding allowed.

Aspen Highlands

Box T, 1600 Maroon Creek Road, Aspen, CO 81612; (800) 356-8811 or (303) 925-5300; lodging, reservations: (303) 925-7077.

Terrain: 552 acres, 23% beginner, 48% intermediate, 14% advanced.

Snowmaking: 110 acres.

Lifts: nine double chairs, two pomas.

Vertical drop: 3,800 feet (1,158 m), the most in Colorado.

Ticket prices: Inexpensive.

Rental equipment and lessons.

Dining: three on-mountain restaurants.

Accommodations: at Highlands (800) 356-8811 or call Aspen and Snowmass numbers above.

Cross-country skiing: see Aspen Mountain.

■ MEGA-RESORTS NEAR DENVER

Developers paid attention to Vail and quickly bunched a batch of resorts within easy driving distance (under two hours) of Denver or other large population centers in Colorado. They learned their lessons well. The resorts get their skiers on the hill as quickly and painlessly as possible. Of course, it also helped that the mountains happen to contain some of the best skiable terrain in the U.S. The following resorts are strategically placed to accommodate a day-trip from Denver or a week of skiing fantasies.

■ BRECKENRIDGE

Eighty-five miles (137 km) west of Denver on Interstate 70 and Colorado 9, Breckenridge is a hybrid combining a gold mining past with a planned skiing future. The town mined gold from 1859 to 1948, decayed, and was revived in 1961 by the Breckenridge Ski Area, now one of the biggest in the state with four mountains plus back bowls. It's sort of strange to walk down the main drag—which is lined with restored and "new Victorians" and see the ski runs behind them—and then visit the back streets and historical displays and get a dose of dilapidated nineteenth century mining history.

Breckenridge Ski Area

Box 1058, Breckenridge, CO 80424; (303) 453-5000; (303) 453-6118 snow report.

Terrain: 112 trails on 1,600 acres; 20% beginner, 31% intermediate, 49% advanced.

Snowmaking: 430 acres.

Lifts: four SuperChair quads, one triple, eight doubles, three surface lifts.

Vertical drop: 3,398 feet (1,036 m).

Ticket prices: Moderate.

Rental equipment, lessons; child care; Kid's Castle on Peak 8, this section of mountain for kids and a restaurant; disabled skiing, call (303) 453-6422.

Dining: five on-mountain restaurants, two at the base.

Accommodations: Breckenridge central reservations (303) 453-2918 in Colorado; nationwide (800) 221-1091.

Cross-country skiing: 23 kilometers of groomed, double-set trails.

Snowboarding allowed; facilities for disabled available.

■ COPPER MOUNTAIN

Located 75 miles (120 km) from Denver on Interstate 70, this area is sprouting into a real resort, complete with condos, restaurants, and other amenities at the base of a great ski complex designed to get you out of your car and onto the mountain as quickly as possible.

Copper Mountain Resort

Box 3001, Copper Mountain, CO 80443; (800) 458-8386 or (303) 968-2882; (303) 968-2100 snow report.

Terrain: 96 trails on 1,330 acres, 350 acres are set aside for guided extreme skiing: 25% beginner, 40% intermediate, 35% advanced.

Snowmaking: 270 acres.

Lifts: two quad chairs, six triple chairs, eight double chairs, four surface lifts.

Vertical drop 2,760 feet (841 m).

Ticket prices: Moderate.

Rental equipment and lessons; day care; 30-acre portion of Union Creek set aside for families and children.

Accommodations: Copper Mountain central reservations (800) 458-8386. Snowboarding allowed.

■ KEYSTONE, NORTH PEAK, ARAPAHOE BASIN, AND OUTBACK

These are four fine hills lurking just over 70 miles (113 km) from Denver on Interstate 70. You pass through the town of Silverthorne before arriving at the ski hills and Keystone Village, which is growing out of the village stage by constantly adding new restaurants, shops, and a variety of condos and places to stay. Keystone is keyed to the beginner and intermediate, while North Peak and the Outback are preferred by experts. Arapahoe Basin caters to snowboarders with a half-pipe for performing all sorts of acts of aerial derring-do.

Keystone Mountain/North Peak/Arapahoe Basin

Box 38, Keystone, CO 80435; (800) 541-3176, (303) 468-2316 general information; (800) 222-0188 (accommodations/reservations); (303) 468-4111 snow report. Ticket prices are moderate and interchangeable at the various slopes.

Keystone Mountain

Terrain: 599 acres: 32% beginner, 57% intermediate, 11% advanced.
Vertical drop: 2,340 feet (713 m).
Lifts: one gondola, two high speed quad chairs, two triples, six double chairs, four surface lifts.
Night skiing; no snowboarding.
Rental equipment and lessons; childcare.
Dining: three restaurants on Keystone Mountain and numerous others at base.
Accommodations: central reservations for Keystone Village and Silverthorne (800) 222-0188.
Cross-country skiing: 18 kilometers of groomed and packed trails near the four resorts, 57 miles of backcountry trails. Ticket prices $7.
No snowboarding.

North Peak

Terrain: 249 acres: 10% beginner, 37% intermediate, 53% advanced.
Vertical drop: 1,620 feet (494 m).
Lifts: one gondola, one quad, one triple.
Snowmaking: 150 acres.
Dining: two on-mountain restaurants.

Arapahoe Basin
Terrain: 490 acres: 10% beginner, 50% intermediate, 40% advanced.
Vertical drop: 1,670 feet (509 m).
Lifts: one triple chair, four double chairs.
Dining: one on-mountain restaurant, one at the base.
Snowboarding allowed.

The Outback
Terrain: 256 acres: 67% intermediate, 33% advanced.
Vertical drop: 1,520 feet (456 m)
Lifts: one high-speed quad.
Snowmaking: 100 acres.
Night skiing: Terrain and lifts variable depending on conditions. Ticket prices
  vary in the inexpensive range, depending upon time skied.

■ WINTER PARK/MARY JANE/VASQUEZ RIDGE

Once no more than a ski hill and some railroad workers' shacks, this area was one
of the state's first ski areas. After more than a half-century it's still going downhill,
which is good, in this case. Paresenn Bowl has become a favorite for intermediate
skiers yearning for the challenge, but not the terror, of ungroomed fresh powder.
Families can also take advantage of lower lift prices when they ski Mini Mountain
and Galloping Goose. The ski train, which has become an institution as well as a
means of transportation, or a 73-mile (117-km) drive from Denver on Interstate
70 and US 40 will deliver you to its 112 trails and all the resort trimmings.

Winter Park/Vasquez Ridge
Box 36, Winter Park, CO 80482; (800) 453-2525, outside Colorado or (303)
  726-5587; (303) 447-6588 Denver direct.
Terrain: 112 trails on over 1,115 acres: 25% beginner, 51% intermediate, 24%
  advanced.
Snowmaking: 260 acres
Lifts: four quad chairs, four triple chairs, 12 double chairs.
Vertical drop: 2,220 feet (677 m).
Ticket prices: Moderate.
Rental equipment and lessons; child care; home to the National Sports Center
  for the disabled, the largest facility of its kind in the nation.
Dining: 12 restaurants scattered on the mountains and at base lodges, from
  full-service dining to cafeterias and pizza. Bar service.

Accommodations: Winter Park central reservations handles bookings for the entire Fraser Valley, (800) 453-2525.

Snowboarding allowed; facilities for handicapped skiers available.

■ HISTORIC HIDEAWAYS

Scattered throughout the central Rockies are a number of resorts with a historical flavor. With the exception of Crested Butte, detailed below, these towns are described here mainly in terms of skiing. To read more of their history see "ROCKY MOUNTAINS" and "SAN JUAN MOUNTAINS."

■ CRESTED BUTTE

Thirty miles (48 km) north of Gunnison, Crested Butte has had its share of gold and silver miners, gunslingers, coal miners, and skiers; and when it comes to Colorado history, Crested Butte has tasted more than a smattering of it all. Although it wasn't a gold or silver boomtown, its location just north of Gunnison made it the logical supply center for the surrounding mining camps.

The town didn't die when the mining camps did; instead, it turned into a mining town itself, thanks to the huge vein of high-grade coal at its back door and the 1881 arrival of the Denver & Rio Grande Railroad. By 1884 Crested Butte had become one of Colorado Fuel and Iron's company towns under the compassionate hand of CF&I owner, John Cleveland Osgood (see "Redstone's Idealist" in "ROCKY MOUNTAINS").

Then we have the outlaws. Or the outlaw legends, at least.

First was Butch Cassidy and the Sundance Kid, *sans* Wild Bunch. In 1902, or so the story goes, the pair entered a local saloon, but robbery wasn't on their mind, a few cold beers were. A few were all they got because a batch of men with badges were coming after them. The pair left town, and since they were running, not riding, and didn't get caught, it's safe to say they kept one foot ahead of the law.

The famous James brothers, Frank and Jesse, also were supposed to be short-time visitors, hiding out for a while in Parlin, outside of Crested Butte, and creating no mischief. Creating some mischief, however, was Billy the Kid, who was alleged to have worked in an outlying sawmill, been fired, held up the next passing stage, and continued down the road into legend.

The Big Mine kept Crested Butte an honest-to-goodness Colorado mining town, prosperous if not exactly booming, until 1953. Then it happened. The Big Mine shut down and everyone expected Crested Butte to join the ghost town parade.

Skiing came to the rescue. Rozeman hill had been hosting skiers since 1951, but it wasn't until 1963 that Crested Butte Mountain opened and created a unique situation when it came to linking a historical town to a ski area: the two weren't linked. Crested Butte Mountain is not, in fact, at Crested Butte's doorstep. It, and its attendant planned village and amenities, are located a couple of miles north of town. The new ski area was an immediate hit with students from Western State College in Gunnision, and helped create the college's unofficial, and we're talking very unofficial, slogan: "Ski Western State and Pick up A Degree in Your Spare Time."

Dashing downhill or traipsing through the trees: Colorado skiing offers it all.

There's a splash of modern action at the entrance to Crested Butte, but once you make a left and turn on to Elk Avenue and start to explore the back streets, of which there aren't too many, things start to look old and settled, ready for the region's famed harsh winters.

Crested Butte has retained its Victorian charm and the influences left by the southern European immigrants who worked the coal mines. It still feels like a small town that is part Victorian mining town and part real town that has kept up with the modern world. It's not full of condos; not every building has been painted or remodeled to appeal to the second home market; and it didn't pave most of its streets until the 1980s. It just happens to have a great ski mountain just up the road.

Mt. Crested Butte

Box A, Mt. Crested Butte, CO 81225; (800) 544-8448 or (303) 349-2222; snow report (303) 349-2323.

Terrain: 85 trails on 1,150 acres, including 550 acres of ungroomed terrain called the "Extreme Limits": 13% beginner, 30% intermediate, 57% advanced.

Lifts: one high-speed quad, two triple chairs, six doubles, four surface lifts.

Vertical drop 3,062 feet (933 m).

Ticket prices: Moderate.

Rental equipment and lessons; child care for infants to three-year-olds.

Dining: three on-mountain restaurants, three at the base.

Accommodations: either at the ski area or in the town of Crested Butte, call (800) 544-8448.

Cross-country skiing: 19 miles (30 km) of groomed track.

Snowboarding allowed.

■ SKI COOPER

The famed Tenth Mountain Division trained here, just 10 miles (16 km) from Leadville, king of the silver cities, with its Victorian allures. Ski Cooper has kept up with the times, and now features Chicago Ridge, a 1,600-acre back bowl just for powder junkies (accessible only by snowcat). It's a pretty long 100 miles (160 km) from Denver over Interstate 70, Colorado 91 or US 24.

Ski Cooper
Box 896, Leadville, CO; (719) 486-3684 reservations; (719) 486-2277 snow
report.
Terrain: 325 acres: 30% beginner, 70% intermediate.
Lifts: one triple chair, one double chair, two surface lifts.
Vertical drop: 1,200 feet (366 m).
Rental equipment and lessons; child care.
Ticket prices: Budget.
Dining: cafeteria at the base lodge.
Accommodations: closest accommodations are in Leadville, (800) 748-2057,
(719) 486-3684, (719) 486-2277.
Cross-country skiing. Snowboarding allowed, snowcat tours to Chicago Ridge
and other backcountry powder hot spots.

■ STEAMBOAT

Way up in the north-central part of the state about 160 miles (260 km) from
Denver via Interstate 70 and US 40, Steamboat was a skiing pioneer, but its main
business was as a regional supply and retail center for surrounding ranchers and
coal miners. The skiing boom didn't destroy those roots, it just led to the present
mixture of skiers and real cowboys the town loves to tout. If you want to be cool,
ski in a cowboy hat.

Steamboat
2305 Mt. Werner Circle, Steamboat Springs, CO 80487; (800) 922-2722 or
(303) 879-6111.
Terrain: 106 trails on 2,500 acres: 15% beginner, 54% intermediate, 31%
advanced.
Snowmaking: 385 acres.
Lifts: one gondola, three quad chairs, five triple chairs, eight double chairs, two
surface lifts.
Vertical drop: 3,600 feet (1,097 m).
Ticket prices: Moderate.
Rental equipment and lessons; child care; instruction for physically and devel-
opmentally disabled, call (303) 879-6111, ext. 531.
Dining: six restaurants ranging from cafeteria to barbecue to gourmet on the
mountain and at the base.
Accommodations: call Steamboat central reservations: (800) 922-2722.

Cross-country skiing: 19 miles (30 km) of groomed trails, call for rates.
Snowboards allowed.

Howelsen Hill

Box 775088, Steamboat Springs, CO 80487; (303) 879-0695,
(303) 879-2043, (303) 879-2170.
Terrain: 100% intermediate.
Lifts: two surface, one double.
Vertical drop: 440 feet (134 m).
Ticket prices: Budget.
Dining: snack bar at base lodge.
Accommodations: see Steamboat.
Night skiing. Bobsled track 4,200 feet (1277 m) open day and night. Five- and
90-meter ski jumps. Cross-country skiing on 6 miles (10 km) of groomed
trails, some open at night.

■ TELLURIDE

This picturesque town in the San Juan Mountains boomed long enough to get a
good shot of Victorian-era buildings, but modern mining left a historic and nasty
tailings pile after its run from 1953 until 1978. The Telluride Ski Area came to
town in 1971 and has since expanded to both sides of Coonskin Mountain, with a
modern, planned resort on the backside, so you can choose from Victorian gingerbread to chrome and glass accommodations.

Telluride

Box 307, Telluride, CO 81435; (303) 728-4424, (303) 728-4431 general info;
(303) 728-3614 snow report.
Terrain: 62 trails on 1,050 acres; 21% beginner, 47% intermediate, 32%
advanced.
Snowmaking: 140 acres.
Lifts: high-speed quad chair (world's longest), six double chairs, two triple
chairs, one poma lift.
Vertical drop: 3,165 feet (965 m).
Ticket prices: Moderate.
Rental equipment and lessons; child care; facilities for disabled.
Dining: seven restaurants scattered throughout the area on the mountain and at
the base lodges.
Accommodations: Telluride central reservations, (800) 525-3455.
Cross-country skiing: more than 31 miles (50 km) of groomed trails.
Snowboarding allowed.

Skiing Genessee Mountain in the old days. (Denver Public Library, Western History Department)

■ ABOUT HOMETOWN SKI HILLS

Hometown ski areas range in size from mere hills with a couple of creaky old lifts to fairly good-sized mountains with lifts and amenities just a notch or two below the big hills. They provide good skiing to the people living nearby and those visitors lucky enough to discover the slower-paced, more intimate ski experience that appeals to families, beginners, and those tired of the crowds.

Most people would be surprised to learn that not every Colorado ski area falls into the mega-resort or historic category. Tucked into the mountains here and there are small ski areas with plenty of great skiing, but not the glitz, promotional muscle, history, and massive mountain operations of the "big guys." Visiting them you'll enjoy the following:

- Being able to ski down the hill without carving turns around other skiers and generally acting like a steroid-crazed halfback executing an open-field punt return.

- Not having to keep looking over your shoulder for fear of being run over by someone skiing like a steroid-crazed halfback executing an open-field punt return.

- Lift lines that don't give you a chance to read a whole chapter of *War and Peace* before you head up the hill.

- Lift ticket prices that don't require notes from your banker and your mother.

- Being able to eat and afford some standard, good old American food, like a hamburger, in the base lodge, instead having to wander around a mall to find a fern-infested "grille" and a ham à la burger served on a croissant costing the same as a good pair of ski poles.

- The feeling that by the end of the day the lift operator is almost family and the rest of the hill's crew does really like having you around and would go out of their way for you.

■ LITTLE HILLS CLOSE TO BIG CITIES

■ ELDORA

The 21-mile (34-km) drive through Boulder Canyon on Colorado 119 is a great drive in itself, then you arrive at Boulder's hometown hill—Eldora—which you can also make in less than an hour from Denver.

Eldora Mountain Resort

Box 430, Nederland, CO 80466; (303) 440-8700 reservations, from Denver (303) 258-7082; (303) 440-8800 snow conditions.

Terrain: 32 trails on 210 acres with 16 trails covering 91 acres available for night skiing: 15% beginner, 85% intermediate.

Snowmaking: 215 acres.

Lifts: five double chairs, two surface lifts.

Vertical drop: 1,400 feet (427 m).

Ticket prices: Budget.

Rental equipment and lessons.

Dining: one on-mountain restaurant, one at base lodge.

Accommodations: closest are in town of Eldora, (800) 422-4629.

Cross-country skiing: 28 miles (45 km) of groomed and backcountry trails.

Snowboards allowed.

■ LOVELAND

Just 56 miles (90 km) west of Denver right on Interstate 70 before the Eisenhower Tunnel is one of Colorado's original ski areas, which has expanded its terrain above timberline. The area's devotees routinely cross-country ski into the deep powder bowls above timberline.

Loveland Basin

Box 899, Georgetown, CO 80444; (303) 569-3203 reservations; from Denver (303) 571-5580.

Terrain: 836 acres: 25% beginner, 48% intermediate, 27% advanced.

Lifts: one quad chair, two triple chairs, five double chairs, one poma, one Mighty-Mite for the ski school.

Vertical drop: 1,430 feet (436 m).

Ticket prices: Budget to Moderate.

Rental equipment and lessons.

Dining: Two cafeterias and three restaurants at the base area.

Accommodations: closest are in Georgetown, 12 miles (19 km) away, (800) 225-LOVE.

Snowboarding allowed.

■ SILVERCREEK

Seventy-eight miles (126 km) from Denver on Interstate 70 and US 40, or just 15 minutes north of Winter Park, SilverCreek emphasizes teaching families how to have fun on skis and gears its tow hills to the student with one of the state's best instructional programs.

SilverCreek Ski Area

Box 1110, Granby, CO 80446; (800) 448-9458 or (303) 887-3384; (303) 629-1020 Denver direct.

Terrain: 25 trails on 208 acres: 30% beginner, 50% intermediate, 20% advanced.

Snowmaking: about 100 acres.

*Winter campers build an igloo by fitting together blocks of
hardened snow. The interior is surprisingly comfortable.*

Lifts: two triple chairs, one double chair, one poma lift.

Vertical drop: 970 feet (296 m).

Ticket prices: Budget.

Rental equipment and lessons a specialty; child care.

Dining: cafeteria at the base lodge.

Accommodations: ski-in/ski-out condos, hotel and motel rooms and nearby guest ranches in the surrounding communities of Granby, Winter Park, and Grand Lake, (303) 627-3324 or (800) 462-5253.

Cross-country skiing: 37 miles (60 km) at nearby Snow Mountain Ranch. Snowboarding allowed.

■ LITTLE HILLS SCATTERED ALL OVER THE PLACE

■ ARROWHEAD

Just west of Vail on Interstate 70, Arrowhead is geared to day-trippers seeking uncrowded, unpretentious family skiing.

Arrowhead Ski Area

Box 69, Edwards, CO 81632; (303) 926-3029 or (800) 332-3029.

Terrain: 178 acres: 30% beginner, 50% intermediate, 20% advanced.

Snowmaking: 43 acres.

Lifts: one high-speed quad chair and one tow.

Vertical drop: 1,700 feet (518 m).

Ticket prices: Budget.

Rental equipment and lessons.

Dining: one restaurant at the base area and one on the mountain.

Accommodations: At the ski area, call (303) 926-8300, or in Vail/Beaver Creek Valley, call the Vail Resort Association (800) 525-3875.

Cross-country skiing: skiing, lessons, equipment rental available through Paragon Guides, (303) 949-4272. No snowboarding.

■ CUCHARA VALLEY

On the east side of San Luis Valley, this resort is only about 75 miles from Pueblo on I-25 and Highway 160. This small ski area is generally geared to beginners and intermediates, although there are a few runs to give an expert a thrill. Lift lines are unheard of.

Cuchara Valley

Box 3, Cuchara Valley, CO 81055; (719) 742-3163, (800) 227-4436.

Terrain: 25 trails on 320 acres: 25% beginner; 75% intermediate.

Snowmaking: 230 acres.

Lifts: one triple chair, three double chairs.

Vertical drop: 1,562 feet (475 m)

Ticket Prices: Budget

Rental equipment and lessons.

Dining: on-mountain restaurant.

Accommodations: limited at the ski area. Closest lodge two miles (3 km) away.

■ MONARCH

Set between Gunnison and Salida on US 50, this resort gets mountains of snow and—thanks to all that soft and dry powder snow, the warm welcome mat that's always out, and the bang for the skiing buck—draws skiers from all over south-central Colorado.

Monarch Ski Area

Number 1 Powder Place, Monarch, CO 81227; (800) 332-3668 reservations; (800) 228-7943 snow report; (719) 539-3573.

Terrain: 54 trails on 637 acres: 28% beginner, 46% intermediate, 26% advanced.

Snowmaking: who needs it when you average 350 inches of snow a year?

Lifts: four double chairs.

Vertical drop: 1,000 feet (305 m).

Ticket prices: Budget.

Equipment rental and lessons; child care.

Dining: cafeteria at the base lodge and a snack bar on the mountain.

Accommodations: The 100-room Monarch Lodge is the only lodge at the ski area, call (800) 332-3668, or call the local chamber of commerce, (719) 539-2068, for information on rooms in Gunnison and Salida.

Cross-country skiing: two miles (3 km) of track skiing. Snowcat skiing: Great Divide Snow Tours, from $20-80 per day.

Snowboards allowed.

■ MOUNTAIN CLIFFE

Formerly known as Conquistador, this small resort west of Pueblo on Highway 95 caters to day skiers and families from the southern portion of the state. Modern, functional on-mountain improvements assure a hassle-free day of skiing without the crowds or pretentiousness of larger resorts.

Mountain Cliffe Ski Resort

1699 Camino, Conquistador, Westcliffe CO 81252, (719) 783-2100, (800) 472-1559; (719) 783-2170 snow report.

Terrain: 17 trails on 160 acres: 25% beginner, 50% intermediate, 25% expert.

Snowmaking: 144 acres.

Vertical drop: 1,200 feet (360 m)

Ticket Prices: Budget

Rental equipment and lessons; child care.

Dining: cafeteria, restaurant, and bar at base.

Accommodations: One 40-room lodge at the base. Call (719) 783-2100 or (800) 472-1559 for information on lodging in Westcliffe, five miles (8 km) away, and surrounding towns.

Cross-country skiing; numerous trails near the ski area.

■ POWDERHORN

Located 35 miles (56 km) from Grand Junction on Interstate 70 and Colorado 65, Powderhorn sits on the flanks of the Grand Mesa, a huge flat-topped mountain, which allows it to receive a steady downpour of light powder. The area draws skiers from across the western slope. Excellent cross-country skiing and snowmobiling can be found in the national forest surrounding the mountain.

Powderhorn Ski Resort

Box 370, Mesa, CO 81643; (800) 876-9337 or (303) 242-5537.

Terrain: over 240 acres: 20% beginner, 80% intermediate.

Snowmaking: 50 acres.

Lifts: one quad, two double chairs, one surface lift.

Vertical drop: 1,650 feet (503 m).

Ticket prices: Budget.

Rental equipment and lessons. Child care.

Dining: restaurant, bar and cafeteria at the base lodge.

Accommodations: limited lodging at the ski area; call (800) 927-6933 or (303) 242-5637 for lodging information in Grand Junction and nearby towns.

■ PURGATORY/DURANGO

Perched in the mountains 50 miles (80 km) north of Durango on US 550, this is the prime ski area and resort for the entire Four Corners region, and has a well earned reputation as a challenging and fun place to ski. It is both a self-contained resort offering lodging, dining, and shopping, as well as a day trip for many in the outlying area.

Purgatory/Durango Ski Area

Box 666, Durango, CO 81302; (800) 525-0892 or (303) 247-9000.

Terrain: 70 trails on 640 acres: 20% beginner, 50% intermediate, 30% advanced.

Snowmaking: over 100 acres.

Lifts: four triple chairs, five double chairs.

Vertical drop: 2,029 feet (618 m).

Ticket prices: Moderate.

Rental equipment and lessons; child care.

Dining: six restaurants ranging from cafeteria to gourmet at the ski area.

Accommodations: eight condo complexes at the ski area; extensive lodging in Durango, (800) 252-0892.

■ SKI SUNLIGHT

About 16 miles (26 km) from Glenwood Springs is my hometown hill, and here's how she works. You take a leisurely drive on a two-lane county road passing a subdivision or two, several ranches, and great mountain scenery. You arrive at the ski area and park. A set of condos is up the hill, a hotel with restaurant and lounge just off to the side. You go to the main lodge, walk up and buy your lift ticket, get on the lift, ride the lift, get off the lift, and start skiing. If you want to dawdle you can get a cup of hot chocolate in the cafeteria or stash something in a locker, or talk shop at the ski shop.

Good skiing, no frenzy, light on the wallet, easy duty.

Ski Sunlight

10901 County Road 117, Glenwood Springs, CO 81601; (800) 445-7931 or (303) 945-7491.

Terrain: 360 acres: 20% beginner, 58% intermediate, 22% advanced.

Snowmaking: 110 acres.

Lifts: one triple chair, two double chairs, one surface lift.

Vertical drop: 2,010 feet (613 m).

Ticket prices: Budget.

Rental equipment and lessons; child care.

Dining: cafeteria at the base lodge.

Accommodations: limited number of condos at the ski area, (800) 445-7931, full range of lodging in Glenwood Springs (800) 221-0098.

Cross-country skiing: 15 miles (24 km) of groomed trails. Snowboards allowed.

■ WOLF CREEK

Set atop the Continental Divide near Wolf Creek Pass between Pagosa Springs and Del Norte on US 160 in the south of the state, this resort gets more snow than any other ski area in Colorado.

Wolf Creek

Box 1036, Pagosa Springs, CO 81147; (303) 264-5629.

Terrain: 700 acres: 20% beginner, 80% intermediate.

Lifts: two triple chairs, two double chairs, two surface lifts.

Vertical drop: 1,425 feet (434 m).

Ticket prices: Budget.

Rental equipment and lessons.

Dining: two cafeterias.

Accommodations: closest lodging is in Pagosa Springs, 23 miles (37 km) west of the ski area, (303) 264-5629.

■ SKIING ADVENTURES

■ CROSS-COUNTRY HUT SKIING

Spending days in the backcountry on your cross-country skis surrounded by nothing more than the beauty of snow-covered scenery is the prime allure of cross-country hut systems. Colorado is home to two of the best hut systems in the nation, which allow you and a few friends to ski away your days in splendid forested silence with only the sounds of your skis and the winter world around you to interrupt your trek.

The Alfred A. Braun Hut System

Colorado's original hut system offers six huts in the Elk Mountains connecting Aspen to Crested Butte. The huts sleep anywhere from seven to 14 skiers.

Box 7937, Aspen, CO 81612, (303) 925-5775 for reservations.
Price: $15 per person, four person minimum.

Tenth Mountain Trail
Commemorating the historic Tenth Mountain Division, this hut system links
Aspen to Vail and Leadville with a string of comfortable huts through some of
Colorado's most striking mountains and valleys.

Tenth Mountain Division Hut Association, 1280 Ute Ave., Aspen, CO 81612,
(303) 925-5775 for reservations.

■ HELICOPTER SKIING
Expert skiers can combine the thrill of cutting fresh tracks through wilderness
powder with the ride of a lifetime via chopper skiing.

Colorado Heli-Ski
Fly into untouched powder territory in the national forests surrounding
Breckenridge, Vail, and Aspen.

Box 64, Frisco, CO 80443, (800) HELI-SKI, (303) 668-5600.
Price: Call for rates on a wide variety of trips.

Telluride Helitrax
Guides take you into the heart of the San Juan Mountains stretching in all
directions from Telluride.

Telluride Helitrax, Box 1560, Telluride, CO 81435, (303) 728-4904.
Price: Call for prices and reservations.

■ SNOWCAT SKIING
For those who like to get to the wild and uncut, yet stay a little closer to the
ground, the solution is to take a snowcat into unscathed skiing terrain.

Chicago Ridge Snowcat Tours
Ride into the heart of over 1,600 acres of Chicago Ridge, atop the Continental
Divide, and plunge into powder you usually only dream about. The views are
worth the ride.

Chicago Ridge Snowcat Tours/Ski Cooper, Box 896, Leadville, CO 80461, (719) 486-3684.
Prices: Call for prices and advanced reservations for full- and half-day rides.

Great Divide Snow Tours

Ride into over 600 acres of untouched terrain that boasts some of the deepest and longest-lasting powder in the state.

Great Divide Snow Tours/Monarch Ski Resort, 1 Powder Place, Monarch, CO 81227, (800) 332-3668, (719) 539-3573.

Steamboat Powder Cats

Travel into the woods two miles (3 km) north of the Steamboat ski area for unmatched powder skiing. Intermediate skiers are welcome and a deluxe overnight trip to a charming mountain cabin is also available.

Steamboat Powder Cats, Box 2468, Steamboat Springs, CO 80477, (800) 288-0543, (303) 879-5188.
Prices: Call for prices, reservations required.

■ SNOWBOARDING

When they first arrived on the slopes, they were regarded as reckless bandits on boards by the purists of Alpine skiing. It went as gospel that their equipment "shredded" and rutted the slopes which had been groomed for graceful turns or unfettered speed. They were shunted off to little sections of the mountain if allowed on the ski hill at all.

They were snowboarders. They were rebels with a powder-hungry cause. Now, thanks to the rapid improvements in their equipment and a change of attitude in the ski industry, they have triumphed.

It took several years for the Colorado ski industry to get over the shock of seeing a "skier" on a single board curving and cutting down the slopes. Now, only Aspen Mountain and Keystone ban snowboarders. Everyone else welcomes them with open arms, instructors, rental boards, and even special sections of the mountain set aside just for snowboarding.

What caused the change? Several things. Cash tops the list. As the number of skiers remained about flat and that of new skiers started to drop, the number of snowboarders zoomed. Typically, the snowboard enthusiasts are young, usually under 25, and hit the mountain a lot. In many respects they are the new class of ski bums: young men and women who take a few years off their regular life to live for snowboarding.

New equipment also helped. The first boards weren't exactly technological marvels, being a bastardization of a surfboard and skateboard with somewhat primitive bindings holding the feet to the contraption. It took practice and skill to learn how to maneuver the brute boards, and getting out of control was part of the process. But improvements come every year. Today's boards and bindings are safe, durable, and responsive to the skier's every whim and knee bend. A good instructor and a few lessons help almost any type of skier, even those in the older crowd, to learn the joys of surfing down the slopes on a snowboard safely and in complete control. The new equipment doesn't "shred" the slopes either.

Instead, most ski areas today openly court snowboarders to "come ride our mountain." They may be seeing the future of skiing, as more and more young people get their first introduction to the delights of carving gentle turns through powder, or bashing the bumps, or back-scratching off jumps, on a snowboard and not skis.

PRACTICAL INFORMATION

■ WEATHER

Here's what you can expect concerning general weather trends when traveling through Colorado. **Eastern plains weather** resembles that of the Midwest. Spring is tornado season, but it's also when the plains start to turn green. Fall harvest season is pleasant and temperate; winter is snowy and windy but mild by Midwestern standards. Summer can be hot (80–90°F or 27–32°C), but verdant greenery on all sides seems to make travel cooler.

In the mountains, summers are made to order, being not too hot in the day (70–80°F or 21–27°C) and cool at night (50–40°F or 10–4°C); however, as soon as the sun goes down so does the mercury, so even in summer bring a jacket. Fall, with its fantastic colors, is a bit unpredictable but not that much hotter or cooler than summer. Winter, of course, is cold and snowy, but that's why you'd come to the Rockies in the winter in the first place.

The Western Slope is a high mountain desert, but it's not Death Valley. Summer temperatures can be in the high 90s (37°C) and occasionally in the 100s (38°C), but again as soon as the sun drops the mercury plunges into the 60–70 range (16–21°C) making for comfortable sleeping. Fall and spring are just a bit cooler all the way around, making them preferred seasons for the locals. Winter is milder than in the mountains, but things still freeze and snow still falls, it just melts faster. The **extreme south of the state,** along the border with New Mexico, can generally be counted on to be hotter and drier than the northern regions.

COLORADO CLIMATE DATA

TEMPERATURES				
PLACE	JULY		JANUARY	
	°F HI/LOW	°C HI/LOW	°F HI/LOW	°C HI/LOW
Aspen	80/45	27/7	34/8	1/-13
Denver	88/57	31/14	42/15	6/-9
Estes Park	79/46	26/8	38/17	3/-8
Grand Junction	94/64	34/18	36/15	2/-9
Lamar	93/63	34/17	45/14	7/-10
Mesa Verde	88/58	31/14	41/19	5/-7
Pikes Peak	48/34	9/1	9/-4	-13/-20

SNOWFALL / RAINFALL				
PLACE	SNOW		PRECIPITATION	
	INCHES/CENTIMETERS		INCHES/CENTIMETERS	
Aspen	138	351	19.4	49
Denver	60	152	15.3	39
Estes Park	37	94	13.8	35
Grand Junction	26	66	8.0	20
Lamar	26	66	14.4	37
Mesa Verde	80	203	17.4	45
Pikes Peak	553	1,405	29.7	75

WORDS OF CAUTION

You can't take the weather for granted in the mountains. Always be prepared, regardless of the forecast, time of year, or the assurances of your companions. Bring along rain or cold-weather gear for even the simplest of outings and be prepared to add or shed layers of clothing as the day progresses.

If you're driving along through the eastern plains in the spring and you see a twister/tornado on the horizon, find a place to hunker down and stay there.

Every couple of winters or so a monster storm settles in and starts snowing so hard and fast you can barely see your hood ornament. Blowing and drifting snow can close the highways crossing the plains and running up and down the Front Range, and Denver's Stapleton Airport sometimes converts itself into a huge hotel. Anyway, if you happen to find yourself staring out of your condo or motel room at just such a blast, chill out. Relax. Snuggle up with another warm body and a snifter of brandy. On the plains, towns hold huge slumber parties in the high school gym. Same goes in the mountains. You're not going to get turned away, you're going to get help. In some cases you can't find the road, much less a town. Park and stay in your car. Highway crews, the state patrol, and other emergency personnel will be looking for you.

■ ACCOMMODATIONS

In Colorado, you will never be too far from basic accommodations. Towns along every interstate and major highway, or near ski resorts or any sort of tourist attraction house your standard string of Best Westerns, stands of condos, or hotel chains in addition to mom-and-pop operations. Therefore, what follows is a select listing of the more interesting, historic, or unique hostelries scattered throughout the state. (Also see "Guest Ranches," following, for information on accommodations far from the beaten path.)

Prices, based on double occupancy, per night, are indicated as follows:

B (Budget) = up to $50; M (Median) = $50 to $100; E (Expensive) = $100 to
$150; L (Luxury) $150 to $200; XL (Extra-luxurious) over $200.

These prices are subject to change and represent a reasonable range, so if you see "B" in this book and get charged $57.49, don't slap the desk clerk.

ALAMOSA
The Cottonwood Inn Turn-of-the-century antiques make this a bed-and-breakfast browser's delight. In town at 123 San Juan Ave., (719) 589-3882. M

ASPEN
Hotel Jerome This recently restored and expanded 1889 jewel is luxurious even by Aspen standards. In the heart of town at 330 E. Main St., (303) 920-1000. XL
Little Nell This mainstay at the base of Aspen Mountain has recently been updated and overhauled into an ultimate modern establishment. 675 E. Durant Ave., (303) 920-4600. Winter: XL; summer: L

Little Red Ski Hause Comparable in decor and decorum to an 1890s' dorm, with 20 rooms, some with private baths. Breakfast is included, and occasionally other meals are offered at a reasonable cost. A good place to meet people if you are vacationing alone. Two blocks from Aspen Mountain at 118 E. Cooper Ave., (303) 925-3333. Winter: M; Summer: B

BOULDER

Goldminer Bed and Breakfast Occupying one of the few original buildings in the old mining town of Eldora, west of Boulder; offers solitude, plenty of outdoor activities, and comfortable rooms. 601 Klondike Ave., Eldora Colorado, (303) 258-7770 or 258-7793. B-M

Hotel Boulderardo Cherry-wood trimmings, stained glass, and other Victorian touches make this 1908 veteran a favorite. The ghost on the fifth floor is pretty harmless, as murdered guest ghosts go. Just off the mall at 2115 13th St., (303) 442-4344. M-E

BRECKENRIDGE

Beaver Run Resort A sprawling complex featuring a variety of hotel rooms and condos that let you ski-in and ski-out onto Peak 9. Also offers a restaurant, bar, deli, and conference facilities. 620 Village Rd., (303) 453-6000. Summer: M; Winter: M-L

Fireside Inn An original Victorian that has been expanded to offer a bed and breakfast experience ranging from full-blown elegant to basic dorm style. In town at 114 N. French St., (303) 453-6456. Winter: B-E; Summer: B-M

Village at Breckenridge A sprawling modern operation that provides a choice of hotel rooms and three types of condos right at the base of Peak 9 at 535 S. Park Rd., (303) 453-2000. Winter: XL; Summer: M-E

COLORADO SPRINGS

The Broadmoor Hotel Opened in 1918, the Broadmoor is a mega-resort complex catering to every visitors' whim from golf to swimming to ice skating. Located southwest of town at 1 Lake Ave., (719) 634-7711; (800) 634-7711. Winter: E; Summer: XL

The Antlers This is a classy, refined, full-service hostelry in the heart of town at the Palmer Center at the corner of Pikes Peak and Cascade Blvds., (719) 473-5600. M-E

Gray's Avenue Hotel One of the original hotels in nearby Manitou Springs, this Victorian-style hotel has great views and is now a comfortable bed and breakfast downtown at 711 Manitou Ave., (719) 685-1277. B

CORTEZ

Stoner Alpine Lodge An attractive new lodge enjoyed by fall-color viewers and cross-country skiers, 14 miles north of Dolores on Hwy. 145, (303) 882-7825. (The ski area associated with this lodge has shut down.) B

CRESTED BUTTE

Claim Jumper Brass beds and other nineteenth century touches make this bed and gourmet breakfast a blast from the past, while the hot tub and sauna let you bask for future ski runs; in town at 704 Whiterock, (303) 349-6471. M

Nordic Inn Nuzzle up to the fireplace in the lobby for après ski relaxing in this comfortable, modern inn at the base of Mt. Crested Butte, (303) 349-5542. Winter: M; Summer: B

CRIPPLE CREEK

Imperial Hotel Golden charms remain via an outstanding collection of antiques that let you glimpse at the past while enjoying present-day services. 123 N. 3rd. St., (719) 689-2922. B

DENVER

Brown Palace A triangular gem that hasn't lost its elegance since opening in 1892. Rooms ring a central atrium and the shining brass and polished surroundings remind guests of golden and silver days, near downtown at 321 17th St., (303) 297-3111. L-XL

Holiday Chalet Stained glass, chandeliers, and a general sense of coming to stay at your refined aunt's house make this one of the city's best bed and breakfast deals, 1820 E. Colfax Ave., (303) 321-9975. B

Loews Georgio Hotel Ultra-modern and dark on the outside, northern Italian on the inside (don't ask me), this is a complete upscale operation at 4150 E. Mississippi Ave., (800) 345-9172. L-XL

Queen Anne Inn This three-story home built in 1879 has ten rooms with various decors. Downtown location; afternoon tea and wine, 2147 Tremont Pl., (303) 296-6666. M-E

Victoria Oaks This Victorian-style residence offers nine rooms, some with shared baths. Free breakfast, as well as afternoon tea, 1575 Race St., (303) 355-1818.

DURANGO

Jarvis Suite Hotel A unique idea: converting a nineteenth-century theater into a set of suites and rooms complete with kitchens and baths and all sorts of combo rates that include either train tickets or lift tickets. In town at 125 W. 10th St., (800) 824-1024, or (303) 259-6190 locally. M-E

Strater Hotel A mixture of history and Victorian charm. Will Rogers, President John F. Kennedy, and western writer Louis L'Amour have all tasted the Strater's charms. Honky-tonk piano pounds from the Diamond Belle Saloon and boos and hisses accompany the summertime melodramas in the Diamond Circle Theatre. In downtown Durango at 699 Main St., (800) 227-4431 in Colorado, (800) 247-4431 nationwide. M-E

EMPIRE

Mad Creek Bed and Breakfast This small Victorian establishment is a perfect place to escape to. In addition to comfortable rooms and great meals, mountain bikes or cross-country skis are part of the deal. 167 Park Ave. (Empire is on Highway 40, about two miles from Interstate 70 exit 232 to Winter Park.) (303) 569-2003. B

ESTES PARK

Aspen Lodge A real "family resort" that offers several family reunion packages. Eight miles south of Estes Park, at 6120 on Highway 7, (303) 586-8133, or (800) 332-6867. E

Riversong Bed and Breakfast This elegant and romantic inn is furnished with antiques; bedrooms have fireplaces, and even sunken bathtubs in some cases. Box 1910, (303) 586-4666. M-E

Stanley Hotel Built by F. O. Stanley, co-inventor of the Stanley Steamer, and opened in 1909, the sprawling, sparkling white, and renovated Stanley of today hosts a summer theater program and other musical events to go with the scenery. Located on a hill above town at 333 Wonderview, (303) 586-3371. M

Telemark Resort Seventeen rustic cabins with screened-in porches and fireplaces, located just west of the Estes Park and bordering the Big Thompson River. Box 100, (303) 586-4343. B-M

Whispering Pines Cottages Fifteen cottages located among the pines along the Big Thompson River. You might even hook a trout from your patio. Box 877, (303) 586-5258. B

GEORGETOWN

Hardy House A Victorian bed and breakfast complete with a parlor and pot-bellied stove and comfortable nineteenth-century furnishings. Full breakfasts served in the winter with lighter fare for the summer. 605 Brownell St., (303) 569-3388. B-M

GLENWOOD SPRINGS

Hotel Colorado Opened in 1893 just across the street from the famous hot springs pool and fashioned after a Medici palace, the recently renovated hotel has hosted presidents, gangsters, and socialites who've come to "take the waters." Located at 526 Pine St., (303) 945-6511. M

Hot Springs Lodge Next to the Hotel Colorado, this modern lodge has tapped into the nearby hot springs to become one of the world's largest geothermally heated buildings. 415 E. 6th St., (303) 945-6571. M

Riverside Cottages Nuzzling up against the banks of the Roaring Fork River just two miles from the hot springs are kitchen-equipped cottages of several shapes and sizes sprinkled over four acres of well-kept grounds, on Old Highway 82 south of Glenwood Springs, (303) 945-5509. M-L

GRAND JUNCTION

The Orchard House Hit at harvest time and you can pick fruit from the orchard alongside this bed and breakfast operation located 20 minutes from Grand Junction on the mesa just above and a bit south of Palisade at 3573 E. 1/2 Rd., (303) 464-0529. B

GRAND LAKE

Grand Lake Lodge Built in 1925 of lodgepole pine, this lodge boasts terrific views of both Grand Lake and Shadow Mountain Lake. There are also 66 cabins and a swimming pool. Box 569, (303) 627-9220, or (303) 759-5848. B

Lemmon Lodge The five-bedroom lodge and 19 cabins (each sleeps four to ten) are situated on secluded banks of the lake itself. The lodge features a sandy beach, as well as a private dock for guests who bring their boats. Box 514, (303) 627-3314 in summer, (303) 595-3733 in winter. M-E

Shadowcliff Lodge This quiet retreat has spectacular views, and each bedroom in the 12- and seven-room lodges offers one dougle bed and two bunk beds, although baths are shared. Perfect for large groups. Box 658, (303) 627-9220. B

GUNNISON

Mary Lawrence Inn A two-story Victorian home stylishly converted into a comfy bed and breakfast in the middle of town, 601 N. Taylor St., (303) 641-3343. M

IDAHO SPRINGS

Indian Springs Resort This nineteenth century resort is still thriving and offers a mineral pool, vapor tunnel, and solitude to bask in. South of town on 302 Soda Creek Rd., (303) 623-2050. B

LEADVILLE

Delaware Hotel A recently restored, 100-year-old building with unique Queen Anne masonry and French mansard design. Breakfast included. 700 Harrison Ave., (800) 748-2004, or (719) 486-1418, locally. B-M

MEEKER

Meeker Hotel The lobby displays the bounty of surrounding forests via the herd of heads mounted on the walls. Big-game animal heads, of course. You can stay in regular rooms, the suite Teddy Roosevelt occupied, or dorm-style rooms. 560 Main St., (303) 878-5062. B

OURAY

The St. Elmo Hotel "Aunt" Kitty Heit built the St. Elmo in 1898 and rarely turned away a hungry but broke miner from her adjoining restaurant, the Bon Ton. The St. Elmo was once bet and lost in a poker game; today it's been turned into a charming bed and breakfast, complete with a good-natured ghost who seems content to rattle dishes. 426 Main St., (303) 325-4951, Winter: B; Summer: M

Wiesbaden Hot Springs Spa and Lodgings Combine a vapor cave, hot springs pool, and massage with comfortable rooms and you have a great stress-reduction package. In town at the corner of 6th and 5th, (303) 325-4347. Winter: M; Summer: E

REDSTONE/MARBLE
Redstone Inn Built by industrialist John Osgood in the early 1900s as a dorm and recreation center for his coal miners, the inn is now a comfortably restored retreat and spa that can't be missed, thanks to its imposing clock tower. 82 Redstone Blvd., (303) 963-2526. B-M

Cleveholm Manor This huge, 42-room, lavishly appointed and decorated Victorian mansion (once the home of industrialist John Osgood) is now a bed and breakfast and available for special events. Located one mile south of Redstone. 58 Redstone Blvd., (303) 963-3463. M-E

SAN LUIS
El Convento Bed and Breakfast This adobe structure in the middle of town across from the Catholic church was first a school, then a convent, before its current incarnation as a bed and breakfast with a downstairs space where local artists work and sell their art. 512 Church Place, (719) 672-4223. B

SILVERTON
The Grand Imperial Hotel The vintage 1880s' cherry-wood back-bar made in London and shipped around Cape Horn is just one of the hotel's many elegant Victorian touches. Built in 1882, the three-story hotel impressed Diamond Jim Brady and Lillian Russell and still shines today. It's the biggest building in town; you can't miss it, (303) 387-5527. B-M

STEAMBOAT SPRINGS
Harbor Hotel Antiques and a 50-year history add character to the Harbor amid the sea of new condos. Characters as diverse as Jack Dempsey and Shirley Temple have liked the place, which has been remodeled, so it's probably got something for everyone. In town at 703 Lincoln Ave., (800) 334-1012 in Colorado, (800) 543-8888 nationwide, (303) 879-1522 from any bar in Steamboat. Winter: M-XL; Summer: B to M

Scandinavian Lodge This Swiss-style lodge offers everything from suites to dorm
rooms. You don't have to ski in, you can drive in on 2883 Burgess Creek Rd.,
(303) 879-0517. Winter: B-E; Summer: B

TELLURIDE

Ice House A modern luxury hotel near downtown with all the amenities a skier or
festival-goer could want. 310 S. First St., (303) 728-6300. Summer: M-L;
Winter: L-XL

Johnston Inn An intimate Victorian, eight-room bed and breakfast with modern
amenities. 403 W. Colorado Ave., (303) 278-3316. M

New Sheridan Hotel Opened in 1895, the Sheridan soon vied with the best of the
nineteenth century's hotels. William Jennings Bryan repeated his impassioned
"Cross of Gold" speech from the hotel to a rapt audience in 1903. Downtown
at 321 W. Colorado St., (303) 728-4351. Call for rates.

San Sofia A modern lavish and large bed and breakfast operation that offers a wide
range of room sizes and styles. It's classy and comfortable. 330 W. Pacific Ave.
(303) 728-3001 or (800) 537-4781. Summer: E; Winter: E-L

Victorian Inn This "new" Victorian built in 1976 offers a sauna and hot tub along
with continental breakfast, in the center of town at 401 W. Pacific Ave., (800)
537-2614, or (303) 728-6601. Winter: M; Summer: B

VAIL/BEAVER CREEK

Lodge at Vail The exterior retains the distinctive European chalet design that was
part of the resort's original allure, while inside is a full-service hostelry. 174 E.
Gore Crk. Dr., (303) 476-5011. Winter: XL; Summer: E

Hyatt Regency Beaver Creek A brand new blend of Alpine and Rocky Mountain
architecture offering ski-in, ski-out convenience at the base of the Beaver Creek
ski area on 136 E. Thomas Place, (303) 949-1234. Winter: XL; Summer: E

Roost Lodge A bit farther out from the middle of town, this is a favorite with
families. 1783 Frontage Rd., (303) 476-5451. Winter: M; Summer: B

WINTER PARK

YMCA Snow Mountain Ranch An entire year-round resort, you can choose between a simple dorm room or a deluxe cabin and partake in everything from
swimming to cross-country skiing. Fourteen miles north of Winter Park Ski
Area, 1344 Grand County Rd. 53, (303) 887-2152. B

Iron Horse Resort Retreat Health club, full hotel trappings, and Winter Park's only ski-in/ski-out hotel located at the base of the Mary Jane and Winter Park hills, in Winter Park, 27 Winter Park Dr., (303) 726-8851. Winter: E; Summer: M

■ GUEST RANCHES

For some, a vacation Out West means a stay at what used to be called "dude ranches," and are now referred to as "guest ranches." Usually isolated oases in classic mountain country, such hideaways can offer everything from a day's horse ride to a week's worth of cozy cabin living and outdoor recreation ranging from fishing to chuckwagon dinners to snowmobiling. Guest ranch getaways are listed under the town(s) they are closest to. The price range given for the guest ranches listed are based on a one-week stay for one person and include three meals a day and use of some of the ranches' amenities, such as horseback riding, pools, saunas, etc. Children's rates are generally $100 to $200 less per week. Group discounts are common. Some ranches charge extra for activities, river rafting, for example, and some don't, so it's best to call in advance and find out exactly what kind of fun is included in the weekly fee. For a complete list of Colorado's Guest Ranches, contact the Colorado Dude and Guest Ranch Association, Box 300, Tabernash, CO 80478, (303) 887-3128, or (800) 441-6060 outside Colorado.

Prices per week, one person, three meals per day:

B (Budget) = up to $500; M (Median) = $500 to $750; E (Expensive) = over $750

ASPEN

T-Lazy 7 Guest Ranch No glitz, no glamor, just neat cabins along Maroon Creek, cross-country skiing, horse trips, and solitude on the edge of the Maroon Bells/Snowmass Wilderness. Open year round. Write 3129 Maroon Crk Rd., Aspen, CO 81611, (303) 925-7254. M

CORTEZ

Lake Mancos Ranch Strategically located between Cortez and Mesa Verde National Park, offering a full slate of outdoor activities, including jeep tours. Open June to November. Write 12161 County Rd. 240, Durango CO 81302, (303) 533-7900, (800) 325-WHOA. E

CREEDE

Wason Ranch Settled along the banks of the Rio Grande River, offering a variety of cabins and great fising, snowmobiling, and cross-country skiing, Just two miles from Creede. Open year round. Write Box 220 Creede, CO 81130, (719) 658-2413. B

CRESTED BUTTE

Harmel's Ranch Resort Between Gunnison and Crested Butte on the Taylor River, offering raft trips, fishing, horses, and cabins and rooms on American or European plan. Open May 15 to November 1. Write Box 944, Gunnison, CO 81230, (303) 641-1740, (800) 235-3402. B

DURANGO

Colorado Trails Ranch Has all the summer fun you could want, from tennis to trout fishing, with special children's programs. Open June through September. Write 12161 County Rd. 240, Durango, CO 81301, (800) 323-DUDE. (There goes my "guest ranch" theory.) M

ESTES PARK

Wind River Ranch Nestled next to Rocky Mountain National Park, this outfit's string of log cabins are a mix of rustic charm and modern convenience. Daily diversions include horseback riding, fishing, hiking, and cookouts. Great food, entertainment, and fine wines finish off the day. Open June through September. Box 3410, Estes Park, CO 80517, (800) 523-4212. E

FORT COLLINS

Sylvan Dale Guest Ranch Gives the feel of a working ranch with its cattle and quarter horses grazing along the Big Thompson River, which you can ride along or fish in. All the basics in a great setting. Open year round. 2939 N. County Rd. 31D, Loveland, CO 80538, (303) 667-3915. M

GRANBY

C Lazy U Ranch Offers everything from live entertainment to a guest "Showdeo." Wranglers take you on trail rides; it also has excellent fishing and rafting, and first-rate accommodations and food. Open year round except October, November, and May. Box 379, Granby, CO 80446, (303) 887-3344. E

MEEKER

Sleepy Cat Guest Ranch Just 18 miles east of Meeker, Sleepy Cat offers unstructured relaxation and great hunting, fishing, and cross-country skiing or snowmobiling. The restaurant is excellent. Open year round. Write 16064 County Rd. 8, Meeker, CO 81641, (303) 878-4413. B

RIFLE

Coulter Lake Guest Ranch About 21 miles northeast of Rifle into the woods, offering everything from fishing to snowmobiling to guided big-game hunts. Open all year except April and May. Write Box 906, Rifle, CO 81650, (303) 625-1473. B

STEAMBOAT

Focus Ranch "So you wanna be a cowboy, huh?" Here's the place. Experienced riders help move cows through the national forest on this working ranch near the Colorado/Wyoming border and milk cows and chickens provide part of the grub. Fishing, hunting, and regular horseback trips also available. Write Focus Ranch, Slater, CO 81653, (303) 583-2410. M

TELLURIDE

Skyline Guest Ranch Lets you enjoy the spectacular San Juan Mountains by jeep, horse, mountain bike, or foot. Exceptional cross-country skiing and classic country lodging. Open year round except April, May, and November. Write Box 67, Telluride, CO 81435, (303) 728-3757. M

VAIL/BEAVER CREEK

Sweetwater Guest Ranch Remote lake and stream fishing, trail rides and hikes combined with modern amenities like a hot tub and heated pool and family-style meals in historic lodge. Open all year except April, write 2650 Sweetwater Road, Gypsum, CO 81637, (303) 524-7949, (800) 321-7639. M

WESTCLIFFE

The Pines Ranch Has the Sangre de Cristo mountains for a backyard and offers modern cabins, fishing, trail rides, pack trips, and family style meals. Open May through mid-November. Write Box 311 Westcliffe, CO 81252, (719) 783-9261, (800) 446-WHOA. M

■ RESTAURANTS

Finding a place to fill your belly is easy anywhere in Colorado. Every small town has at least a couple of cafés or a motel restaurant that will stave off hunger. The same goes for towns along major highways and interstates, and around tourist attractions. Thus, the following list includes a selection of the state's more interesting, famous, or generally great restaurants.

Restaurants in many ski resorts are closed in the spring off-season (April to May or even June) for varying lengths of time depending on the owner's whim, balance sheet, or need for recuperation. Call ahead to see if the boss is back from Cabo San Lucas yet and ready to get back in the kitchen.

Prices per complete meal (entrée, drink, dessert or appetizer):
B (Budget) = under $10; M (Median) = $10 to $20; E (Expensive) = $20 and up.

ALAMOSA
Laura's Soft Spoken Restaurant Ample lunches and dinners make this a locals' favorite. Ask about the name and you'll get several great stories. 801 State Ave., (719) 589-6769. B-M

ASPEN
Abetone Ristorante Almost the unanimous choice for ultimate Italian cuisine, star gazing, and fine wine from an extensive wine cellar. Downtown at 650 Hyman Ave., (303) 925-9022. Closed in spring. E

Asia Mandarin and Szechuan Chinese food served in an expanded and renovated Victorian which also offers patio dining in the summer, 132 Main St., (303) 925-5433. Closed in spring. B-E

Crystal Palace Theatre Restaurant Mixes a little political parody via live, sarcastic dinner theater, with dinner entrées. Downtown at 300 E. Hyman Ave., (303) 925-1455. E

Flying Dog Brew Pub This micro-brewery (brew brewed on the premises) serves it up with lunch and dinner. Standard fare, with the exception of prime organic Limousin beef which it uses in its beef dishes. 424 E. Cooper St. (downstairs), (303) 925-7464. M-E

Kenichi The sushi bar is great, but the real attraction is the unique, East meets West dinner entrees which tastefully blend Japanese cuisine with the California style of haute cuisine pioneered by Wolfgang Puck. A treat for eye and palate. 533 E. Hopkins, (303) 920-2212. E

Krablonik Specializing in wild game dishes such as moose, deer, caribou, elk, antelope, etc. Dog sled rides add to the mystique. Located about a mile (two km) from Snowmass Village on the Divide Road, (303) 923-3953. Open for lunch and dinner in winter and dinner and Sunday buffet in summer. E

Wienberstube Old world European decor, charm, and food have made this a mainstay with locals and visitors alike for breakfast, lunch, and dinner. 633 Hyman Ave., (303) 925-3357. B-E

Woody Creek Tavern Basic burgers, booze, and Mexican food for lunch and dinner is the closest thing Aspen has to a neighborhood tavern. Located about three miles (five km) before the Snowmass Ski Area off Highway 82 in the Woody Creek Trailer Park, (303) 923-4585. B

BOULDER

Dot's Diner Breakfast and lunch fans groove on the authentic red-eye gravy and grits. Just off the mall at 799 Pearl St., (303) 449-1323. B

Falafal King Great Greek and Mediterranean food with the gyroes the real heroes of the place On the Pearl Street Mall at 1314 Pearl St., (303) 449-9321. B

Flagstaff House Perched above the city, offering elegant four-star dining and a great view. West on Baseline up Flagstaff Mountain, 1138 Flagstaff Rd., (303) 442-4640. E

Last American Diner Burgers, dogs, BLTs, malts, meatloaf and other almost forgotten diner delights precariously brought to you all day by a roller-skating staff. 1955 28th. St., (303) 447-1997. B

Pasta Jays Super pasta and Italian lunches and dinners served up at a sidewalk café on the Mall, 925 Pearl St., (303) 444-5800. B

Sink A legendary CU watering hole that has whetted the whistles and withstood generations of undergrads. Features a full bar, live music, pizza and burgers, and munchies. 1165 13th. St., (303) 444-7465 (SINK). B-M

BRECKENRIDGE

Breckenridge Brew Pub A variety of fresh-brewed brewskies add extra flavor to standard burgers and pub-like lunch fare and nightly dinner specials. 600 Main St., (303) 453-1550. B

Horseshoe II Restaurant Upscale American food for breakfast, lunch, and dinner and a great old restored barroom, 115 Main St., (303) 453-7463. B-M

CARBONDALE

Village Smithy The locals' favorite for fast, filling breakfast and lunches served in a comfortably remodeled old home with patio seating in the summer. 26 S. Third St., (303) 963-9990. B

COLORADO SPRINGS

Broadmoor Hotel The eight restaurants tucked into the Broadmoor provide a day-long choice of settings and food ranging from an English Pub to elegant gourmet dining (ties and dresses, please) to international cuisine. Southwest of town off Interstate 25 to Highway 122, 1 Lake Ave., (800) 634-7711. B-E

Judge Baldwin's Brewing Company Fresh-brewed beer and a selection of soups, sandwiches, and salads for lunch and dinner, in the Antlers Hotel, Pikes Peak and Cascade, (719) 473-5600. B

Giuseppe's Old Depot Housed in a renovated train station, train fans and Italian-food fanatics will like everything from the lunches and dinners to the atmosphere and pasta. Downtown at 10 S. Sierra Madre, (719) 635-3111. B-M

Wade's Pancake House One of Wade's variety of pancakes and waffles, which can number up to 20 depending on the will of the batter beater, will surely be your favorite flapjack for breakfast, lunch, or dinner, 3708 Galley St., (719) 597-7578. B

CORTEZ

Francisca's Traditional Mexican food, family atmosphere, and sopapillas to die for, downtown at 123 E. Main St., (303) 565-4093. B-M

Stromsted's A consistently good steakhouse with fresh seafood and summertime barbecue action on the deck. 1020 S. Broadway, (303) 565-1257. M

CRAIG

Signal Hill Featuring steaks and prime rib in a rustic old ranch house, 2705 W. Victory Way, (303) 824-6682. M-E

The Galaxy Watch cowboys wield chopsticks on great Chinese lunches and dinners, 524 Yampa Ave., (303) 824-8164. B

CRESTED BUTTE

Penelope's American and Continental cuisine nightly in classy Victorian setting at 120 Elk Ave., (303) 349-5178. M

Gourmet Noodle Homemade pasta and Italian cuisine in a stylish old home at 411 S. 3rd. St., (303) 349-7401. Closed in the spring. M

Wooden Nickel Enjoy beers, burgers, prime rib, and shrimp around the big fireplace, 222 Elk Ave., (303) 349-6350. Closed in the spring. B-M

DENVER

Buckhorn Exchange Specializes in wild game and exotic meat dishes—elk, deer, pheasant, alligator, etc., at 1000 Osage St., (303) 534-9505. M-E

Healthy Habits As the name implies, healthy food you can proudly offer to your vegetarian friends along with healthy food for meat eaters. Served in a serve-yourself buffet style. 865 S. Colorado Blvd., (303) 733-2005. B

Joe's Buffet (say Buff-it or you'll be tossed out immediately.) Undecorated authentic Mexican food, 753 Santa Fe Dr., (303) 571-5637. B

Tante Louise Restaurant Intimate Friday lunches and nightly dinners featuring contemporary American cuisine with innovative light sauces in restored turn-of-the-century bungalows, 4900 E. Colfax, (303) 355-4488. E

DOWNTOWN DENVER
(SIXTEENTH STREET MALL AND LARIMER SQUARE)

Little Russian Café Russian fare such as beef stroganoff, stuffed cabbage, and more, 1424-H Larimer St., (303) 595-8600. M

The Market Feels like a mix between a bustling European coffee house and old general store. Featuring flavored coffees and home-made pastries, sandwiches, and hot meals all day long, patio dining, and a store section where you can buy goodies in bulk. 1445 Larimar St., (303) 534-5140. B

Morton's of Chicago Steaks, steaks and more steaks is what Morton's has staked its reputation on, and it's worked for years. The best in town, say many. 900 Auraria Pkwy., (303) 825-3353. E

Palace Arms Restaurant In the historic Brown Palace Hotel, coat and tie required for ultra-deluxe dining all the way around at 321 17th St., (303) 297-3111. E

Wynkoop Brewing Company A classic brew pub serving lunch, dinner, and Sunday buffet along with its variety of newly brewed brews. On the bottom of the three-story fun house is the Wynkoop Cabaret Theater, featuring all manner of live performances, while the top story is home to Wynkoop Billiards, offering over 20 tables and a deli. 1634 18th St., (303) 297-2700. M

DURANGO

Henry's at the Strater Hotel Breakfast, lunch, or dinner inside this historic hotel include specials such as a Sunday brunch and a summertime all-you-can-eat prime rib buffet, 699 Main St., (303) 247-4431. B-M

The Edgewater Dining Room at the Red Lion Inn On the banks of the Animas River, offering simple breakfast and lunch fare on the patio, more elaborate dinners and a Sunday brunch, 501 Camino del Rio, (303) 259-6580. B-M

Griego's Get ready for this: a drive-in Mexican restaurant in an old A&W with good food and sweat-producing green chile. 2603 N. Main Ave., (303) 259-3558. B

Durango Diner Basic breakfast, lunch, and locals chewing the fat and chowing down. Gotta love it. 957 Main Ave., (303) 247-9889. B

FORT COLLINS

Nico's Catacombs Upscale American and Continental dinners and an extensive wine cellar in a refined setting. 115 S. College Ave., (303) 482-6426. E

Silver Grill Café Locals' hangout for breakfast and lunch. Are the cinnamon rolls good? Well, they crank out 8,000 a month and have a cinnamon roll award on the wall. 218 Walnut St., (303) 484-4656. B

FRISCO

Golden Annie's Fine fajitas, barbecue ribs, and fresh seafood make this the spot for aprés-ski dinner in the winter or patio lunches aprés boating on Dillon Reservoir in the summer. 603 Main St., (303) 668-0345. B-M

Moose Jaw The local hangout for pool, big burgers and fries, along with the usual assortment of saloon eats. 208 Main St., (303) 668-3931. B

GEORGETOWN

The Ram Bar and Restaurant A cozy establishment that hasn't been restored to the point of losing its Victorian character. General fare for lunch and dinner at 606 6th St., (303) 569-3263. B-M

GLENWOOD SPRINGS

Bayou Funhouse Cajun dinners (motto: Food So Good You'll Slap Yo Mamma); ask for "The Abuse Room" in winter, the patio in summer. Located in West Glenwood, (303) 945-1047. M

Daily Bread Bakery/Café Offering breakfast/lunch and all-natural homemade baked goods made fresh daily. Downtown at 729 Grand Ave., (303) 945-6253. B

Florindo's Fine Italian Cuisine Real Italian food prepared by real Italian owners who really came out West from New York. Everything, from the pasta to the veal, is saucy and scrumptious. Dinners nightly and lunch during the week. 721 Grand Ave., (303) 945-1245. B-M

Restaurant Sopris Consistently good continental cuisine in a spacious, gracious setting, about five miles (eight km) south of Glenwood on Highway 82, (303) 945-7771. M-E

GRAND JUNCTION

Enstrom Candies is a local operation famous for its Almond Toffees, which are sold everywhere in town.

Far East Authentic Cantonese, Szechuan, and Mandarin dishes for lunch and dinner served in a palatial setting, in town at 1530 North Ave., (303) 242-8131. B-M

G. B. Gladstones A little too fern-filled, but good American lunch and dinners, between town and the airport at the corner of 12th Street and Patterson Drive, (303) 241-6000. B-M

Good Pastures Healthy food that tastes good for breakfast, lunch, or dinner, by the airport, 733 Horizon Dr., (303) 243-3058. B-M

GUNNISON

Cattleman Inn The two restaurants in the inn serve breakfast, lunch, and dinner, with steaks and prime rib the big draws, in town, 301 W. Tomichi Ave., (303) 641-1061. B-M

Mario's Pizza The pizzas and Italian food here have kept generations of college students alive, 213 W. Tomichi Ave., (303) 641-1374. B-M

IDAHO SPRINGS

Beau Jo's Could just be the best pizza joint in the state, featuring five types of crusts and innumerable toppings limited only be your imagination and willingness to see what will fit on a pizza. You can get one-, two-, and five-pound pizzas, carried by very strong wait people. 1517 Miner St., (303) 567-4376; from Denver, 573-6924. B-M

LAKE CITY
Lake City Café & Bar They like to joke about serving their fellow man, but offer the basics like fast breakfasts, burgers, pizza, and steaks, at the corner of 3rd and Gunnison, just off town square, (303) 944-2733. B-M

LEADVILLE
The Grill Just one of four fine Mexican restaurants in town, 715 Elm St., (719) 486-9930. B

LOUISVILLE
People come from Denver, Boulder, and Rome to eat the homemade Italian food at the two following restaurants:
The Blue Parrot Café, 640 Main St., (303) 666-0677. M
Colacci's 816 Main St., (303) 673-9400. M

MEEKER
Sleepy Cat Guest Ranch Just 18 miles (29 km) east of town, and worth the drive. A bar full of real cowboys, tables in cozy little rooms, lots of hunting trophies, and good beef, pork, and lamb. Open daily in summer, weekends in winter. (303) 878-4413. M

MONTROSE
Glen Eyrie Fine dining in the middle of meat-and-potatoes country; Sunday brunch. 2351 S. Townsend Ave., (303) 249-9263. M

NEDERLAND
Pioneer Inn A mingling of old hippies, cowboys, and yuppies enjoying standard American fare for lunch and dinner in a rustic setting. First St. (you can't miss it), (303) 258-7733. B-M

OURAY

Bon Ton Restaurant Located in the historic St. Elmo Hotel, northern Italian food is the big draw, along with the colorful Victorian atmosphere. 426 Main St., (303) 352-4951. M

The Outlaw Steak and seafood are the order of the day, with a outdoor barbecue and lunch available in the summer. The Duke (John Wayne) left his hat here during the filming of "True Grit," so now everyone does. 610 Main St., (303) 325-4366. M

Silver Nugget Café Belly up to the counter at this all-American café where unpretentious food, coffee, and conversation replace "atmosphere," 740 Main St., (303) 325-4100. B

PUEBLO

Gaetano's Restaurant Italian food in a classy setting at 910 Hwy. 50 West, (719) 546-0949. M

Gus' Restaurant All-day Dutch lunch: they spread out the goodies, you grab as much as you can, including huge schooners of beer. 1201 Elm St., (719) 542-0756. B

Ianne's Pizzeria The "grinder" sandwich with hot peppers is a legend. 515 W. Northern Ave., (719) 542-5942 or 543-3230. B-M

The Renaissance This restored old church is now home to a classy restaurant offering an array of five-course American meals. Located at 217 E. Routt Ave., (719) 543-6367. M-E

REDSTONE

Redstone Inn Sunday buffet is the summer treat in this historic Tudor-style inn, while the Grille and Redstone Room are open all year. 82 Redstone Blvd., (303) 963-2526. B-M

SILVERTHORNE

Sunshine Cafe Great bakery and a variety of healthy yet tasty food for breakfast, lunch, and dinner. Homemade cookies Mom would be jealous of. Summit Place Shopping Center (right beside the Silverthorne exit off Interstate 70), (303) 468-6663. B

SILVERTON

French Bakery Restaurant The name says it all: a great bakery and eating establishment on the ground floor of the Teller House Hotel. 1250 Greene St., (303) 387-5423. B

STEAMBOAT SPRINGS

L'Apogee Contemporary and classic French cuisine with a wide choice of wine in cowboy country and a more eclectic menu in the adjoining Harwig's Bar and Grill, in town at 911 Lincoln St., (303) 879-1919. M-E

Mattie Silk's Candle-lit dining on veal, seafood, lamb, and steaks with 50 imported beers in a building named after an infamous lady of the evening. On Mt. Werner at Ski Time Square, 1890 Mt. Werner Rd., (303) 879-2441. M

Shack Quick and tasty breakfast and lunch, in town at 740 Lincoln Ave., (303) 879-9975. B

TELLURIDE

Floradora Quick lunches and a full dinner menu offering standard American fare. The hand-squashed burgers and steaks are a hallmark. 103 W. Colorado Ave., (303) 728-3888. B-M

La Marmotte Fine country French cuisine featured nightly for dinners. 150 S. San Juan St. (303) 728-6232. M-E

Powderhouse A wide range of dinner entrees from wild game to pasta to seafood to steak in an upscale setting. 222 W. Colorado Ave., (303) 728-3622. B-M

Silverglade The specialty of the house is fresh seafood with a full menu as complement. Lunch and dinner in the summer with dinners only in the winter. 115 W. Colorado Ave., (303) 728-4943. M

VAIL/BEAVER CREEK

Beano's Cabin Take a sleigh in the winter or a horse and buggy in the summer to partake of nouvelle and continental cuisine on Beaver Creek Mountain, reservations only, (303) 949-9090. Closed in the spring. E

Gashouse Appropriately titled, since this homey establishment used to be a gas station. Where the locals go to escape the glitz of Vail and Beaver Creek. Features great lunch burgers and dinners of baby-back ribs, steak, and seafood. 34185 Hwy. 6 (in the heart of Edwards, 13 miles from Vail and four miles from Beaver Creek), (303) 926-3613. B-M

Gasthof Gramshammer Continental cuisine in one dining room and wild game in another make the Gasthof stand out. 231 E. Gore Creek Dr., Vail, (303) 476-5626. M-E

Mirabelle's The best French food in the region, if not the state, resides in this rambling, renovated farmhouse, 55 Village Crk. Rd., Beaver Creek, (303) 949-7728. (Closed in the spring.) E

Sweet Basil Noted for homemade desserts and an eclectic dinner menu featuring creative American cuisine. Lunches are mainstream. At 193 E. Gore Creek Dr., Vail, (303) 476-0125. B-M

WINTER PARK

Crooked Creek Saloon American breakfasts, lunches, and dinners by the Fraser River, 401 Zerex Ave., Fraser, (303) 726-9250. B-M

■ CASINOS

Three historic mining towns tucked just behind the Front Range and two Ute Indian reservations in the southwest are home to limited stakes gambling in Colorado. There is a $5 limit on bets, but you can still spend all day slinging quarters down slot machines or playing poker and blackjack until your rear end or wallet wears out. Following are a few of the more interesting or unique casinos which offer more than the standard line of slot machines and games of chance.

BLACK HAWK

Black Forest Inn and Otto's Casino Actually a successful German restaurant before gambling arrived, the Inn embraced gaming but kept cranking out the kraut and other German delights as well as wild game dishes. The kid's arcade and ice cream parlor are nice touches for harried parents. 260 Gregory St., (303) 279-2333, or (303) 582-9971.

Gilpin Hotel A three-story, red-brick landmark since 1869, the gambling onslaught meant the end of lodging, but provided enough capital to spruce up the old place without destroying its Victorian charm. The Mineshaft Bar provides live entertainment. 111 Main St., (303) 582-1133.

CENTRAL CITY

Bullwhackers Casino A brand-new, thoroughly modern casino that offers all the creature comforts any gambler could want, including transportation to and from Denver. 130 Main St., (303) 271-2500 or (800) 426-2855.

Glory Hole Saloon and Gaming Hall An ore cart full of authentic gold ore greets you when you enter this remodeled historic establishment. Besides the usual slots and poker and inexpensive food, there's live entertainment and a beautiful century-old bar worthy of your attention. 131 Main St., (303) 582-1171.

Long Branch Saloon and Casino Sidle up to the bar and mount a saddle instead of a barstool to enjoy the slightly corny cowboy-and-Indian aura in this small, laid-back casino whose walls are festooned with Western paraphernalia and whose Muzak consists of Country-and-Western tunes. The second floor features a cafe and poker room. 123 Main St., (303) 582-1171.

Teller House Casino The Teller House's former claim to fame was the "Face on the Barroom Floor," a painting of a misty-eyed beauty drawn by a forlorn lover who allegedly dies after completing his masterpiece. The artwork still adorns the floor of the Teller House Bar, one of the few spots without slots, as do a number of murals depicting Greco-cheapo nudes. The Lillian Gish Atrium Restaurant, tours of the historic Teller House and the Teller Opera House, which still hosts a full gamut of summer opera, make this more than a single-bet casino. 120 Eureka St., (303) 279-3200.

CRIPPLE CREEK

Bronco Billy's Sports Bar and Casino This cramped little operation still has the feel of a small-town bar and restaurant, despite the incessant clanging of slot machines. There's good food at cheap prices with plenty of local banter to go along with it. 232 E. Bennett Ave., (719) 689-2030.

Imperial Hotel Gambling was merely added to his old hostelry which still features 26 rooms and an outstanding collection of antiques. 279 E. Bennett Ave., (719) 689-7777.

Phoenix House A one-stop operation offering bed and breakfast accommodations, the usual casino action, live music, several restaurants, and an art gallery all housed in a unique building that blends mostly old Victorian styling with a few modern touches. 232 E. Bennett Ave., (719) 689-2030.

Wild Wild West Gambling Hall and Brewery Beer brewed on the premises is the big draw here, no pun intended. The combo brew-pub/casino is outfitted with walls covered with antiques and features a second-floor dance hall, poker room, and bar. 443 E. Bennett Ave., (719) 689-3736.

IGNACIO

Sky Ute Convention Center Casino Located on the Southern Ute Indian Reservation, this small, modern casino offers card games, bingo, and slot machines. One mile north of Ignacio on Highway 172, (303) 563-4531.

TOWAOC

Ute Mountain Casino Located amidst the stunning scenery of the Ute Mountain Indian Reservation, this modern casino features all the gambling favorites plus dining and the array of activities available in the Four Corners region. Towaoc (11 miles south of Cortez on Highway 160/660), (303) 565-8800 or (800) 258-8007.

■ NATIONAL FORESTS

In Colorado, the U.S. Forest Service operates 400 campgrounds featuring 8,000 spots to pitch your tent or park your RV. Fees are required at some campsites, but not all.

Most of the campsites operate on a first-come/first-served basis. If you don't want to risk driving all day only to arrive at a campsite where you are last-come/not-served, you can reserve a site by calling (800) 283-CAMP.

The problem with the reservation system is that when you call you will be talking to someone staring at a computer screen—not a campground. Therefore, before you make your reservations, it's worth your time to call or write for information about the specific forest you plan to visit. The staff members at each forest's headquarters can can give you up-to-the-minute information about the pluses and minuses of their campsites and provide the latest information about such things as road closings, fire danger, the best and worst times to visit, easy access points, and maybe even some attractions you weren't aware of.

Arapaho and Roosevelt National Forests, 240 W. Prospect Rd., Fort Collins, CO
80526; (303) 224-1100

Grand Mesa, Uncompahgre, and Gunnison National Forests, 2250 U.S. Highway 50, Delta, CO 81416; (303) 874-7691

Pike and San Isabel National Forests, 1920 Valley Dr., Pueblo, CO 81008;
(719) 545-8734

Rio Grande National Forest, 1803 W. U.S. Highway 160, Monte Vista, CO
81144; (719) 852-5941

Routt National Forest, 29587 W. U.S. Highway 40, Suite 20, Steamboat Springs,
CO 80487; (303) 879-1722

San Juan National Forest, 701 Camino Del Rio, Durango, CO 81301;
(303) 247-4874

White River National Forest, Old Federal Building, Ninth St. and Grand Ave.,
Box 948, Glenwood Springs, CO 81601; (303) 945-9895

■ NATIONAL PARKS, MONUMENTS, AND HISTORIC SITES

The National Park Service oversees Colorado's eight national parks and monuments, which combined handle a yearly average of over 500,000 overnight visitors, including campers, backpackers, and RVers. It is probably a good idea to make reservations at the national parks and monuments well in advance of your visit. The number for reservations is (303) 969-2000.

For the latest information about specific parks and monuments, it's best to contact the people at the site. The addresses and phone numbers below will help you do that.

National Park Service Regional Headquarters, Box 25287, Denver, CO 80225;
(303) 969-2000

Bent's Old Fort National Historic Site, 35110 Hwy. 194 East, La Junta, CO;
(719) 384-2596

Black Canyon of the Gunnison National Monument, Box 1648, Montrose, CO
81401; (303) 240-6522

Colorado National Monument; (303) 858-3617

Curecanti National Recreation Area; (303) 641-2337
Dinosaur National Monument; (303) 374-2216
Florissant Fossil Beds National Monument; (719) 748-3253
Great Sand Dunes National Monument; (719) 378-2312
Hovenweep National Monument; (303) 529-4465
Mesa Verde National Park; (303) 529-4465
Rocky Mountain National Park; (303) 586-2371

■ STATE RECREATION AREAS

Barbour Ponds State Recreation Area; (303) 669-1739
Bonny State Recreation Area; Park (303) 659-6005
   Nature Center (303) 659-1160
Boyd Lake State Recreation Area; Park (303) 669-1739
   Marina (303) 663-2662
Chatfield State Recreation Area; Park (303) 791-7275
   Marina (303) 794-8508, Livery (303) 978-9898
Cherry Creek State Recreation Area; Park (303) 690-1166
   Marina (303) 690-1211
Crawford State Recreation Area; (303) 921-5721
Eleven Mile State Recreation Area; (719) 748-3401
Harvey Gap State Recreation Area; (303) 625-1607
Highline State Recreation Area; (303) 858-7208
Island Acres State Recreation Area; (303) 464-0548
Jackson Lake State Recreation Area; Park (303) 645-2551
Mancos Lake State Recreation Area; (303) 883-2208
Navajo Lake State Recreation Area; (303) 883-2208
Paonia State Recreation Area; (303) 921-5721
Pueblo State Recreation Area; Park 561-9320
   North Marina 547-3880, South Marina
Ridgeway State Recreation Area; (303) 249-7812
Rifle Gap State Recreation Area; (303) 625-1607
Spinney Mountain State Recreation Area; (719) 748-3401
Steamboat Lake State Recreation Area; (303) 879-3922

Sweitzer Lake State Recreation Area; (303) 874-4258
Trinidad State Recreation Area; (719) 846-6951
Vega State Recreation Area; (303) 487-3407

■ STATE PARKS

Colorado operates 38 state parks, with camping facilities available at 26 of them.
For reservations, call (800) 365-2267.
Barr Lake State Park; (303) 695-6005
Castlewood Canyon State Park; (303) 688-7505
Eldorado Canyon State Park; (303) 494-3943
Golden Gate State Park; (303) 592-1502
Lathrop State Park; (719) 738-2376, 493-1623
Mueller Ranch State Park ;(719) 687-2366
Pearl Lake State Park; (303) 879-3922
Picnic Rock; (303) 493-1623
Rifle Falls State Park; (303) 625-1607
Roxborough State Park; (303) 973-3959
State Forest; (303) 723-8366
Staunton Ranch State Park; (303) 289-5801, ext. 265
Sylvan Lake State Park; (303) 625-1607

■ EVENTS

Pick a month, any month, and someone is having fun somewhere in Colorado.
Below is just a simple surface scratching of the yearly events which run the gamut
from unique and unusual to traditional to trendy on the Colorado calendar.

JANUARY
Aspen: The Aspen/Snowmass Winterskol celebration, a five-day extravaganza of
fireworks, parades, all manner of ski races, and an impressive torchlight descent
down Aspen Mountain.
Breckenridge: Ullrfest and World Cup Freestyle honor Ull, the Norse god of
snow, with a parade, fireworks, torchlight night skiing, and the best pro
freestyle skiers in the nation.
Denver: The National Western Stock Show, largest stock show in the U.S., 23 days
of rodeos, and a month's worth of all the cowtown ambiance you can handle.

Meeker: Two types of snow travel are highlighted: the Meeker Massacre Sled Dog Race and the White River Rendezvous Devil's Hole Hill Climb for snowmobiles.

FEBRUARY

Breckenridge: Mardi Gras comes to the mountains during the Annual Fat Tuesday Celebration, featuring Cajun cahoots.

Delta: North Fork Snowmobile Races and Snowdeo celebrates snowmobiling fun.

Steamboat Springs: Annual Winter Carnival—the oldest winter carnival west of the Mississippi—features a band on skis, ski jumping, ski jouring (skiers being pulled by horses), and more.

Vail: The Vail/Beaver Creek Coors Light Mountain Man Triathlon, wherein those with large muscles and a brain that blocks pain compete in cross-country skiing, speed skating, and snowshoeing all in one day.

Walsenburg: Ground Hog Brunch at the Walsenburg golf course lets you munch while watching for a certain furry shadow.

MARCH

Craig: Greek Festival. This northeastern Colorado town dines on *souvlaki, dolmathes,* and *baklava* before dancing Greek folk dances.

Denver: Colorado Ballet begins its month-long run at the Denver Auditorium Theater.

Denver: St. Patrick's Day Parade, allegedly the second longest in the nation, due in part to the 5,000 horses.

Monte Vista: Monte Vista Crane Festival celebrates the whooping and sandhill cranes returning to the valley for spring. Guided wildlife tours and lectures are included.

San Luis: Stations of the Cross. A Good Friday observance of the traditional Stations of the Cross, which are represented by sculptures along a trail outside of town. (In April when Easter is.)

Silverton: Fencing Tournament, and we're not talking barbed wire, we're talking rapiers and sword swingers.

Springfield: Spring Equinox Festival. During spring and autumn equinox, the sun turns Crack Cave into Colorado's version of Stonehenge and shines into the cave to reveal the ancient Ogam calendar and writings linked to Celtic roots in fourth-century Erie.

Vail/Beaver Creek: Beaver Creek American Ski Classic, hosted by former President Gerald Ford, highlights the Legends of Skiing Competition, honoring past national and world champs.

APRIL

Copper Mountain: The Hot Shot Eenie Weenie Bikini Ski Contest lets 25 men and 25 women strip down to the least amount of clothing weather will allow for one final race down the slopes.

Denver: Opera Colorado starts its six-week run as the only opera company performing opera-in-the-round in the Boettcher Concert Hall.

Colorado Springs: Easter Sunrise Service at the Garden of the Gods.

Georgetown: Poverty Ball. Held after April 15. Attire: old rags. Food: stew and bread.

Kit Carson: Annual Mountain Man Rendezvous takes you back in time to the days when men matched the mountains by featuring period dress, black powder shooting, and displays of the cooking and crafts of yesteryear.

Rocky Ford: Peony Festival and Fun Day. Why they decided to combine an onion- eating contest with a peony fest is beyond me, but they did. Maybe you eat peonies last.

MAY

Antonito: Cumbres and Toltec Scenic Railroad Season Opening.

Boulder: Bolder Boulder 10-K, one of the nation's premier 10- km road races.

Boulder: Kinetic Conveyance Sculpture Race features the weirdest human-powered vehicles ever to traverse land and water.

Burlington: Longhorn Cattle Drive, when cowboys and longhorn cows fill the streets, turns nostalgia for the legendary cattle drives into reality, at least for a day.

Cripple Creek: Donkey Derby Days. Donkey races for all ages (donkeys and humans, we assume), greased pig chase, and need we go on.

Cuchara: Cuchara Valley Cowboy Arts Festival celebrates all things cowboy, from the rustic to the artistic.

Denver: Cinco de Mayo converts the 16th Street Mall into a huge Mexican fiesta replete with food, dance, and costume.

Durango: Annual Iron Horse Bicycle Classic draws over 2,000 mountain bikers and road racers for three days of pedaling.

Fort Garland: Rendezvous of Cultures reunites the Hispanic, Indian, and Anglo influences which converged on the San Luis Valley in the mid-1800s.

Grand Junction: The ten best junior college baseball teams in the nation compete in the JUCO Junior College World Series.

Ignacio: Annual Bear Dance begins a three-day spring celebration marked by traditional Ute dancing, costumes, singing, and ceremonies.

Julesburg: Pony Express Re-Ride. Watch aerobic pony express riders change horses in a heartbeat, hold on to the mail pouch, and keep on going without missing a step.

Leadville: Annual Great Peaks Quadathlon combines cross-country skiing, bicycling, running, and kayaking.

Pueblo: Annual Governor's Cup Regatta. A sailboat race around Pueblo Reservoir.

Telluride: Telluride Mountain Film Festival features outdoor, adventure, and mountain films.

JUNE

June means summer which means town festivals and county fairs throughout Colorado. Usually named after a historic event or long-gone local product (Strawberry Days), the civic fests feature parades, kids games, rodeos, arts and crafts fairs, food, and entertainment. At county fairgrounds around the state, everything from roses to rutabagas are being judged; local 4-H kids and their animals are on display; and grandstands are packed for quarter horse races and rodeos. If you happen to hit a town and the park is full of people, a parade is in progress, or there seems to be an unusual number of farm animals around, you're probably in the middle of such an event and should consider stopping for a taste of local fun and lore.

Aspen: The Aspen Music Festival and School begins its nine-week run, with performances of everything from opera to jazz to symphonies in the Wheeler Opera House and the Music Tent.

Bent's Old Fort: "Voices Under the Wind," a theatrical presentation of the region's history and life at the fort begins its six-week run.

Central City: Lou Bunch Day celebrates the town's last madame with bed races and a formal costume ball.

Cortez: Arts and Crafts Fiesta brings Native American and other artists from throughout the Southwest to display and sell their wares.

Delta: "Thunder Mountain Lives Tonight," and for six more weeks. This theatrical enterprise includes Ute dancers, gunslingers, fur traders, and other scenes from Colorado's pioneer past.

Denver: Capitol Hill People's Fair brings over 500 arts and crafts booths, live entertainment on three stages, and thousands of people to Civic Center Park.

Glenwood Springs: Strawberry Days is the state's oldest civic celebration and offers arts and crafts booths, entertainment, a parade, and free strawberries and ice cream.

Greeley: Denver Broncos Training Camp. It's more fun to watch the fanatics, er, fans, who flock to watch their heroes prepare for the upcoming season.

Larkspur: Renaissance Festival revives the sixteenth century, complete with jousting, every weekend through July.

Pagosa Springs: Mountain Man Rendezvous re-creates the famous extravaganzas that marked the fur-trapping trade.

Salida: FibArk Boat Races. The longest and oldest downriver kayak race in America, with raft races and other entertainment tossed in.

Telluride: The Telluride Bluegrass Festival, a weekend of fiddling, fun, and fandangos.

Trinidad: Santa Fe Trail Festival, a two-day celebration of history and art.

JULY

Aspen: Dance/Aspen starts its six-week run of performances by nationally-known dance companies, ranging from classic to modern to avant-garde.

Boulder: Colorado Shakespeare Festival, performed under the stars, ranks among the nation's top three Bard bashes. Dance and music festivals also fill the month.

Breckenridge: Bach, Beethoven, and Breckenridge is a combination of classical concerts and workshops that runs for a full month.

Carbondale: Carbondale Mountain Fair presents fine food, live entertainment, and a juried selection of the finest professional art and handmade crafts in any single festival.

Central City: Central City Opera Festival, held in the restored opera house, runs through August with classic opera performed in English.

Colorado Springs: Colorado State Games. The finals in 30 different sports open to Coloradoans of all ages and abilities.

Denver: Colorado Indian Market brings over 400 Native Americans from over 90 tribes to town with their traditional dances, dress, arts and crafts, weaving and sculpture.

Florissant: 1880's Picnic on the Hornbeck Homestead at the Florissant Fossil Beds National Monument.

Greeley: Greeley Independence Stampede features the largest Fourth of July rodeo, preceded by a week's worth of barbecues, parades, and family-oriented fun.

Idaho Springs: Gold Rush Days. Watch mucking and drilling contests and try your hand at panning gold.

La Junta: Bent's Old Fort Fur Trade Encampment and Old Time Fourth of July lets you relive the excitement of the fur-trapping era in the authentically restored fort.

Lake City: Alfred Packer Trial. Watch the trial of the famed Colorado cannibal as presented by the Western State College Drama Department. Runs through August.

Las Animas: The Annual Las Animas Silly Homemade River Raft Race decorates the Arkansas River with what else but silly homemade rafts.

Manitou Springs: Chevrolet Pikes Peak Hill Climb. Over 60 professional race car drivers twist up the 12 miles (19 km) of gravel to the top of Pikes Peak in this Race to the Clouds.

Pueblo: National High School Rodeo Finals brings the best high school bronc busters, steer wrestlers, ropers, and overall rodeo hands to town.

Steamboat Springs: Rodeo hits town as cowboys and broncs tango every Friday and Saturday night for a thirteen-week run.

Vail Valley: Bravo Colorado Music Festival brings together chamber, orchestral, and jazz music in various locations in Vail and Beaver Creek.

Winter Park: Winter Park Jazz Festival combines headline jazz artists playing outdoors and food and crafts booths.

AUGUST

Castle Rock: International Golf Tournament at the Castle Pines Golf Club is the PGA's only Colorado stop.

Central City: Central City Jazz Festival brings to town the best jazz jammers from the U.S. and Europe.

Cortez: Notah Dineh trading Post Indian Dance and Sing celebrates traditional Navajo dress, dance, and song.

Golden: Coors Annual Schuetzenfest Black Powder Competition, a five-day boomer with 200 sharpshooters blasting away in a single shot target shoot using black powder rifles.

Grand Junction: Annual Hilltop Renaissance Fair lets knights errant and ladies-in-waiting play Middle Ages, complete with period costumes, artists, food and entertainment.

Grand Junction: Palisade Peach Festival celebrates the area's celebrated peaches.

Kiowa: Colorado Day Ice Cream Social. Kiowans celebrate Colorado's statehood by dishing out free ice cream.

Leadville: Annual Boom Town Days Celebration brings back the silver boom with a drilling contest and 22-mile (35-km) pack burro race over a 13,000-foot (3,967-m) mountain.

Leadville: Leadville Trail 100. People actually run 100 miles (160 km) at 10,000 feet (3,048 m) above sea level. Spectators free, runners insane.

Montrose: Annual Black Canyon Horse and Mule Race Meet. Yes, mules can run, proving burros aren't the only four-legged Colorado athletes.

Pueblo: The Colorado State Fair. About two weeks of agricultural ecstasy where everything from strawberry preserves to peaches vie for blue ribbons. Parades, professional rodeo, big-name country-western artists, and nights of carnival lights make this the fairest fair in this fair state.

Vail: Vail Annual Jerry Ford Invitational golf tournament brings top pro golfers and celebrities to the valley's links.

SEPTEMBER

Aspen: Coors/Aspen Ruggerfest: International rugby teams hit town and each other in this three day bash.

Beecher's Island: Beecher's Island Reunion is a remembrance of the Battle of Beecher's Island, one of the last between whites and Native Americans. Attractions include a black powder shoot, crafts, and games.

Denver: Festival of Mountain and Plain . . . A Taste of Colorado, a great excuse to gorge yourself on every type of food imaginable.

Estes Park: Annual Scottish-Irish Highland Festival, a celebration of all things Scottish and Irish including authentic Celtic music and athletic competitions, kilts, and that drink that Scots like to drink.

Ignacio: Southern Ute Tribal Fair, with traditional games, exhibits, and ceremonies.

La Junta: Early Settlers' Day is one of the most popular events in southeast Colorado. Over 140 arts and crafts booths, beer garden, fiddling contests, barbecue, and more.

Leadville: St. Patrick's Day Practice Parade. Great excuse for green beer.

Loveland: Annual Stone Age Fair presents displays of ancient Indian artifacts and art with archaeologists there to explain what they mean.

Meeker: Border Collie National Finals. The world's best sheep dogs and handlers attempt to corral ornery Colorado sheep.

Montrose: Annual Native American Lifeways at the Ute Indian Museum, a cultural fair of Native American arts, crafts, and cuisine.

Steamboat Springs: Annual Steamboat Mountain Road Race and Vintage Auto Race and Concours d'Elegance. Vintage motorcycles and autos challenge a two-mile (three-km) course and restored exotic sports cars are displayed.

Telluride: Telluride Film Festival, with premieres and oldies (fee) and the Telluride Hang Gliding Festival (free) keeping the town hopping.

Yuma: Ole Threshers Day. Demonstrations of old wheat threshers, corn huskers, and other farm equipment and activities trace the history of farming.

OCTOBER

Durango: Western Arts, Film, and Poetry Gathering combines lectures, demonstrations of cowboy skills, and readings from real cowboy poets.

Fort Morgan: Western Barbecue Cookoff runs. The best barbecue cooks in the area gather to get sauced, barbecue style.

DECEMBER

Aspen: Aspen Highlands, Playboy Magazine Winter Carnival. You can figure this one out on your own.

Bent's Old Fort: Christmas 1846, which is just what it says, a frontier Christmas celebration.

Burlington: Carousel and Old Town Christmas. The Burlington Carousel, a National Landmark, is the center of this celebration, also featuring costumed Victorian carolers, and treats.

Denver: Parade of Lights. Brightly lit floats and bands converge on the downtown Civic Center, and the Denver City and County Building is set aglow with colored light in every nook and cupola.

San Luis: Fiesta de Nuesta Senora de Guadalupe. A fiesta of music and prayer dedicated to the Virgin of Guadalupe.

San Luis: Las Posadas is a two-week re-enactment of the journey of Mary and Joseph in search of a room for the Christ Child.

San Luis: Los Pastores, a medieval morality play.

Pueblo: Posata. A processional with a living nativity scene and music and song.

■ GOLF COURSES

Most Colorado towns and resorts have at least a nine-hole golf course somewhere in proximity. The following, however, are 18-hole layouts offering either good golfing, great views, or both. Most of the resort courses in the middle of the Rockies open in May, with those in the west and south and even Front Range courses offering almost year-round golfing.

ASPEN/SNOWMASS

Aspen Golf Course has great views and a challenging layout with lots of hidden ditches and lakes, (303) 925-2145.

Snowmass Club Golf Links are more expensive and less challenging than the Aspen 18, but the setting is stunning, (303) 923-3148.

BRECKENRIDGE

Breckenridge Golf Club is the only publicly owned Jack Nicklaus-designed course in the world. It plays through the natural terrain, even a beaver pond, and is infested with trees. Reservations suggested, (303) 453-9104.

BOULDER

Flatirons Golf Course is not only popular, but scenic and challenging, thanks to lots of lakes and trees. Call for tee times, (303) 441-7851.

CASTLE ROCK

Castle Pines Golf Club, home of the PGA International Golf Tournament, challenges the pros, so you can imagine what it does to the rest of us.

COLORADO SPRINGS

Patty Jewett Golf Course is definitely mature, since it was built in 1898 and was the first golf course west of the Mississippi. Located in the middle of town with a great view of Pikes Peak, it offers 27 holes. (719) 578-6825.

COPPER MOUNTAIN

Copper Creek Golf Course, a Perry Dye design, has the highest altitude of any PGA course in the nation and great views of the Tenmile Range. Reservations suggested, (303) 968-2339.

CRESTED BUTTE

Skyland Resort is tucked into the base of Mt. Crested Butte and surrounded by high-country scenery, which helps keep your mind off the battle its 18-hole layout presents. (303) 349-6129.

DENVER

With over 20 public links to choose from, Denver is not lacking for hacking. **Arrowhead Golf Club,** with 76 sand traps and six lakes, not to mention scrub oak and the rock formations of Roxborough Park, is a dandy. Designer Robert Trent Jones, Jr. claims this course is among his favorites. Reservations suggested, (303) 973-9614. **Meadow Hills Golf Course** isn't as challenging or expensive, but is still a good play, with plenty of mature trees and geese creating most of the obstacles, (303) 690-2500. **Wellshire Golf Course** is full of trees and very long (over 6,500 yards), but at a mile high you can slash away and hope for altitude assistance to improve your score, (303) 757-1352.

DURANGO

Hillcrest Golf Course, on the Fort Lewis College Mesa, gives you a peek at the La Plata Mountains, and some good mountain golfing. (303) 247-1499.

GRAND JUNCTION

Tiara Rado Golf Course is a young tough near the entrance to the Colorado National Monument, assuring nice views. (303) 245-8085.

GRAND LAKE

Grand Lake Golf Course, on the western edge of Colorado National Park, has tight fairways and tons of trees, so you have to keep it on the straight and narrow or bring lots of balls. But at an altitude of 8,400 feet (2,550 m), things really fly. (303) 627-8008.

RIFLE

Rifle Creek Golf Course is at the base of Rifle Gap, where artist Cristo hung a short-lived red curtain from rim to rim. The 18-hole layout is short, but steep, and tricky. (303) 625-1093.

STEAMBOAT SPRINGS

Sheraton Steamboat Golf Club, designed by Robert Trent Jones, Jr., is one of the toughest in the state, regardless of the views of Mt. Werner and the Yampa River Valley. Reservations are suggested. (303) 879-1391.

PUEBLO

Pueblo West Golf Club, the second highest rated course in the state, is a good test of all your golfing skills, cursing included. (719) 547-2280.

VAIL/BEAVER CREEK/EAGLE

Packed with four quality courses, here are just two treats.

Vail Golf Club, a municipal course, is flank to shank with the Gore River and Vail Mountain and hosts the Gerry Ford Invitational. Call for tee times, (303) 479-2260.

Beaver Creek Resort Golf Club offers limited public tee times, but it's worth the wait to tangle with this rolling, sand-trapped terror at the base of the Beaver Creek ski hill. Reservations suggested, (303) 949-7123.

■ HUNTING AND FISHING INFORMATION

For hunting, the state is divided into over 100 "game management units," and in many cases restrictions are numerous and somewhat complicated. That's where the men and women at the Colorado Division of Wildlife (DOW), who are charged with maintaining and improving the state's abundant supply of wildlife, come into play. They want your Colorado hunting or fishing trip to be a booming success. You see, their budget is completely funded through hunting and fishing license fees, so they pay attention. That doesn't mean they neglect non-game species. Indeed, Colorado was one of the first states in the nation to use a voluntary state income tax check-off system to fund a wide range of DOW propagation and protection programs for the state's non-game animals.

The DOW produces a number of comprehensive brochures which outline in detail every aspect of the state's hunting and fishing regulations and rules. These informational gems are a good place to start when planning a hunting trip.

The following list will put you in touch with DOW officers in the field who have been monitoring the wildlife situation with a watchful eye.

MAIN REGIONAL FIELD OFFICES

Denver Headquarters and Central; 6060 Broadway, Denver, CO 80216; (303) 297-1192

Northeast; 317 W. Prospect Ave., Fort Collins, CO 80526; (303) 484-2836

Northwest; 711 Independent Ave., Grand Junction, CO 81505; (303) 248-7175

Southeast; 2126 N. Weber, Colorado Springs, CO 80907; (719) 473-2945

Southwest; 2300 S. Townsend Ave., Montrose, CO 81401; (303) 249-3431

FISHING
(all prefixes 303)
General; 291-7533
Metro Denver/Foothills; 291-7535
Northeast Colorado; 291-7536
Northwest Colorado; 291-7537
Southeast Colorado; 291-7538
Southwest Colorado; 291-7539

HUNTING
(all prefixes 303)
Deer, elk, antelope; 291-7529
Small game; 291-7546
Upland game; 291-7547
Waterfowl; 291-7548
Camping; 291-7532
Maps; 291-7540

The DOW also publishes *Colorado Outdoors,* a bimonthly, full-color magazine "dedicated to the conservation and enjoyment of Colorado outdoors—its animals, fish, soil, forests, prairies, and waters." For a subscription, write to *Colorado Outdoors,* 6060 Broadway, Denver CO 80216, or call (303) 291-7469 for a subscription or sample copy.

■ OUTFITTERS AND GUIDES

Another group quite interested in the success of your hunting, fishing, and floating adventures consists of the private outfitters and guides who take sportsmen into the woods. For information call the Colorado Outfitters Association in Aurora at (303) 751-9274.

■ AMERICAN INDIAN INFORMATION

From the magnificent cliff dwellings of the Anasazi to the present-day life of the Utes, Colorado is a storehouse of historical and contemporary Native Americana. The following national parks, museums, and cultural centers have preserved part of that culture.

Anasazi Heritage Center, 27501 Hwy. 184, Dolores, CO 81323;
    (303) 882-4811.
Colorado Historical Society,1300 Broadway, Denver, CO 80303;
    (303) 866-3682.
Denver Art Museum, Department of Native Arts (exhibits only), 100 W. 14th.
    Ave. Pkwy., Denver, CO, 80204; (303) 575-2793.
Denver Museum of Natural History, 2001 Colorado Blvd., Denver, CO 80205;
    (303) 322-7009.
Koshare Indian Museum, Inc., 115 W. 18th, La Junta, CO 81050;
    (719) 384-4411.
Mesa Verde National Park, Mesa Verde National Park, CO 81330;
    (303) 529-4465.
Southern Ute Tourist Center, Box 550, Ignacio CO 81137; (303) 4531.
University of Colorado Cortez Center, 25 N. Market St., Cortez, CO 81321;
    (303) 565-3414, (1-800) 346-6528.
Ute Indian Museum, 17253 Chipeta Dr., Montrose, CO 81401;
    (303) 249-3098.
Ute Mountain Ute Indian Tribal Parks, Box 52, Towaoc, CO 81334;
    (303) 565-3751.

■ TOURS

DENVER

Byers-Evans House A post-World War I home, complete with upper-crust trappings. Open daily except Tuesday, fee. 1310 Bannock St. (303) 623-0709.

Grant-Humpreys Mansion A 42-room, Beaux Arts mansion, complete with columns and detailed terra-cotta balustrades at all levels. Open Tuesday through Friday, fee. 770 Pennsylvania St., (303) 894-2506.

Pearce-McAllister Cottage is an example of Colonial Revival architecture which houses the Museum of Miniatures, Dolls, and Toys. Open Wednesday through Sunday, fee. 770 Pennsylvania St., (303) 322-3704.

Molly Brown House Museum is the lavishly appointed Victorian mansion from which the Unsinkable one launched her attack on Denver society. Open daily, fee. 1340 Pennsylvania St. (303) 832-4092.

GOLDEN

Adolf Coors Company offers tours of its beer-brewing facility, which was started by 21-year-old Adolf in 1873 and is now the largest single beer plant in the nation. Open daily except Sundays and holidays, free. 13th and Ford, (303) 277-BEER.

LEADVILLE

Healy House and Dexter Cabin preserves the genteel nineteenth century setting enjoyed by the town's non-married, thus unsullied, schoolmarms. **Dexter Cabin** is an old hunting cabin complete with trappings where nineteenth century men could smoke, chew, and discuss life in general. Open daily from Memorial Day to Labor Day, fee. 912 Harrison Ave., (303) 670-1686.

Matchless Mine, a multi-million-dollar producer in its heyday, is where Baby Doe Tabor spent the final 36 years of her life, holding onto the Matchless and waiting for the silver boom that never returned. Open from June to Labor Day. Fee. One mile east of town on 7th Street.

Tabor Opera House, was Horace Tabor's crowning cultural jewel that hosted the most renowned entertainers of the late 1800s. Its finery is slowly being restored from the small fees which allow visitors to tour the entire operation, from lobby to dressing rooms. Open in the summer. 815 Harrison Avenue.

PUEBLO

Rosemont Victorian House Museum is 24,000 square feet of the finest Victorian architecture in the state. Turrets, chimneys, ten fireplaces, and a 10,000-gallon water tank in the attic are just some of the delightful aspects of this monument to Victorian craftsmanship. Varying summer and winter hours, fee. 419 W. 19th St., (719) 545-5290.

SOUTHEASTERN PLAINS

Bent's Old Fort was once the hub of the buffalo trading empire and a welcome stop on the Rocky Mountain Branch of the Santa Fe Trail. The reconstructed fort's guides are in period dress and host a series of events. Open year round, except for winter holidays; fee. Located west of La Junta on Highway 194, (719) 384-2596.

SOUTHERN COLORADO

Fort Garland consists of six one-story buildings around a parade ground that Commander Kit Carson once oversaw. Restored dioramas and artifacts give a taste of military life on the frontier. Open Memorial Day through Labor Day; fee. Located 25 miles (40 km) east of Alamosa off Highway 160, (719) 379-3512.

■ HISTORIC RAILROADS

Narrow-gauge tracks laid precariously along mountainsides, over trestles, or though rolling forests still carry sturdy steam locomotives and their string of passenger cars, reminding visitors what the world was like before the automobile and freeway. Plumes of steam spewing from the smokestack, sparks, and soot spraying the summer air with their unique smell mark the passage of three of Colorado's most famous, scenic, and delightful historic train rides.

The Georgetown Loop Railroad winds its way back to glory days of Colorado's gold boom by taking travelers on an hour-long, steam-powered ride. Starting from Georgetown, the narrow-gauge tracks cross the rebuilt 95-foot (29-m) high Devil's Gate Bridge (called the Eighth Wonder of the World when it was completed in 1888), then take 14 twisting turns before hitting Silver Plume. A brief rest and you're back aboard for the return trip which closes the loop. The rolling stock, engines, and restored passenger cars (some of which are open to the mountain air, so don't forget a jacket), are immaculate and the crews enthusiastic and helpful. You can board at either Georgetown, an hour's drive west from Denver on Interstate 70, or Silver Plume, another half hour away on the interstate. **Season and Information:** Trains run every day during June and July, and on Saturdays and Sundays during September. Box 217, Georgetown, CO 80444; (303) 569-2403 from Georgetown/Silver Plume; (303) 670-1686, from Denver.

Lebanon Mine and Mill Tour lets you delve even deeper into the golden era by taking you inside an old mine and mill, accessible only by train, which you can do as a part of the Georgetown Loop trip or independently. Be sure to bring a jacket (the mine is a constant 44 degrees (7°C) and walking shoes for this hour and a half tour. Reservations are also suggested if you want to combine the tour and train ride. **Schedule and information:** see "Georgetown Loop Railroad," above.

Durango & Silverton Narrow Gauge Railroad takes you 45 miles (72 km) through the heart of southwestern Colorado's stunning San Juan National Forest and past remnants of the state's mining past and living reminders of its mining present. Over $300 million in gold and silver were hauled on the narrow-gauge tracks in mining's heyday, and those days can now be relived in a number of ways on the current train. A choice of authentically restored 1880 passenger cars is available, ranging from the opulent private Cinco Animas car (for charter only) to standard covered coach to an open-air gondola car. Refreshments are served in the Alamosa Parlour Car. Along the way hearing the shriek of the steam whistle, seeing abandoned mine sites, and miles of roadless, virgin forest make for an unforgettable journey. The entire trip from Durango to Silverton takes most of a day, so many opt for staying the night in Silverton, which started as and remains a mining town, and returning to Durango the next day. **Season and information:** Mid-June to late October, depending on the length of trip. Reservations are strongly recommended. Call for an order form/brochure and then pick up your tickets in advance, especially if you are planning a fall trip to view the spectacular fall foliage. For information: 479 Main Ave., Durango, CO 81301, (303) 247-2733.

Cumbres & Toltec Scenic Railroad, the longest and highest narrow-gauge line in North America, stretches 64 miles (102 km) from Antonito, Colorado, to Chama, New Mexico. From Antonito, the train starts a slow chug up the rolling high country, passing through the dramatic Toltec Gorge of the Los Pinos River before cresting out at a heady 10,015 feet (3045 m) atop Cumbres Pass. Then it's all downhill, at a four-percent grade, into Chama. The trip along rivers and over mountains has made many agree that the Cumbres & Toltec was one of the most spectacular feats of mountain railroad building ever undertaken. Located along the isolated Colorado/New Mexico border, the train is off the beaten track, but once you get on its tracks, you can rest assured it's well worth it. Coming from Colorado, you can take US 285 south from Denver through Alamosa to the Antonito station. From Santa Fe, hit 285 north to Espanola, then U.S. 84 to the Chama station. The enclosed coaches feature windows that can be open or closed, weather allowing. A completely open sightseeing coach is available to all, with on-train refreshments. Cars are not heated, so be prepared with your own warmth. The train stops in Osier for lunch, or you can hop off at Osier and head back to where you started. **Season and information:** June to mid-October. For information: Antonito Depot, Box 668, Antonito, CO 81120, (719) 376-5483, Chama Depot, Box 789, Chama, NM 87520, (505) 756-2151.

Cripple Creek/Victor Narrow Gauge Railroad takes you on a four-mile round trip through the gold town of Cripple Creek and includes a stop at the famous Molly Catherine Mine. **Season and information:** Memorial Day until mid-October. Box 459, Cripple Creek, CO 80813, or call (719) 689-2640.

Blackhawk & Central City Narrow Gauge Railroad takes travelers on a short haul, a bit over a mile (two km), down the valley from Central City using an original Colorado and Southern steam engine that was revived after a 46-year rest and rust stop on a local hillside. **Season and information:** daily trips, June through September, weekend trips through October. Box 13558, Denver CO 80201, (303) 433-7872.

Leadville Colorado and Southern Railroad runs from Leadville to the Climax Mine, giving riders a panoramic view of this once booming valley of silver. **Information,** 326 E. 7th. St., Leadville, CO 80461, (719) 486-3936.

Manitou & Pikes Peak Cog Railway is a modern people-mover that makes a three-hour round trip from Manitou Springs to the top of Pikes Peak. Gaining

8,000 feet (2,700 m) in altitude during the nine-mile (14-km) trip through aspens and pines to timberline, once atop the peak you can see the purple mountains' majesty and amber waves of grain that inspired Katherine Lee Bates to pen "America the Beautiful." **Season and information:** May through October with hourly departures during peak (that's not a pun) seasons. Contact either Cog Road Depot, 515 Ruxton Ave., Manitou Springs, CO 80829, (719) 685-5401; or Box 1329, Colorado Springs, CO 80901.

Royal Gorge Scenic Railway snakes along the top of the imposing Royal Gorge, in modern, open-air cars and stops for peeks over the edge that make you want to get back in you seat. **Information:** Box 1387, Canon City, CO 81212, (719) 275-5485.

Royal Gorge Aerial Tram and the **Royal Gorge Incline Railway** will give you two views of this monstrous crack in the earth spanned by the world's highest suspension bridge. Up to 35 passengers without a fear of heights can look down 1,200 feet (366 km) into the bottom of the gorge from the safety of the comfortable tram cars chugging across the top of the gorge. For those who want to take a closer look, the railway, steepest in the world, takes you right to the bottom. **Season and information:** Open year round, depending on weather. Royal Gorge Bridge Co., Box 594, Canon City, CO 81212, (719) 275-7507.

■ SHOPPING

You don't have to go to an upscale ski resort to wear the numbers off your credit card during a go-for-broke shopping binge. If you're the member of the "Shop 'till You Drop Society," the following select shopping spots will have you dropping in no time.

Cherry Creek Shopping Center Denver's prestige mall features all the big-name high-fashion department and specialty stores, from Neiman Marcus on down. A relaxing respite from the mall crawl is the Tattered Cover Bookstore (2955 E. First Ave.), which, with three stories packed to the gills, is one of the nation's largest. Cherry Creek is located south of downtown at the corner of University and First Avenue and covering enough space to wear out any pair of loafers (shoes, that is).

Larimer Square and Sixteenth Street Mall Downtown Denver's showcase urban renewal and historic preservation projects, both areas offer an eclectic array of shops ranging from the silly to the practical to the tacky. Great people watching in the summer from the numerous outdoor cafes. Both malls are located in the heart of downtown Denver. The Sixteenth Street Mall is closed to cars from Market Street to Broadway. Larimer Square is a block from 16th on Larimer Street.

South Broadway When Denverites want an antique, they head to South Broadway, home to a crazy-quilt collection of antique and collectible shops, some random second-hand stores, and a jarring dose of low-budget used car lots. The antiques are the key and the shops run from small storefront operations to warehouse-size stores.Prime antiquing on South Broadway can be found in about the first 15 blocks directly south of the Broadway exit from Interstate 25.

Silverthorne Factory Stores Over 50 factory outlet stores offer bargains on everything from Nike shoes to VanHeusen clothing. Silverthorne stores are located right at the Silverthorne exit off Interstate 70, about 70 miles west of Denver.

Castle Rock Factory Shops Same drill as at Silverthorne: 60 stores devoted to a single line of clothes or shoes, all at factory discoujnt prices. Located at the Castle Rock exit off Interstate 25, about 30 miles south of Denver.

■ INFORMATION SOURCES

Weather Reports
Denver: (303) 398-3964.
Statewide: (303) 639-1515.

Road Conditions
Denver and west: (303) 639-1111
Denver and east: (303) 639-1234

STATEWIDE TOURIST/PROMOTIONAL ORGANIZATIONS

Colorado Ski Country USA is the promotional association for all of the state's ski areas. It produces a slick, 100-page magazine describing every ski area, how to get there, and listings of accommodations and other nearby amenities. Call (303) 837-0793 for more information.

Colorado Tourism Board will send you the official state vacation guide, a 130-page magazine describing the state and its attractions. Included in the guide are phone numbers and addresses for everything from government offices to all the state's chambers of commerce and national parks and recreation areas. To order, call (800) 433-2656.

OUTDOOR RECREATION ORGANIZATIONS

Colorado Campground and Cabin Resort Association (commercial), Boulder, (303) 499-9343.

Colorado Cross-Country Ski Association, Winter Park; (303) 887-2152.

Colorado Dude/Guest Ranch Association, Tabernash; (1-800) 441-6060.

Colorado Golf Association, Englewood; (303) 779-4653

Colorado Llama Packers Association, Clark; (303) 879-9044.

Colorado Outfitters Association, Aurora; (303) 751-9274.

Colorado River Outfitters Association, Buena Vista; (303) 369-4632.

Colorado Snowmobiling Association, Grand Lake; (303) 627-8101.

Colorado Tennis Association, Denver; (303) 695-4116.

RECOMMENDED READING

■ HISTORY

Borland, Hal. *High, Wide, and Lonesome.* Philadelphia, New York: J. B. Lippincott Company, 1956.

Fay, Abbott. *Ski Tracks in the Rockies: A History of Skiing in Colorado.* Evergreen, CO: Cordillera Press, Inc., 1984.

Fradkin, Philip L. *A River No More: The Colorado River and the West.* Tucson, Arizona: University of Arizona Press, 1984. How the state and its mighty Colorado River have become interwoven into the politics and problems of the West.

Neihardt, John G. *Black Elk Speaks.* New York: William Morrow & Co., 1932.

Parkman, Francis. *The California and Oregon Trail.* New York: Thomas Y. Crowell & Co., 1849.

Ubbelohde, Carl, Maxine Benson, and Duane A. Smith. *A Colorado History.* 6th ed. Boulder: Pruett Publishing Co., 1988.

Vandenbusche, Duane. *A Land Alone, Colorado's Western Slope.* Boulder: Pruett Publishing Co., 1980.

Note: Caroline Bancroft is Colorado's best-known and most prolific citizen historian. She has written dozens of short histories, pamphlets, and profiles on almost every aspect of the state and its many colorful characters. Her efforts afford the visitor a quick, colorful glimpse into the state's past.

■ GUIDEBOOKS

Borneman, Walter R., and Lydon J. Lampert. *Climbing Guide to Colorado's Fourteeners.* Boulder: Pruett Publishing Co., 1989.

Borneman, Walter, R. *Colorado's Other Mountains: A Climbing Guide to Selected Peaks Under 14,000 Feet.* Evergreen, CO: Cordillera Press, Inc., 1984.

Cahill, Rick. *Colorado Hot Springs Guide.* Boulder, Colorado: Pruett Publishing Company, 1986.

Caughey, Bruce, and Dean Winstanley. *The Colorado Guide: Landscapes, Cityscapes, Escapes.* Golden, CO: Fulcrum, Inc., 1991.

Fidler, John, and M. John Fayhee. *Along the Colorado Trail.* Englewood, CO: Westcliffe Publishers, 1992. Over 120 photos accompany text that guides you along the 470 miles of hiking on the Colorado Trail.

Gray, Mary Taylor. *Colorado Wildlife Viewing Guide.* Helena, MT: Falcon Press, Inc., 1992. Photos, maps, and illustrations of the state's wildlife and where to go to see them.

Keilty, Maureen. *Best Hikes with Children in Colorado.* Seattle: The Mountaineers, 1991.

Litz, Brian. *Colorado Hut to Hut: A Guide to Skiing and Biking Colorado's Backcountry.* Englewood, CO: Westcliffe Publishers, 1992. Color photos, topo maps, and advice on hut-hopping Colorado style.

Rye, David. *Colorado's Guide to Fishing.* Denver: Mountain Peaks, Inc., 1991. If there's a fish in water, this book will show you where it is and how to catch it.

Wilson, D. Ray. *Colorado Historical Tour Guide.* Carpentersville, IL: Crossroads Communications, 1990. The state's every visible historical site, plaque, museum, digging, or roadside attraction.

■ FICTION

Abbey, Edward. *The Monkey Wrench Gang.* Philadelphia: J. B. Lippincott Co., 1975. The seminal work on acting out the West's eco-outrage.

Cather, Willa. *Song of the Lark.* Boston and New York: Houghton Mifflin Co., 1932.

Guthrie, A. B., Jr. *The Big Sky.* Forward by Wallace Stegner. Boston: Houghton Mifflin Co., 1952. The best novel written about Mountain Men, their way of life, and the mountains which provided their livelihood.

Michener, James A. *Centennial.* New York: Random House, Inc., 1974. Michener applies his exacting research and storytelling gifts to Colorado's vibrant past.

I N D E X

COMPASS AMERICAN GUIDES

Comprehensive, literate, and beautifully illustrated guides to the individual cities and states of the United States and Canada, Compass American Guides are unparalleled in their cultural, historical, and informational scope. They are to the 1990s what the WPA guidebook series was to the 1930s — insightful, resourceful, and entertaining.

"Each [Compass American Guide] pairs an accomplished photographer with a writer native to the state. The resulting pictures and words have such an impact I constantly had to remind myself I was reading a travel guide."

— National Geographic Traveler

"You can read [a Compass American Guide] for information and come away entertained. Or you can read it for entertainment and come away informed . . . an informational jackpot."

—Houston Chronicle

"Wickedly stylish writing!"

—Chicago Sun-Times

Compass American Guides are available in general and travel bookstores, or may be ordered directly by calling 1-800-733-3000; or by sending a check or money order, including the cost of shipping and handling, payable to: Random House, Inc. 400 Hahn Road, Westminster, Maryland 21157. Books are shipped by USPS Book Rate (allow 30 days for delivery): $2.00 for the 1st book, $0.50 for each additional book. Applicable sales tax will be charged. All prices are subject to change. Or ask your bookseller to order for you.

"Books can make thoughtful (and sometimes even thought-provoking) gifts for incentive travel winners or convention attendees. A new series of guidebooks published by Compass American Guides is right on the mark." —Successful Meetings magazine

Consider Compass American Guides as gifts or incentives for VIP's, employees, clients, customers, convention and meeting attendees, friends and others. Compass American Guides are available at special discounts for bulk purchases (100 copies or more) for sales promotions or premiums. Special editions, including personalized covers, excerpts of existing guides, and corporate imprints, can be created in large quantities for special needs. For more information, write to Special Marketing, Fodor's Travel Publications, 201 E. 50th St., New York, NY 10022; or call 800/800-3246. Inquiries from the United Kingdom should be sent to Fodor's Travel Publications, 20 Vauxhall Bridge Rd., London, England SW1V 2SA.

A R I Z O N A
2nd Edition
Author
Lawrence Cheek
Photographer
Michael Freeman
1-878-86732-6

$16.95 Paper 288 pp.
($22.50 Canada)

"This is my kind of guidebook."

—David Laird, *Books of the Southwest*

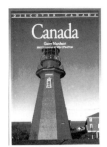

C A N A D A
1st Edition
Author
Garry Marchant
Photographer
Ken Straiton
1-878-86712-1

$14.95 Paper 320 pp.
($19.95 Canada)

"*Canada* goes a long way in presenting this country
in all its complex, beautiful glory." — *Toronto Sun*

H A W A I ' I
1st Edition
Author
Moana Tregaskis
Photographers
Wayne Levin & Paul Chesley
1-878-86723-7

$15.95 Paper 364 pp.
($19.95 Canada)

Also available in a hardcover
edition:
1-878-86724-5
$22.95 ($29.00 Canada)

"A fine guide and a welcome addition to travel
collections."   —*Library Journal*

1993 Award of Merit—Hawai'i Visitors Bureau

L A S   V E G A S
3rd Edition
Author
Deke Castleman
Photographer
Michael Yamashita
1-878-86736-9

$16.95 Paper   304 pp.
($22.50 Canada)

"Visiting this neon oasis has been made much more
interesting thanks to Deke Castleman's *Las Vegas*."

— *Travel & Leisure*

N E W   M E X I C O
1st Edition
Author
Nancy Harbert
Photographer
Michael Freeman
1-878-86706-7

$15.95 Paper 288 pp.
($19.95 Canada)

Also available in a hardcover
edition:
1-878-86722-9 $22.95
($29.00 Canada)

"Bold yet artful in its photography. "

— *Albuquerque Journal*

S A N   F R A N C I S C O
& T H E   B A Y   A R E A
2nd Edition
Author
Barry Parr
Photographer
Michael Yamashita
1-878-86716-4

$14.95 Paper 396 pp.
($19.95 Canada)

"*San Francisco* tackles the 'why' of travel to that city as
well as the nitty gritty details." — *Travel Weekly*